‖‖‖PERSPECTIVES
‖‖ ON CRIME AND JUSTICE

Joseph A. Schafer,
Series Editor

Dilemma of Duties

The Conflicted Role of Juvenile Defenders

Anne M. Corbin

Southern Illinois University Press
Carbondale

Southern Illinois University Press
www.siupress.com

21 20 19 18   4 3 2 1

Publication of this book has been underwritten by the Elmer H. Johnson and
    Carol Holmes Johnson criminology fund.

Cover illustration: desk scene with juvenile and lawyer. Courtesy of Douglas
    William Jones

Library of Congress Cataloging-in-Publication Data
Names: Corbin, Anne M., author.
Title: Dilemma of duties : the conflicted role of juvenile defenders / Anne M.
    Corbin.
Description: Carbondale, Illinois : Southern Illinois University Press, 2018. |
    Series: Perspectives on crime and justice | Includes bibliographical references
    and index.
Identifiers: LCCN 2017045407 | ISBN 9780809336647 (paperback) | ISBN
    9780809336654 (ebook)
Subjects: LCSH: Right to counsel—United States. | Defense (Criminal
    procedure)—United States. | Juvenile justice, Administration of—United
    States | Juvenile delinquents—Legal status, laws, etc.—United States.
    | Trial practice—United States. | BISAC: LAW / Criminal Law /
    Juvenile Offenders. | SOCIAL SCIENCE / Criminology.
Classification: LCC KF9646 .C665 2018 | DDC 345.73/08—dc23
LC record available at https://lccn.loc.gov/2017045407

To the amazing juvenile defenders who participated in this study and those who support them. To my mentor, Dr. Jon B. Gould, for his tireless encouragement of all my professional endeavors. To Dr. Christopher E. Smith, for his endless advocacy of my vision and projects. And to my husband, Christopher G. Clow, for his unflinching companionship and patience.

Contents

Charts

Tables

*M*ore *than fifty* years after the anniversary of *In re Gault* (1967), the US Supreme Court case establishing the right to counsel for juveniles, the state of juvenile defense in the United States remains a quagmire of conflicting policies and practices. Although the landmark Supreme Court decision established that children accused of crime have the same right to counsel as adults, the nature of juvenile defense has been shown to be inconsistent among the states. According to reports from nearly half of them, the quality of juvenile defense also shows inconsistencies, mostly due to role confusion and role conflict. Identifying a single juvenile defense area of study as more worthy than another is nearly impossible, given the critical worth of *all* child welfare topics. However, to date very little of the juvenile defense conversation has involved a scientific focus on the *juvenile defender role*. There has been even less focus on juvenile defenders' lived experiences of the advocate role and the obstacles they face carrying out the role in a context of vacillating support, even half a century after *Gault*. The need for this focus is more critical than ever, given the increasingly arbitrary and punitive practices of modern juvenile courts and despite their espoused best-interests mission and duty to uphold the due process rights set out in the US Constitution and subsequent US Supreme Court decisions.

Without detracting from the importance of the needs of the clients whom juvenile defenders aim to serve, this book aspires to lend voice to the defenders themselves. It seeks to shed light on the unfortunate but unmistakable gap between the mission they swear to undertake and that which they are expected to pursue. A solid understanding of juvenile defender role meaning, challenges, and conflicts is a necessary component to making good on the promise of *Gault*. This book intends to lay the foundation for such an understanding. It is dedicated to juvenile defenders and their noble efforts to fill a conflicted role in the face of seemingly universal contention.

Dilemma of Duties

Introduction

Imagine you have been appointed one of a number of supervisors at a playground where your chief responsibility is to make sure your assigned children get their fair share of time on the jungle gym. The jungle gym, as you might recall from childhood, is a webbed frame of interwoven metal rods that can reach heights well above a child's head. Your assigned children get ten full minutes on the jungle gym, but it is up to them to determine how they stay on it without touching their feet to the ground, because doing so automatically ends their time on the equipment. Also imagine that there are land mines on the ground beneath the jungle gym, only a few of which you know about. Recall that your job is to ensure that your kids get their full ten minutes on the jungle gym without disqualifying themselves, so you have to be able to communicate with them and counsel them as to the potential pitfalls of swinging to a bar that is too near the ground. You must also argue on their behalf against adults trying to pull them off before their time is up. You have multiple kids on the jungle gym, and the reality is, they are *kids*. They are absorbed in the task at hand of grappling with one metal rod or another, hanging upside down, getting turned around, probably not hearing what you are saying or forgetting what you say from one minute to the next, and possibly doubting you really care if they fall or not. So, you try to get closer to them so you can hold their attention, but you notice that despite your careful stepping you occasionally set off land mines, jeopardizing yourself and your little charges. Land mines. At a playground. Under a jungle gym meant to be an instrument of growth and learning for children.

While the playground supervisor analogy might not perfectly align with the juvenile defender role, there are enough parallels to provide the reader with some sense of what an attorney faces when attempting to fill this critical role. Juvenile defenders must often serve as their clients' voices to the court, a context that can present them with a level of hostility beyond what is expected in the normal course of an adversarial contest.

The defense attorney role in juvenile courts has been the source of considerable debate since juveniles' right to counsel was first established in 1967 (*In re Gault*). This book discusses an empirical investigation of juvenile defender role meaning and the nature, extent, and impact of role conflict among juvenile defenders in a jurisdiction that has officially clarified the role. The investigation utilized data derived from in-depth interviews of juvenile defenders from a state on the East Coast previously the subject of juvenile defense assessment. Even though the book does not introduce readers to the study's details until chapter 3, it presents participant quotes—referenced by participant number (e.g., Participant 001)—in earlier chapters to illustrate relevant concepts. The book begins with a brief history of the juvenile defender role and the controversy currently surrounding its meaning. It will then introduce the problem of the role and role conflict among juvenile defenders and discuss the scholarship addressing these issues. A brief description of the investigation's methods and target questions is followed by a presentation and discussion of its main findings. The book concludes with a discussion of the findings' implications and directions for future research.

Much of the debate about the juvenile defender role has centered on the *advocate*, as opposed to the counselor, components of the role. For the duration of the book, the juvenile defender role is presumed to refer more to the advocate role than to the counselor role. The counselor role is equally critical to juvenile defense but is not as central to this study's investigation. The debate has also centered on the extent to which attorneys should represent their juvenile clients' *expressed* interests or *best* interests. In other words, should attorneys advocate for the interests they believe their clients should have (best interests) or for the interests actually articulated by the clients (expressed interests)? Before delving into the crux of the juvenile defender role debate, a brief definition of the role's official components is useful.

The *Modern Rules of Professional Conduct* provides guidance on all lawyers' two-part role: adviser (or counselor) and advocate (American Bar Association [ABA], 2013, pmbl. § 2). The rules state that an attorney, as an adviser or counselor, provides "an informed understanding of the client's legal rights and obligations and explains their practical implication" and, as an advocate, "zealously asserts the *client's position* [emphasis added] under the rules of the adversary system" (pmbl. § 2).

The distinction between the adviser/counselor role and the advocate role is an important one when considering the expressed-/best-interests advocacy dilemma (hereinafter referred to as *conflicting-client-interests dilemma*). This book suggests that this dilemma, addressed more thoroughly in chapter 2, is the foundation of role conflict for juvenile defenders. The counselor component is here briefly illustrated, but the advocate component of the attorney role will be addressed more fully in chapter 1, since it is the most central component to this book and the study described herein.

An attorney's counselor role as a necessary and distinct component of his or her larger attorney role resonates with professional rules and practicing attorneys. It also resonates with juvenile defenders. Consider the following. Regardless of clients' ages, an attorney would not allow them to determine what legal tactics he or she should use since they have not had legal training or professional experience. That attorney would also not expect them to provide themselves with legal counseling for the same reasons. This expectation would make even less sense if the clients were juveniles, who lack life experience and have the status of minors. Juvenile clients might be experts of their own lives and circumstances, but they have not dedicated any significant amount of time to the study of law or preparation for law practice. It therefore seems unreasonable and irresponsible to expect attorneys to relinquish their counseling and strategizing responsibilities to any client, let alone their juvenile clients.

The juvenile defender's counselor role can be broken down into two major categories: advice/strategy and persuasion. One juvenile defender (Participant 005) concisely explained, "Your client gets to make the ultimate decision as to where you go with the case. As I tell a lot of my clients: you get to decide practical, I get to decide the tactical." This is a critical distinction to make, especially for legal representatives for children. As discussed more thoroughly later in this introduction, children make unique clients because of their lack of life experience and less developed decision-making capacity. It is therefore reasonable for juvenile defenders to *not* prioritize a client's expressed wishes when it comes to their counselor function.

Since North Carolina attorneys made up the sample for the study presented in this book, a comment about the state's juvenile representation guidelines is useful. The "performance guidelines" in the *North Carolina Juvenile Defender Manual* address this counselor role nuance to some extent in that they provide that if there is an "absolute impasse as to tactical decisions [at adjudication], the juvenile's wishes *may* [emphasis added] control" (Newman, Grine, & Zogry, 2008, p. 17). The guidelines do not provide direction on this conflict at any other stages of the process except to say that such "tactical disagreements ... do not justify withdrawal from a case" (p. 2). The guidelines might be written this way to provide some protection to defenders who choose to defer to their clients' expressed interests when it comes to tactical decisions. This implies that they might have the choice *not* to when it comes to tactical decisions. More broadly, the guidelines specify that juvenile defenders must treat their juvenile clients just as they would their adult clients (p. 1), and legal counseling and strategy are unlikely areas for even adult clients to take the lead. Also, since *expressed* interests refer to the "stated desires of the juvenile client about the direction and objectives of the case" but *not* to the tactics used to pursue that direction or those objectives, it stands to reason that participants are justified in not deferring to their child clients' expressed interests when it comes to strategy (p. 1). The following excerpt is illustrative.

> I think even in the more technical aspects of performing your job—whether it's pre-adjudication, whether it's filing motions—at every point I feel that you should be explaining the law to your clients.... There will certainly be points where in my experience [clients] will almost always defer to your judgment because we're attorneys and because they don't really know what a motion means or they may not understand what precedents there are when it comes to a specific legal aspect of their case. But, I still feel that as an attorney and advocate I don't generally file anything and then try to explain it to the client later [as,] "Well, this is what I did and here's why." (Participant 022)

Participant 022's comments address more than just strategy. He also makes an important point about the need to *explain* the law to clients, another task involved in the counseling function of the juvenile defender role. Juvenile defenders therefore also view their legal counselor function as including the use of persuasion to convince clients to change their interests when defenders think it would benefit their clients. Participant 014 sheds light on this dynamic:

> So there's the counseling aspect ... when I'm talking to my juvenile clients.... We'll talk about what their expressed interests are and what I may think their best interests are. After we've had that conversation and if they are adamant in going a certain route, their expressed interests, well, I've satisfied myself and my ethical obligations to counsel them as far as the process, outcomes, and things like that so that now I can go full force and try to accomplish their expressed wishes, even if I personally think that's the worst thing that could happen to them. (Participant 014)

Considering Participant 014's comments, it would seem that when it comes to the counselor role, juvenile defenders do their best to inform their clients of relevant information and options, even when clients' expressed interests conflict with what is in their best interests, creating a conflicting-client-interests dilemma. They also might attempt to convince a client to change his or her mind. However, once juvenile defenders inhabit the advocate role, they tend to defer to clients' expressed interests if clients are unwilling to be persuaded to change their interests.

To further illustrate, imagine a fourteen-year-old young man—let's call him Max—is caught with a group of friends shoplifting DVDs from Walmart. None of them is pointing fingers at the others, and none of them is making a "responsible" (that is, guilty) admission. Max is your client, and as a seasoned defense attorney you know that you can convince the (tough) judge that given his age and station in life, he was merely following along with the crowd. You also know that if you offer the judge a "responsible" admission and get your client to agree to a "forbidden-friends clause" in his disposition (sentencing) report, your client can avoid a harsher punishment. This clause would mean that Max could not socialize with the group of friends he was with when they were caught shoplifting. Despite your best efforts to convince Max that agreeing to the clause would be the least restrictive (and least damaging) outcome for him, he is adamant that he will not agree to distance himself from these friends. In order to adhere to your ethical duties, you *must* argue to exclude the forbidden-friends clause from the disposition report, even though you are completely certain that its inclusion would help mitigate the negative impact of the legal proceedings on your client's life. According to your professional ethics guidelines, that is simply not your call.

Imagine also that Max's home life lacks stability and healthy relationships. Perhaps he has only one parent at home and a couple of siblings who also require that single parent's attention, creating a lot of sibling rivalry. He struggles with feeling like he does not belong anywhere, but he feels a sense of belonging with this particular group of friends. So, Max has found the social acceptance and confidence in himself that he lacks at home in this group of young men, filling a basic human need, namely a sense of belonging. Unfortunately, with this affiliation comes susceptibility to antisocial behavior and rendering vulnerable his previously good legal standing. As a developing member of society, Max needs to fulfill his need for belonging somewhere, but he also needs to remain clear of criminal convictions in order to protect his future. It is easy to see how a juvenile defender might struggle with the conflicting-client-interests dilemma despite the professional rules. Any caring adult is likely to understand what a struggle this could be for a juvenile defender. At the same time, without the mandate that juvenile defenders treat juveniles the same as adults by prioritizing clients' *expressed* interests, they run the risk of confusing their clients with something like the following message:

> You are here in court because you broke a rule and society expects you to behave in certain ways that we adults tell you about because we know better and we want you to act like an adult, the way we do. I am also supposed to follow a

rule that requires me to do what you tell me to do because I am your lawyer and you can trust me, even though it is likely that you have been betrayed by other adults during your short life. If I don't agree with what you want me to do on your behalf, I am going to go ahead and do what I think is best anyway, even though doing so breaks the rule I am supposed to follow to help you and breaks your trust in me after I have assured you that I am your lawyer and will do what you ask of me (within the parameters of the law). You are just a kid. You don't know what you want and you don't matter. But, yes, you're supposed to follow rules, and now not only are you in trouble because you didn't follow the rules, but I am yet another adult who is not going to hear your voice and treat you like you matter because you're just a kid. So, after I've betrayed you by breaking my own rules and the rules of this court that we all expect you to comply with, society is going to expect you to still keep following rules and trusting adults after this is all over.

This is arguably the unspoken message juveniles processed in the court system receive when they have defenders who substitute their clients' interests with what they believe is best for their clients. One could also argue that juveniles end up in the court system as a result of inconsistent messages from other people about their personal worth or the worth of the rules by which members of society must play. Their commitment to group values is clearly already tenuous, so communicating to them this kind of message is certainly *not* going to increase their likelihood of committing to those values. In fact, it is likelier to *decrease* their commitment to group values. If we expect juveniles to adhere to the rules of society, it is incumbent upon us to make absolutely sure that those tasked with holding them accountable for their behavior are allowed and enabled to do the same as well. This is especially true when it comes to those tasked with giving juveniles voice to the system at large. The research at the heart of this book demonstrates very clearly that juvenile defenders' efforts to appropriately serve as their clients' voices to the justice system are often unnecessarily impeded. This reality naturally hampers the efficacy of the system itself, calling into question the system's credibility and legitimacy and raising the following questions: Do juveniles not deserve better? Can we not do better?

The conflicting-client-interests dilemma can be argued to represent quintessential role conflict for juvenile defenders since the clients themselves are the center of conflicting expectations and the defenders are obligated to prioritize the clients' *expressed* interests. The dilemma asks what happens when clients express an interest that is not what is best for them and they cannot be persuaded to change their interests. At this point juvenile defenders truly face a dilemma, especially once they take on their *advocate* role, where they are supposed to serve as the client's *voice* to the legal system. It is important to reiterate that this book's focus is on the advocate component of the juvenile defender role. Unlike when juvenile defenders inhabit their counselor role, while in the advocate role defenders are ethically required to defer to their clients' expressed wishes. Recall that in North Carolina, juvenile defenders are also required to treat their child clients the same as they would treat their adult clients. However, prior research and the present study demonstrate that this is not so easily accomplished and sometimes is not accomplished at all. Before addressing the research in more depth, however, further discussion of the juvenile defender role debate is necessary.

Again, a critical aspect of the juvenile defender role debate is the question of whether juvenile defenders should advocate for the *expressed* interests of their clients (prioritizing clients' expressed wishes), as required by the American Bar Association's *Model Rules of Professional Conduct*, or for clients' *best* interests (prioritizing what the defense attorney believes is best for his or her clients even if it conflicts with clients' expressed wishes), as do other juvenile court functionaries (Henning, 2005). This book directly addresses the role's meaning by examining juvenile defender interviews illustrating how defenders view their role and its requirements, particularly with regard to this expressed-/best-interests dichotomy.

Lawyers' professional behavior is governed by the *Model Rules of Professional Conduct* published by the American Bar Association. Its preamble states, "As advocate, a lawyer zealously asserts the *client's* [emphasis added] position under the rules of the adversary system" (ABA, 2013, pmbl. § 2). And Rule 1.2a states that "a lawyer shall abide by a client's decisions concerning the objectives of representation and, as required by Rule 1.4, shall consult with the client as to the means by which they are to be pursued." This rule also asserts, "A lawyer shall abide by a client's decision whether to settle a matter. In a criminal case, the lawyer shall abide by the client's decision, after consultation with the lawyer, as to a plea to be entered, whether to waive jury trial and whether the client will testify."

It seems clear that the *Model Rules* requires a lawyer to inform his or her clients of their options and the consequences of those options, but ultimately that attorney must advocate for clients' *stated* interests. In other words, the advocate function of the defense attorney role is to serve as the *client's* voice to the justice system. However, there is an added element of complexity when the client is a child who might not have the same maturity or decision-making capacity as an adult. Nevertheless, the *National Juvenile Defense Standards* indicates that juvenile defenders should also apply the *Model Rules'* mandates to their child clients. For example, Standard 1.2, "Elicit and Represent Client's Stated Interests," gives these guidelines:

a. Counsel may not substitute his or her own view of the client's best interests for those expressed by the client;

b. Counsel may not substitute a parent's interests or view of the client's best interests for those expressed by the client;

c. Where counsel believes that the client's directions will not achieve the best long-term outcome for the client, counsel must provide the client with additional information to help the client understand the potential outcomes and offer an opportunity to reconsider; and

d. If the client is not persuaded, counsel must continue to act in accordance with the client's *expressed* [emphasis added] interests throughout the course of the case. (National Juvenile Defense Center [NJDC], 2012, p. 18)

While there has been extensive discussion of the juvenile defender role and its requirements in the *legal* literature, there is little evidence of empirical investigation into this topic in the social science literature. Moreover, the existing empirical literature on the juvenile defender role is limited, for the most part, to descriptive accounts of rates and types of representation (such as public defender, contract counsel, retained counsel; see, e.g., Feld, 1988; Green & Dohrn, 1995); ABA/NJDC assessments of the nature and quality of representation in several states, with samples and methodology described only superficially (Puritz & Sterling, 2010); and more sophisticated multivariate analyses of the impact of representation on juvenile case outcomes (Burruss & Kempf-Leonard, 2002; Feld, 1988). The present investigation fills a critical gap in the social science literature by directly addressing the juvenile defender role and examining role incumbents' lived experiences.

Scholars have frequently observed that juvenile defenders are confused about their role (Henning, 2005; Puritz & Sterling; 2010; Scali, Tandy, Michel, & Pauluhn, 2013), that their role tends to be constrained by other courtroom actors, and that, as a result, they tend to be marginal players in the courtroom (Stapleton & Teitelbaum, 1972; ABA Juvenile Center & New England Juvenile Defender Center, 2003; Grindall & Puritz, 2003; Puritz & Sterling; 2010; Scali et al., 2013). The current literature also refers to *role conflict* among juvenile defenders. Role conflict has been defined in the organizational literature as "a situation that results when role expectations are inconsistent, as when a supervisor sends employees mixed messages about their roles" (Levy,

2010, p. 292). For instance, imagine you are a juvenile defender representing a young man of fourteen who has been charged with drug possession (see the "James" vignette in appendix E). During the course of your short-lived case preparation, you discover that James is an addict. You know James needs treatment for his addiction but can afford it only if he is adjudicated delinquent or responsible. You also discover that the evidence collected against him was illegally obtained. You know there is a good chance that a motion to suppress the illegally obtained evidence would succeed and James could go free, but if it does, James will not get treatment for his addiction. Your professional rules of ethics expect you to file the motion to suppress, unless James does not want it. If James properly understands your role, he will expect you to file the motion to suppress by virtue of the fact that he has expressed a desire for you to do so. The prosecutor, judge, and court counselor (social worker/probation officer/court professional who is tasked with discerning the juvenile's best interests) all expect you to help James get treatment for his addiction. You might even feel *internal* role conflict as you consider your ethical duties to serve as James's voice and your role as an experienced adult who would naturally like to help a child in need. These role expectations are inconsistent and are likely to present you with *role conflict*.

There has been very little focused and systematic investigation of the extent to which juvenile defenders experience role conflict, how they respond to it, and how it affects the quality of their representation. The present study seeks to remedy this lack by investigating role meaning and the nature, extent, and impact of role conflict among juvenile defenders who practice in a jurisdiction where their role is clearly defined, presumably eliminating role confusion that might lead to role conflict.

This study seeks to examine the juvenile defender *advocate* role and role conflict by analyzing qualitative data systematically gathered from a sample of active role incumbents (juvenile defenders). Understanding how juvenile defenders define their role and experience and cope with role conflict provides valuable insights into the role in the context of the modern-day juvenile court. It also provides insights about the juvenile justice system, especially with regard to its role in upholding juveniles' due process rights. These insights have important implications for the training, policy, and practice of juvenile court functionaries and for the efficacy, credibility, and legitimacy of the juvenile justice system itself.

1. History of the Juvenile Defender Role

*W*hen considering why the right to counsel exists, one might summon up images of the hapless victims of the Salem witch trials in colonial New England. A number of individuals, mostly women, were adjudicated guilty and summarily executed on mere suspicion of "cavorting with the devil" (e.g., taking a walk in the woods, having a mole on their torsos, disagreeing with a town elder) (Rosenthal, 1995). Hindsight, a handy thing called social science, and sociopolitical progress have allowed us to reflect on this period in American history to see how defenseless these convicted "witches" were. Even now it is easy to see how vulnerable anyone would be without the assistance of counsel to help respond to criminal charges. More recent examples can be drawn from cases taken on by the Innocence Project, a widely recognized nonprofit legal organization dedicated to exonerating wrongfully convicted individuals, often through discrediting eyewitness testimony or by applying new technical advances (such as DNA testing) to previously collected evidence. Even though the American justice system is designed to prevent innocent people from getting punished, they still get punished. The justice system is a powerful machine, and most people are neither criminal procedure experts nor skilled enough to engage in an adversarial contest with criminal procedure experts (the prosecutor and criminal court judge) on their own. One could therefore argue that any adult brought to a criminal court's attention is vulnerable. The same could be said for juveniles in this position, but incredibly more so.

Because of US Supreme Court rulings like *Miranda v. Arizona* (1966) and the popular media, the constitutional right to the assistance of counsel for accused persons has become widely recognized. Specifically, two of the *Miranda* warning's four components address the right to counsel. While the first two parts address the right to remain silent, the third informs arrestees that they have the right to counsel, and the fourth informs them that if they cannot afford counsel, it will be appointed to them by the government (*Miranda v. Arizona*, 1966). This warning is so well known, due to its frequent use in the media and the popularity of stories in the justice genre, that a recent Supreme Court case addressed the question of whether it was still necessary for law enforcement agents to articulate it (*Dickerson v. United States*, 2000). The Court ultimately decided that the *Miranda* warning was still necessary to communicate basic rights to those in police custody and subject to police questioning, so it is likely that the right to counsel will continue to play a large role in popular media as well as in justice system practice.

Despite this wide recognition of the right to counsel, a large gap still appears to exist between those entitled to the assistance of counsel and those who actually receive assistance of counsel, particularly when it comes to juvenile defendants (referred to hereinafter as "respondents" to reflect the juvenile court culture). Even though *access* to counsel for juveniles does not squarely fall within the scope of this book, a discussion of the role of counsel is incomplete without acknowledging that access to counsel is an issue. This is particularly true because much of what is known about juvenile respondents' access to counsel has revealed critical information about the current meaning of the juvenile defender role. As with many justice system practitioners, the juvenile defender role has seen changes over the course of time. Unfortunately, the changes have not been sufficient for the role to fully meet its intended potential.

The role of counsel for juveniles has been a source of confusion and controversy throughout the juvenile justice system's short history. What began as an informal process over a century ago and involved a judge who put himself in the shoes of the parents, doling out *rehabilitative*—not punitive—guidance to children and their parents, did not even include legal counsel (Mennel, 1972). In contrast, the juvenile justice system in the twenty-first century involves more punishment outcomes and encompasses more previously dismissed behaviors than ever before (Birckhead, 2010). Given the progress made in applying due process rights to adults facing criminal charges, particularly with regard to the right to counsel (*Gideon v. Wainwright*, 1963), one might expect the same to be true for juvenile respondents. Unfortunately, reality does not match this expectation, and modern assessments of juvenile respondents' access to counsel indicate that such access is still sorely lacking.

More specifically, the defense counsel role for juveniles was not officially recognized as valuable or necessary until the mid-1960s, more than half a century after the juvenile court system was established. In fact, it was not recognized until five years after adults' right to counsel was established. Furthermore, despite the landmark *In re Gault* ruling (1967) officially recognizing the role as important and necessary, and more than fifty years of practice, the role still appears to be not only misunderstood but also viewed as somewhat superfluous (see, e.g., Grindall & Puritz, 2003).

Juvenile Justice Origins

Considering that the Sixth Amendment right to counsel for a criminal defendant does not attach until the minute the government begins adversarial proceedings against an arrestee, the following history will focus on the post-arrest period. This period begins with arraignment, when formal charges are read to the defendant, and ends with the disposition or sentencing phase (*Powell v. Alabama*, 1932). Even though the widely recognized *Miranda* warning provides that an arrestee has the right to counsel once he or she is in custodial interrogation (i.e., does not feel free to leave police custody and is subjected to police questioning), this right is not automatic as it is during adversarial proceedings (*Miranda v. Arizona*, 1966). Police custodial interrogation occurs as part of an *investigation* where the arrestee's involvement in criminal activity is still in question; in other words, the state has not yet elected to press charges. So, during custodial interrogation an arrestee must ask for an attorney but can choose to informally engage in custodial interrogation without one. Once charges are formally read, the Sixth Amendment right to counsel automatically attaches, and defendants should have counsel present (*Powell v. Alabama*, 1932).

The juvenile defender role was not a part of the first juvenile court in the United States when it opened in 1899 (Mennel, 1972). Before that time, youths accused of criminal acts were treated like adults; they were presumed to be rational actors who had chosen to commit a crime and were therefore as culpable as adults for their misdeeds. So, clearly there was no place for a juvenile advocate before the original juvenile courts were established (Mennel, 1972). There was presumably no consideration of the child's brain development, cognitive ability, nutrition, or parenting style. There would also have been no trips to the principal's office, no school resource officer, and no diversion programs (e.g., to divert youthful offenders from the juvenile justice system; Shelden, 1999), such as there are in many jurisdictions today.

During the juvenile court system's initial development, social reformers embraced the notion that juvenile offenders were immature, vulnerable, and malleable (Bishop & Feld, 2012). They also viewed juvenile crime as caused by factors over which the offender had no control, such as neglectful parenting and exposure to deviant role models. These ideas—that young offenders were immature, that their offending was largely a function of external influences, and that corrective treatment could effect a cure—provided the philosophical foundation for the juvenile court (Bishop & Feld, 2012). This philosophical foundation is referred to as *parens patriae*—the state as parent—and was conceived as a protective and benevolent institution serving the best interests of the child (Platt, 1977).

In the parens patriae scheme, where the child is viewed as in need of the court to serve as a benevolent parent substitute, there seemed to be no need for the assistance of counsel or other due process protections since the ultimate goal of the court was rehabilitative, not punitive (Birckhead, 2010). In fact, the central feature of the juvenile hearing was a casual conversation between the judge, the youth, and his or her parents, which has been described as "a combination of instruction, lecture, and counseling" (p. 971). The child was questioned by the judge and encouraged to talk freely so that the court might gain insight into his or her problems and needs. The judge was assisted in that effort by the probation officer, who might tell the judge what the child (unrepresented) and the parents had revealed during intake interviews. Not surprisingly, "judges evinced active hostility to the participation of lawyers" (Feld, 1999, p. 68). And, "although judges could not banish a lawyer from the courtroom altogether, they did not consider his presence either appropriate or necessary" (Rothman, 1980, p. 216). This hostility is no surprise given that the court was initially not so concerned with a determination of the child's guilt or innocence through an adversarial process; instead, the court preferred a process that was much more casual, administrative, and inquisitorial (Birckhead, 2010).

For nearly three-quarters of a century the juvenile court had functioned largely unnoticed, without successful challenge to the constitutionality of its loose standards and lack of regularized procedures. This came to an end in the 1960s and early 1970s when the US Supreme Court recognized that the juvenile court's rhetoric of compassionate care was in stark contrast to the arbitrary and punitive realities of its practices (Bishop & Feld, 2012).

In the landmark decision *In re Gault* (1967), the Supreme Court described the lawless and unbridled discretion of the juvenile judges as "a poor substitute for principle and procedure," likely to result in arbitrary adjudications of delinquency and loss of liberty (pp. 18–19). The Court ruled that, in light of the liberty interests at stake ("comparable in seriousness to a felony prosecution," p. 36), any child facing the prospect of incarceration was entitled to a panoply of criminal procedural rights—the right to notice of the charges against him or her, the right to counsel, the privilege against self-incrimination, the right to compulsory process (e.g., to have witnesses subpoenaed), the right to confront and cross-examine adversarial witnesses—in order to ensure accurate fact-finding and to protect the child from erroneous conviction. Importantly, the Court observed that children needed counsel in order "to cope with the problems of law, to make skilled inquiry into the facts, to insist upon regularity of the proceedings, and to ascertain whether [they have] a defense and to prepare and submit it" (p. 36).

In re Gault established a right to counsel for juveniles, but it did not specify exactly what that role should entail. Since the Court was silent on these details, one might have assumed the Court's intent to create the exact same protections for juveniles as had been created for adults. However, the 1971 Supreme Court decision *McKeiver v. Pennsylvania* cast doubt on this assumption. In *McKeiver*, the Court was asked to extend the right to a jury trial to juvenile respondents. It declined to do so, asserting that, although fundamental fairness demanded accurate fact-finding, this could be ensured as well by a judge as by a jury. In contrast to its decision in *Gault*, the *McKeiver* court revived the image of the sympathetic, paternalistic juvenile court judge and disregarded concerns that juvenile courts' best-interests orientation could compromise accurate fact-finding (Feld, 2012, p. 679). Fearful that the addition of the right to a jury trial "might well destroy the traditional character of juvenile court proceedings" (*McKeiver*, 1971, p. 540, quoting the Pennsylvania court), the US Supreme Court refused to extend the right to jury trial in order that juvenile courts might remain "informal enough to permit the benefits of the juvenile system to operate" (p. 539, quoting the Pennsylvania court).

The *McKeiver* decision likely created a great deal of confusion for juvenile defenders. It appeared to recognize that due process protections for juvenile respondents were not *exactly* the same as for adult defendants. It also endorsed the value of the parens patriae orientation, possibly further obscuring the already unclear juvenile defender role. This pair of decisions seems to have sent juvenile defenders a mixed message: juvenile court should be like adult court in terms of due process protections, such as the right to counsel, but should retain its informal, paternalistic approach in terms of the fact finder. The confusion surrounding the true definition of the juvenile defender role is not unlike that surrounding defense attorneys who represent the mentally ill. Cohen describes these advocates as "stranger[s] in a strange land without benefit of guidebook, map, or dictionary" (1965, p. 424). The result for both types of clients could be the same: "free citizens of a free country are frequently deprived of their liberty for [sometimes] an indefinite duration" (p. 424). Considering the impressionable nature of juveniles and their vulnerable social standing, this result could have disastrous long-term effects for them.

Defining the Juvenile Defender Role

Legal scholars have criticized the Supreme Court for failing to adequately define the role of counsel for juveniles (e.g., Fedders, 2010). In reaffirming the parens patriae model, the 1971 *McKeiver* court seemed to actively encourage the paternalistic bent of juvenile court judges and court functionaries. This raises an important question: What role must defense counsel play in a system that embraces punitive outcomes but remains at least nominally committed to serving the *best* interests of the child?

The Supreme Court in its *Gault* decision did not define the juvenile defender role (Shepard & Volenik, 1987), leaving juvenile defenders to wonder how they were supposed to navigate the best-interests orientation of the court while serving in what was officially an expressed-interests advocate role. For instance, were they supposed to explain the proceedings to child clients in a largely disinterested and objective manner? Serve as independent advocates for the best interests of the child (i.e., the guardian ad litem function)? Serve in the exact same capacity as criminal defense attorneys for adults, working to minimize the probability and severity of coercive state intervention? Advocate for child clients' expressed interests (that is, what the child expressly states that he or she wants), even if these interests conflicted with defenders' view of what was in child clients' best interests? Advocate for their clients' expressed interests at every stage of the proceedings, or shift to best-interests advocacy at a particular stage (such as at sentencing)?

Even though each of these functions had been identified as the most appropriate for juvenile defenders as of the early 1980s (Shepard & Volenik, 1987), a professional and academic consensus has since developed. Juvenile defenders are expected to act as zealous advocates for the *expressed* interests of their clients at *all* stages of the juvenile process (Henning, 2005). This means that, as far as the juvenile defense attorney's advocate role is concerned, the child's stated wishes are paramount, and the defense attorney, as the child's zealous advocate, is ethically obligated to use any legal means necessary to advocate for those expressed interests.

Zealous advocacy is the standard that attorneys are expected to meet when representing their clients (Schmidt, Reppucci, & Woolard, 2003). It requires the attorney to encourage the client to actively participate in the trial process by making decisions about the direction of his or her case with the attorney's guidance. The zealous advocacy model presumes client capacity, or "adjudicative competence" (p. 176), and relies on children's capacity to participate in legal situations beyond mere "legal competence" (p. 177). Adjudicative competence requires that a client be able to "understand and consult with his/her attorney, factually and rationally understand the charges against him/her, and aid his/her lawyer in creating the defense" (p. 176). However, effective participation involves abilities beyond adjudicative competence, such as the ability to make decisions, "foresee the consequences of multiple options," and weigh these options' "probability of occurrence and subjective desirability in making a decision" (p. 176, citing Grisso, 1997). The extent to which children have adjudicative competence and can effectively participate in their own defense is a critical question when it comes to juvenile defense. Yet despite its importance, this particular question is beyond the scope of the present study, which focuses on the manifestations and impact of role conflict on the role incumbents as opposed to their clients.

A Call for Justice (Puritz, Burrell, Schwartz, Soler, & Warboys, 1996/2002), a joint report of the ABA Juvenile Justice Center, the Juvenile Law Center, and the Youth Law Center, reveals an expectation of zealous (expressed-interest) advocacy for juvenile defenders. According to Henning (2005), this expectation is also a point of consensus among "numerous scholars and leaders in the juvenile justice community" (p. 246).

Despite this consensus, studies have shown that the right to counsel has been implemented unevenly both among the states and across counties within states ("A Call for Justice," Puritz et al., 1996, as cited in Puritz et al., 2002). Courts in many jurisdictions have been shown to actively discourage juveniles from invoking their right to counsel, either by telling them that they do not need counsel because nothing of consequence will happen to them or by assuring them that the judge will look after their interests (Puritz et al., 1996/2002). For example, Feld's study of rates of juvenile representation in Minnesota revealed that rural counties had rates of representation as low as 19 percent, while large urban jurisdictions appointed counsel for juveniles at rates of 90 percent or greater (1989). In addition, the quality of representation has often been shown to be poor. A possible indication of the low quality of counsel can be seen from Lawrence (1983), who surveyed juvenile defense attorneys and found that 61 percent reported spending a total of two hours or less on case preparation.

In 1993, the ABA's Juvenile Justice Center conducted a national assessment of access to counsel and quality of representation for juveniles. The report, "A Call for Justice," indicated that numerous dedicated attorneys labored under tremendous systemic burdens—such as very high caseloads—that compromised their ability to provide quality representation to youth. Many attorneys rarely filed pretrial motions, and a number of them avoided post-dispositional issues entirely (Puritz et al., 1996/2002). Two early in-depth studies of juvenile court proceedings showed that trials were rare and most were "marginally contested" and marked by "lackadaisical defense efforts—including making few objections, rarely calling defense witnesses, perfunctory cross-examination of prosecution witnesses, and either no, or very sketchy, closing arguments" (Ainsworth, 1990, pp. 1127–1128, citing a Boston assessment by Finkelstein, Weiss, Cohen, & Fisher, 1973, and a New York assessment by Knitzer & Sobie, 1984). The New York assessment estimated that only 5 percent of all juvenile trials involved what could be considered "effective representation" by defense attorneys (Moss, 1987, p. 29).

The quality of legal representation for juveniles is influenced by many factors, including the poorly delineated role of defense counsel. However, even in jurisdictions where the role is very clearly defined, it is likely that role confusion and conflict still exist and affect quality of counsel. These issues were central to this study.

This chapter has been primarily concerned with illustrating the background against which the juvenile defender's role operates and how it has come to exist. In brief review, the earliest versions of the juvenile justice system did not have a place for juvenile defenders. The process of making a young person officially accountable for his or her offending behaviors was relatively informal. In addition, the outcome involved the provision of paternal guidance for the child and his or her parents, not punishment. Given the US Supreme Court's reasoning behind the conditions necessary to trigger the right to counsel (*In re Gault*, 1967), such as the possibility of government-administered punishment, it makes sense that early juvenile courts overlooked the need for defense counsel. However, as the juvenile court judges increasingly applied punishments to juvenile respondents, the need for defense counsel became more and more apparent. This was especially true once *In re Gault* was decided. A main area of concern for juvenile justice policy analysts, practitioners, and researchers is that half a century after this landmark case, juveniles still do not have access to effective assistance of counsel. Again, even though this gap in counsel is not the central focus of this book, it is a key component of its primary concern, the role conflict that juvenile defenders experience. Chapter 2 addresses the current nature of the juvenile defender role as well of some of the stumbling blocks its incumbents face.

2. The Modern-Day Juvenile Defender

Do you remember the last time you started a new job? Or, perhaps starting a new job is something that lies in your future. How long did it take you to fully learn the different facets of your new role? What information about your new role did you bring to your first day, and how long was it before something happened or someone said something that contradicted your expectations of your new role? When you start your next new role, how will you handle it when what you expect your role to entail is contradicted by what other people tell you your role entails? And, what if the expectations others have of you in your role conflict with each other? What if these others have relatively equal authority over you? How easily will you decide whose expectations to meet? Will you experience any negative effects as a result of the conflicting expectations?

Any time someone begins a new job, that person and his or her supervisor must reasonably expect the newcomer to undergo a learning curve. This means a delay between the individual's first day on the job and when he or she is able to expertly carry out the job's tasks. Naturally, part of what is responsible for this delay is the difference in skill level and familiarity with the position's parameters and duties. Another factor that plays into this delay is the difference between the newcomer's *expectations* of the job and the job's *realities*. This book is, in large part, about the *mismatch between expectations and realities* of the juvenile defense attorney role.

Try to imagine what it would be like to engage in a professional endeavor to which you have dedicated several years, and likely several thousands of dollars, only to have what you expected to be true about your position turn out to be incorrect. Naturally, there is a certain amount of unmet expectations in every professional role. But, imagine if the gap between your expectations and the reality of your role were partly due to others' misunderstanding of your role and that their misunderstanding unnecessarily interfered with your success in your role. Worse yet, imagine that this unnecessary interference cost the future chances of survival of some of society's most vulnerable citizens, a result you likely worked very hard to avoid. Or, imagine the interference reduced your chances of positively influencing a life that appeared, at the very least, to be going in the wrong direction. In practical terms, it is possible the interference even contributed to recidivism (in other words, reoffending) of juvenile offenders, if it reduced the effectiveness of juvenile defense attorneys who are supposed to lend credibility to the justice system by serving as a check on state power abuses. In order to fully consider these questions, a close examination of the current role of these attorneys is in order.

The literature on the juvenile defender role largely consists of legal analyses and is often focused on the ongoing debate about the *type* of advocacy that juvenile defenders should provide for their clients. The traditional zealous (that is, expressed-interests) advocacy model is endorsed by many leading juvenile justice figures and scholars (Birckhead, 2010; Buss, 1995, 1998; Guggenheim, 1984; Henning, 2005; Marrus, 2003; Mlyniec, 1995; Stranger, 1996). Moreover, by the early 1980s, a professional consensus had developed that defense attorneys owe their juvenile clients the same duty of loyalty they owe their adult clients (again, expressed-interests advocacy) (Henning, 2005). Attorneys' professional rules of conduct clearly support the expressed-interests advocate model. As described in the introduction, section 2 of the preamble to the American Bar Association's *Model Rules of Professional Conduct* states, "As advocate, a lawyer zealously asserts the *client's* position [emphasis added] under the rules of the adversary system" (ABA, 2013). And, as previously stated, the *National Juvenile Defense Standards*, specifically Standard 1.2, requires attorneys to do the same for their juvenile clients (NJDC, 2012).

If you are a juvenile brought to the attention of the juvenile justice system for having committed an act that society deems so offensive that your behavior requires formal scrutiny, in order for the justice system to be effective, you need to be able to buy into the idea that society's rules are worth following and that society is correct in requiring you to follow them. The justice system must have legitimacy and credibility in your eyes, or you will not learn your lesson from your experience in the justice system, regardless of whether you receive a second chance (rehabilitation) or punishment. In other words, when you are brought under the scrutiny of the justice system and told that you have an advocate, someone who will serve *you* as *your voice* to the court, there is a good chance that the system will cease to have legitimacy and credibility in your eyes if that one person standing in for you does not actually assert *your* interests but substitutes his or her own views of what he or she thinks your interests should be instead. You might feel rather dismissed as a person, something you might already feel and which might have contributed to what brought you to the justice system's attention to begin with. What is more, you are unlikely to benefit from the system that you find lacks credibility and ultimately might not contribute to its mission of preventing your recidivism.

Zealous advocacy of the client's interests is what adult defendants are expected to receive and for the reasons herein described. Despite the fact that juveniles are less experienced than adults and might not fully understand the world enough to know what their interests are, if the justice system breaks its promise to provide them with an advocate, a voice, for their interests, juveniles are unlikely to grow a sense of faith in the justice system. They are likewise apt to reinforce their own conclusion that society's rules are not worth following because society itself is not doing so.

Now that there is a clear idea of what the role for juvenile defenders is *supposed* to be, it is critical to point out that the role is not carried out in a vacuum. Naturally, it is carried out among other juvenile justice system practitioners, including one—the prosecutor—whose specific goal it is to compete with the juvenile defender in an adversarial contest. However, the challenges a juvenile defender faces in carrying out his or her role do not always come only from the prosecutor, and when they do, they are not always limited to the bounds of an adversarial contest.

Duty versus Context

Notwithstanding the modern trend of information processing and telecommuting, nearly all professional roles exist in some kind of context that presumably supports the role and its goals. It is not unreasonable to assume a criminal court functions in the same way. The purpose of this court is to provide a forum in which formalized procedures ensure that an adversarial contest results in an outcome establishing the extent of an individual's legal responsibility for his or her alleged criminal behaviors. As will be emphasized throughout this book, juvenile defenders appear to encounter unexpected tensions between their role duties and the context in which they carry out their duties.

What happens when the context appears to lack support for, or even seems to purposely interfere with, the professional role's intended purpose? This question represents this book's general foundation. What happens if a juvenile court's practitioners, particularly the judge, exhibit hostility or unnecessary resistance to the efforts of the one practitioner who is constitutionally mandated and who is responsible for ensuring due process? Does this hostility persist even more than half a century after the US Supreme Court firmly established juveniles' right to counsel? Scholarly investigations into this question covering the last thirty years reveal that, unfortunately, it is.

Not many empirical investigations into the question of access to counsel for juveniles exist, and even fewer address the extent to which juvenile defenders encounter hostility toward their efforts to carry out their duties. Naturally, it takes time for new justice policies to filter through to the courts after they have been established, so this literature examination draws from work published as early as 1970 (Fox), a mere three years after the *In re Gault* decision. Unfortunately, investigations into juveniles' access to counsel from the 1980s and 1990s and into the new century uncovered the same problems.

A simple key-term search for juvenile justice literature easily reveals Barry C. Feld as a prolific scholar on a variety of related issues, including access to counsel. He has noted a large number of unrepresented youth and "continuing judicial hostility to an advocacy role" in what are referred to as traditional rehabilitation-oriented, or parens patriae, juvenile courts (1993, p. 223). In 1988 he argued that in the twenty years since the *Gault* decision, the "promise of legal representation remains unrealized" (p. 394). Even when juveniles had counsel, effectiveness was often compromised by various factors, including "role ambiguity created by the dual goals of rehabilitation and punishment" (1993, p. 225). It is important to note here that role *ambiguity* relates more to role expectations that are not clearly defined, whereas role *conflict* refers to clearly defined but conflicting role expectations. Several scholars suggest that counsel's role is compromised by such factors as the judge's hostility toward adversarial (defense) attorneys, defense attorneys' internalization of the court's rehabilitation mission, and pressures to be cooperative emanating from others in the courtroom (Clarke & Koch, 1980; Feld, 1989; Fox, 1970).

More recent work by Kristin Henning, also a prolific juvenile justice scholar, particularly with regard to legal nuances and ramifications, includes a discussion of the disparity between policy and practice in the juvenile courts. She identifies a "deeply entrenched history of paternalism in the juvenile justice system" as a source of attorney role conflict (2005, p. 260). In discussing the expert impressions of legal scholars and the findings of seven state assessments, she reflects that even defense attorneys who want to respect the expressed interests of their clients are confronted with "tremendous systemic opposition from judges, prosecutors, and probation officers who expect defense counsel to participate as part of the juvenile justice team" (p. 260, citing Stewart et al., 2000 [TX]).[1]

Juvenile defenders might experience this opposition, particularly from a judge who is essentially their de facto supervisor, when they insist on arguing against a component of the disposition report. Recall the example of the forbidden-friends clause from the introduction. Imagine that despite this defender's best efforts to be heard on behalf of his client, the judge summarily cuts him off during his argument and expresses overt hostility toward the defender's other clients in future cases. Since many juvenile defenders also represent adult clients and in some jurisdictions face the same judge for different cases, this kind of scenario is not entirely improbable. The extent to which scenarios like this occur is unclear based on the existing research, making the present study all the more necessary. However, the extant research has recognized that juvenile defenders do actually depart from their role and has suggested three major contributing factors: (1) the stage of the juvenile justice process at which juvenile defenders are viewed as most likely to depart from their role (that is, the sentencing phase, where the court's rehabilitative mission most runs counter to juvenile defenders' expressed interests), (2) role ambiguity or confusion (where juvenile defenders are unclear about their duties), and (3) pressure from the court culture for defenders to abandon their expressed-interests duties in favor of the court's best-interests approach (where the court context interferes with the juvenile defenders' duties).

The Disposition (Sentencing) Stage

The juvenile justice process follows a progression of steps similar to that of the adult system. However, it differs in ways that are reflected in the nature and language of the proceedings. A major difference can be seen in how a juvenile comes to the justice system's attention in the first place. For instance, when a law enforcement officer (such as a school resource officer) files a petition against a juvenile alleging that he or she has committed a criminal act, the juvenile may be either "detained" (R. Waldrop Rugh, personal communication, July 27, 2016) instead of arrested or diverted from the court using something referred to as a "behavior contract" (Participant 011). This behavior contract provides for the juvenile to engage in services that are deemed necessary by juvenile justice professionals, typically the court counselor (the equivalent of a juvenile social worker or probation officer). To be sure, one of the major differences between the adult and juvenile justice systems is that the juvenile has a higher chance of being diverted from court and provided with necessary services; in other words, a juvenile facing charges for an offense does not always mean he or she will go to court (Participant 011). However, if the juvenile does not comply with the diversion's conditions (the behavior contract), the charges that resulted from the petition will come to the court to be prosecuted (Participant 011).

The very first step in bringing a juvenile to the juvenile justice system's attention typically involves some form of *intake*. However, if a juvenile is charged with an offense and does not get diversion, a petition to bring the juvenile to the attention of the court system is filed, which serves to establish the jurisdiction of the court over the juvenile, notify the juvenile's parents, identify the reason for the court appearance, and officially charge the minor with an offense. Once the petition has been filed, the next two major stages are adjudication and disposition (R. Waldrop Rugh, personal communication, July 27, 2016).

A defense attorney might come into the picture during the period of time between the filing of the petition with the court and the adjudication hearing. In some jurisdictions—like North Carolina—where juveniles are automatically considered indigent, the court, as a matter of course, will appoint counsel to juveniles for whom a petition is filed. If a juvenile's parents prefer to pay for an attorney themselves, they can retain counsel with an attorney of their choice. Otherwise, the defense attorney will be notified of the appointment and must undertake efforts to procure information regarding the petition and his or her new client. Gaining access to new clients can be a challenge for some defense attorneys for a number of reasons that run the spectrum from a client's lack of personal transportation to a client's being officially detained. While beyond the scope of this book, defense attorneys' access to their juvenile clients is currently a very controversial, and worthy, topic. Nevertheless, juvenile defenders do what they can to communicate with their clients in order to prepare them for adjudication.

During adjudication, like during a trial, the court expects to hear from both the prosecutor and the defense attorney a version of events surrounding the offense for which the juvenile has been charged. Each will present evidence and/or witnesses to the court addressing the respondent's responsibility (R. Waldrop Rugh, personal communication, July 27, 2016). Unlike in adult court, the juvenile judge will also expect to receive a sentencing, or disposition, report from the one juvenile court practitioner with no real parallel in the adult court system: the juvenile probation officer, or court counselor.

The court counselor is a juvenile court workgroup member responsible for focusing on the best interests of the juvenile respondent and relaying to the court for the purposes of disposition what he or she believes are recommendations that take into account the best interests of the child. Judges are known to rely heavily on the court counselor's report, presumably in large part because this professional's main focus is getting to know the child and delving into the child's life in order to determine what factors contributed to the offending behaviors. The court counselor is also tasked with being well versed in available remedies for any number of issues juvenile respondents might face so that he or she can adeptly make recommendations in the disposition report. This practitioner is typically college educated and might have a background in criminal justice and/ or social work (R. Waldrop Rugh, personal communication, July 27, 2016).

Finally, the disposition stage occurs after the judge has adjudicated the child as responsible for the charges listed in the petition. This is typically viewed as the final stage of the juvenile justice process. Although adjudication *could* be appealed after the case is over, appeals for juvenile cases do not happen often (Participant 011). During this stage the judge, pursuant to the rehabilitative mission of the juvenile justice system, will take into consideration the seriousness of the juvenile's offense, the circumstances surrounding the events leading up to the offense, and the factors believed to play a role in the juvenile's life and decision-making behaviors. To this end, the judge will rely, often heavily, on the court counselor's report. The judge will also consider any additional information provided by the victim, the juvenile's family members, and the juvenile himself or herself. Finally, the judge will sentence the juvenile to a set of conditions by which he or she must move forward in order to make up for the offense. Examples include maintaining a C average in school, performing a set number of hours of public service, adhering to a curfew, undergoing psychological or substance abuse therapy, paying a set amount of money to a victim as restitution, or, in more serious cases, serving a set number of months/years in a juvenile detention center.

The disposition phase presumably reflects the rehabilitative mission of the juvenile justice system by "sentencing" juveniles to experiences that provide them with opportunities to learn from their mistakes and improve their decision-making skills. However, the juvenile justice literature indicates that, especially since the 1990s, this mission has been largely forsaken for a more punitive one that mirrors the adult justice system (Birckhead, 2010; Singer, 1997). Given this shift and the US Supreme Court's recognition that punitive outcomes for anyone facing criminal charges merit the constitutionally guaranteed assistance of counsel throughout the justice process, ensuring that the juvenile defender role is carried out without unnecessary hindrance is more critical than ever. This is especially true when it comes to the disposition phase of the juvenile process. At the same time, because this phase was originally intended to embody the spirit of juvenile justice's rehabilitative mission, vestiges of this mission might create undue obstacles for juvenile defenders attempting to ethically carry out their duties. An examination of current scholarship addressing the disposition phase helps to clarify.

Legal scholars who have directly addressed the juvenile defender role have recognized the inconsistencies inherent in the role, the need for consensus about the role, and the role's unique challenges, one of which is confusion about the nature of the role at disposition. The argument that child respondents require the assistance of counsel during the adjudication process, where their legal responsibility, and possibly future, is determined might be more compelling than that supporting their need for a zealous advocate once they have been convicted. This is especially true if the court espouses a rehabilitative, or best interests of the child, mission. It is more difficult to argue that juvenile respondents, now convicted of an offense, still require the effective assistance of a zealous advocate at the disposition (sentencing) phase because the court espouses that it seeks only to provide the child with treatment for a problem that has come to the court's attention. Despite this difficulty, some legal scholars have deftly made this argument.

Legal scholars maintain that even at sentencing, juveniles still need someone to serve as their voice to the court; they also need to be able to make autonomous, though well-counseled, decisions about their cases. For examples, Fedders notes that juveniles do not enjoy a constitutional right to represent themselves, making the effective assistance of counsel when under the justice system's authority all the more critical (2012). Fedders points out that abdicating the authority to make these decisions to a parent or defender would devalue the rights themselves. This is another example of where *best-* and *expressed-*interests advocacy diverge. Juveniles need to make the decisions since they are the clients, but they are inexperienced and already presumably poor decision-makers, so having the counsel of an attorney is critical. Even though the disposition phase appears to be the end of the road for the juvenile justice process, it could be the beginning of a new road for the juvenile, an outcome intended by the system's espoused rehabilitative mission. That the system's *practiced* mission appears far more punitive makes the need for assistance of counsel at this phase even *more* important, not less.

Another way to examine the problem posed by the disposition phase is to examine some of the alternatives to prioritizing the juvenile's expressed interests. For instance, neither the juvenile respondent's parents nor the juvenile defender should be granted the authority to make the child's decisions for him or her, regardless of what these adults view is in the juvenile's best interests. Fedders argues that substituting the client's autonomous decision-making with parental or defender decision-making merely replaces the court's paternalism with another's (2012). This ultimately deprives the juvenile of his or her constitutional right to counsel *and* places the defender at odds with the ethical duty to advocate for the client's expressed interests. Practically speaking, it also prevents a critical development opportunity for juveniles to experience the empowerment of standing at the helm of their own fate while benefiting from the counsel and guidance of a seasoned adult. This is an experience juveniles might have missed out on in their tender years that, some could argue, possibly contributed to their poor decision-making to begin with.

Taking this last point to the next logical step implies a vicious cycle. Juveniles are presumably in front of the judge because they exercised poor decision-making. They are brought to the attention of the court so they can recognize they have acted inappropriately and are made aware that they must learn to make better decisions. Developmental psychology scholars widely recognize the diminished decision-making ability of young persons (Steinberg & Schwartz, 2000). The court's job, especially considering its rehabilitative mission, is not merely to point this out to juveniles. It is also not merely to mandate programs it deems appropriate for children to improve their behavior and decision-making. The court must also recognize that juveniles' time in court provides a *series of decision-making opportunities* designed to empower them to learn how to make good decisions. The defense attorney's job is to serve as the juveniles' guide, counselor, and voice to the court during this process. However, if the defender is expected to disregard clients' expressed wishes in favor of what he or she, or another adult, deems is in their best interests, the juveniles are deprived of this critical practice. Society is best served when justice systems work to reduce recidivism and when they have credibility and legitimacy. The disposition stage might be perceived as the last opportunity to communicate to the juveniles that while they have made some poor decisions requiring formal and official intervention, they are still members of our society worthy of all the constitutional rights and protections accorded adults. That message has the chance of leaving a lasting impression on juveniles given their potential for growth as they move forward.

Despite these arguments in favor of the need for a zealous advocate at the disposition stage of the juvenile justice process, and despite discernible recognition of this need in the legal scholarship, court decisions have not been so clearly supportive. For example, Henning discusses a confusing Illinois Court of Appeals decision (*In re RD*, 1986) that held that counsel for juvenile respondents must simultaneously advocate for clients' rights (i.e., client-directed, expressed-interest advocacy) yet propose dispositions (sentencing options) reflecting clients' best interests, whether or not those clients agree (2005). This decision supports the possibility that some attorneys and judges might view the proper role of defense counsel to be different at different stages of the juvenile process. This might be particularly true of the disposition stage, where the focus shifts from adjudication of responsibility (adversarial process) to determination of outcome (theoretically treatment, not punishment). This issue is discussed more fully in chapter 5.

Other contributing factors to the apparent gap in legal representation for juvenile respondents might involve the way the role itself is perceived. For instance, juvenile defenders might have mixed expectations about the role or might be confused about what is expected of them in the role. A brief discussion of the literature addressing these factors is essential.

Role Ambiguity and Confusion

The legal scholarship and a number of reports by various professional law organizations demonstrate that juvenile defenders exhibit a fair amount of role ambiguity and confusion. For example, the New York State Bar Association conducted an examination of the juvenile defender role in the mid-1980s (Knitzer & Sobie, 1984). It reported that despite the guidance provided in professional rules that lawyers should represent their clients' *expressed* interests, most lawyers serving juveniles defined their role as representing their clients' *best* interests (Moss, 1987). A disturbingly small percentage of attorneys, 15 percent, likened their role to that of a defense attorney for adults, as delineated in the professional rules (Moss, 1987). More recently, Buss (2000) has asserted that the current consensus is that juvenile defenders must take direction from their juvenile clients as if they were adults (expressed-interests advocacy). This consensus comes from the US Supreme Court and the delinquency bar (that is, lawyers' professional associations, like the American Bar Association or any state's bar association). However, as illustrated by the state assessments introduced earlier, juvenile courts in practice do not share this view (Buss, 2000). The professional consensus is clearly inconsistent with the juvenile court's rehabilitative mission and raises the question of whether lawyers' professional standards and the juvenile court's rehabilitative mission are ultimately irreconcilable. While not at the heart of the problem herein discussed, this possibility is briefly discussed in the chapters that follow.

Implications of Best-Interests Juvenile Defense

So, what is wrong with juvenile defenders taking a best-interests approach with their clients? Quite a bit, in fact. If the juvenile court system's rehabilitative orientation contributes to an expectation that defense attorneys must advocate for their clients' best interests, as appears to be the case in many jurisdictions, this expectation could place defense attorneys at odds with their ethical duties. However, little is known about juvenile defenders' experience of such an expectation or how it impacts their view and pursuit of zealous advocacy.

Juvenile defense attorneys face special challenges when they inhabit the traditional zealous (expressed-interests) advocate role with their clients because they operate in a system that prioritizes respondents' *best* interests. Even though the desire to push all juvenile justice practitioners into complying with the status quo of prioritizing a child's best interests might resonate with many at first blush, looking more deeply into the repercussions of falling in line with the juvenile court culture has serious ramifications for the child and the juvenile justice system itself. An example of a conflict between expressed and best interests is illustrative.

Recall the scenario where Max, the respondent, has been charged with shoplifting DVDs from Walmart. Imagine that he expresses to his counsel, whose professional duty requires her to advocate for her client's expressed interests, that he does not want to be barred from associating with the friends with whom he was arrested for shoplifting. Imagine that the court counselor assigned to the case has written a report suggesting that the juvenile not associate with these particular friends in order to avoid their presumably bad influence. This is an especially important component of the court counselor's report if the respondent's defense is that he was merely following the crowd at the time of the offense. Based on the court counselor's recommendation and the respondent's proffered defense, the court might include a forbidden-friends clause in its disposition plan.

In her traditional zealous advocate role, the defense attorney assumes her client has the capacity to consider and articulate his own interests. She also must have fulfilled her counselor role by presenting and explaining all relevant options and anticipated outcomes to her client. If Max, after having been counseled, still will not agree to the forbidden-friends component of the plea agreement, the defense attorney *must* advocate for its removal, even if she believes those friends are a bad influence on Max and it is in Max's best interests not to associate with them.

In this scenario the juvenile defender faces two alternatives to requesting removal of the forbidden-friends clause—one that does not violate her ethical mandate of zealous advocacy and one that does. The juvenile defender could consider that Max's lack of experience in life and court prevents him from seeing the situation realistically. She might then, as part of her counselor function, attempt to convince him to reconsider his position regarding his friends or strongly urge him to accept the judge's recommendation to include the forbidden-friends clause. As long as she ultimately pushes to have the clause removed if Max is *not* persuaded, she is still complying with her ethical duties. However, she is not complying with them if she disregards Max's wishes altogether and accepts the disposition plan as is when Max makes his disapproval evident. This would be the epitome of a best-interests approach to this particular scenario, and her behavior would *not* comport with a zealous advocate's duties because she has not advocated for his expressed interests.

If the defense attorney were to take a best-interests role in this situation, she would be substituting *her* idea of her client's interests for his expressed interests. She would be in violation of her ethical duty to provide Max with zealous advocacy of his expressed interests, essentially weakening the impact of her role and his due process protections. Ethical dilemmas like these might be unique to juvenile defenders and can occur as a result of the mixed messages juvenile defenders receive about their role. Exploring how juvenile defenders view their role and experience role conflict is central to this book. In order to assist the reader in visualizing the nature of the juvenile defender role, it is essential to discuss modern-day state reports.

State Assessments of the Juvenile Defender Role

Throughout the course of the last fourteen years, access to and quality of legal representation for juveniles has been assessed in twenty-one states. These assessments were conducted by the ABA's Juvenile Justice Center or by the National Juvenile Defender Center in the following states: Colorado, Florida, Georgia, Illinois, Indiana, Kentucky, Louisiana, Maine, Maryland, Mississippi, Missouri, Montana, Nebraska, North Carolina, Ohio, Pennsylvania, South Carolina, Texas, Virginia, Washington, and West Virginia. They were conducted to (1) determine whether youth in the selected jurisdictions had "meaningful access to counsel in delinquency proceedings," (2) "highlight systemic barriers to quality representation," and (3) "provide recommendations for improv[ement]" (Puritz, Walker, Riley-Collins, & Bedi, 2007, p. 15).

All twenty-one assessments appear to have utilized essentially the same methodology, slightly tailored to the individual jurisdictions.[2] The published reports describe their methodology in a remarkably similar way with only slight variations and limited detail. These assessments applied a "well-tested and highly structured methodology" (Scali et al., 2013, p. 13 [MO]). Data collection for all jurisdictions included surveys and interviews of a variety of juvenile court stakeholders, courtroom observations, documentary analysis, and facility visits. In addition, an "investigative team of experts in juvenile defense" conducted courtroom observations and collected statistical data on the status of the municipalities' children (p. 13).

Unfortunately, there is insufficient detail on survey and interview content, making it difficult to determine if the investigators sought to directly assess role problems faced by juvenile defenders. There is also no information available on survey samples, sampling methodologies, or the number of defense attorneys interviewed in each jurisdiction.[3]

Despite these limitations, the findings shed much-needed light on the current nature of juvenile defense in the jurisdictions assessed. They suggest that a great deal of confusion about the defense attorney role exists in *every* state examined. Almost every report provided the same conclusion, written in almost exactly the same way, indicating that despite the efforts of some zealous advocates, systemic barriers render the juvenile defender role insignificant.[4] These barriers thwart juvenile defenders' efforts to zealously advocate, and some defenders resign themselves to an "insignificant" role (Cumming, Finley, Hall, Humphrey, & Picou, 2003, p. 71 [MD]). Some defenders remain zealous advocates despite the odds that they might not be successful in their efforts; others, however, have accommodated the notion that the juvenile defense attorney plays an insignificant role in juvenile court (Albin, Albin, Gladden, Ropelato, & Stroll, 2003, p. 7 [MT]; Cumming et al., 2003, p. 71 [MD]; Kehoe & Tandy, 2006, p. 10 [IN]; Grindall & Puritz, 2003, p. 45 [NC]; Crawford, Dohrn, Geraghty, Moss, & Puritz, 2007, pp. 5–6 [IL]).

These and other reports note a lack of zealous advocacy among juvenile defenders.[5] For example, the Kentucky assessment showed that "trial practice and preparation for disposition hearings in juvenile court were weak and showed an overall lack of advocacy efforts" (Puritz & Brooks, 2002, p. 1). The Illinois assessment stated that "[a] child is also guaranteed the right to . . . zealous advocacy during the sentencing phase . . . [and] . . . the quality of advocacy at this critical stage [is] lacking" (Crawford et al., 2007, p. 4). The Mississippi assessment found that "across the state, investigators observed that the level of advocacy provided for indigent youth in Mississippi was less than zealous" (Puritz et al., 2007, p. 8). Nebraska's assessment revealed that even though "instances of juvenile defenders providing diligent, creative, client-centered advocacy for their young clients" occurred, "this level of practice was not the norm" (Beck, Puritz, & Sterling, 2009, p. v), and "in general, defense representation was well-meaning, and even caring, but not necessarily client-centered or zealous" (p. vi).

Multiple assessments reported that zealous advocacy is strongly discouraged in juvenile courtrooms (see, for example, Stewart et al., 2000 [TX];

Puritz & Sun, 2001 [GA]; Calvin, 2003 [WA]; and Scali et al., 2013 [MO]). For instance, the Texas assessment reported, "Defenders are systematically discouraged from providing adequate representation" (Stewart et al., 2000, p. 18). The Georgia assessment noted that "the nonadversarial culture of the juvenile court undoubtedly affects the level of zealous advocacy that lawyers feel they can engage in" (Puritz & Sun, 2001, p. 31). Washington's investigative team found that defenders experience a "subtle form of pressure" from courts to be team players such that "the value of 'getting along' with others in the court system hurts a juvenile's prospects for zealous defense" (Calvin, 2003, p. 32). Missouri's assessment noted that most of its counties "exert[ed] both covert and overt pressure for attorneys to minimize zealous advocacy and work with the judge and the [probation officer]" (Scali et al., 2013, p. 38) and that "the culture of many of the juvenile courts discourages formal assertion of legal issues and encourages hallway conversations to resolve legal questions" (p. 46).

All twenty-one reports identified either judges or the juvenile court culture as a barrier or negative influence, depressing the availability and/or quality of counsel.[6] For example, the Illinois report revealed that judges often expressed relief that "'the attorneys have not been defense zealots in juvenile cases'" (Crawford et al., 2007, p. 63). The Missouri report noted the existence of "a court culture that appeared to exert pressure on defenders to work as a team with other stakeholders" (Scali et al., 2013, p. 38). This report further revealed that "even when attorneys have the opportunity to be advocates, their voices are often ignored," with one defense attorney stating, "'In juvenile court, I am not more than a potted plant,'" and another sharing, "'There is not a lot I can do . . . it's essentially standing next to someone while they get sent to DYS [state incarceration facility] for petty nonsense'" (p. 52). The Mississippi assessment found that "the culture of the juvenile court, and other barriers . . . affect the quality of representation of Mississippi youth" (Puritz et al., 2007, p. 15). The Nebraska assessment concluded that "law violation proceedings are infused with an informal, non-adversarial nature that facilitates less than zealous defense advocacy" (Beck et al., 2009, p. 56). The West Virginia investigative team found that "a pervasive lack of legal advocacy permeates the juvenile court" because of the courthouse "emphasis on the importance of civility" and the "unwritten rule that [defense counsel] should not be 'too adversarial or too aggressive'" (Puritz & Sterling, 2010, p. 5). Finally, the South Carolina report described that "the conformist culture of the court" indicates that a "misunderstanding of the juvenile defender's role seem[s] to create overwhelming pressure for the juvenile defender to be a 'team player'

. . . often prioritizing this goal ahead of zealous advocacy" (Scali, Song, & Puritz, 2010, p. 22).

In sum, all of the state assessments documented inconsistencies in the expectations of the juvenile defender role that *still* exist in the new century.[7] It is problematic, however, that there are not more, and not more informative, empirical studies of the juvenile defender role. The study at the center of this book sought to fill some of this gap. In order to set the stage for the context in which the study was conducted, a discussion of the present-day nature of juvenile defense within the study's jurisdiction is useful.

Juvenile Defense in North Carolina

The study at the center of this book sought to examine the juvenile defender role in North Carolina as well as the nature, extent, and impact of the role conflict that juvenile defenders experience there. Unlike adult defendants, child respondents cannot waive their right to counsel. North Carolina legislatively abolished such a waiver in the Juvenile Code Revision Committee of 1979, making the presence of juvenile defenders in North Carolina's juvenile courts all the more necessary. In North Carolina, children are presumed indigent because they are not expected to earn their own money with which they could pay for an attorney. Thus, counsel is automatically appointed for each child when a delinquency petition is filed with the court. Children or their parents *can* hire retained (private) counsel if they wish; there is no official rule prohibiting parents from changing the appointed attorney to retained counsel (E. Zogry, personal communication, September 4, 2013).

Several state assessments have so far been briefly highlighted to tell the story of the modern-day juvenile defender's understanding of his or her role. A more detailed discussion of the North Carolina assessment, published in 2003, is necessary to provide the reader with a better context in which to understand the study that is presented in later chapters. The North Carolina assessment involved a collaborative effort among the ABA Juvenile Justice Center, the Southern Juvenile Defender Center, the National Juvenile Defender Center, and the North Carolina Office of Indigent Defense Services (Grindall & Puritz, 2003). The assessment included a cross-sectional analysis of eleven North Carolina counties, including urban, suburban and rural areas, and a variety of defense systems. Data collected were

> statistics on population, racial composition, and income . . . for each county
> . . . data on juvenile [delinquency variables such as complaints, admissions,

intakes, arrests, etc.] . . . survey questionnaires [content neither published nor released upon request] . . . interviews (pursuant to standardized protocols) [details neither published nor released upon request] . . . [courtroom observations] . . . facility [tours] and documentary [and statistical] evidence [details neither published nor released upon request]. (Grindall & Puritz, 2003, p. 12)

Phone calls were used to follow up when information needed elaboration or clarification. Interviews and conversations were conducted with an unspecified number of judges, juvenile public defenders, court appointed counsel, prosecutors, court personnel and administrators, court counselors, case managers, mental health experts, school resource officers, detention center personnel and administrators, service providers, key state stakeholders, policy advocates, and children and parents (p. 12). These efforts resulted in a report that reflected many of the same role issues described in other state reports.

The scope of the North Carolina assessment is very impressive. Unfortunately, like the other assessments, it offered insufficient detail on the methods used, including the specific questions used in the interviews. My attempts to learn more about the survey and interview measures were unsuccessful. Moreover, the number of juvenile defenders interviewed and the methods by which they were sampled are unknown. Nevertheless, the findings of the assessment provide a healthy foundation for a study of juvenile defender role conflict experiences.

The North Carolina assessment concluded that "a misapprehension of the *role* [emphasis added] of defense counsel in juvenile proceedings" was thought to contribute to the "uneven state of defense representation observed in North Carolina" (Grindall & Puritz, 2003, p. 2). Some juvenile defenders were so peripheral to the process that they appeared to play *no role* whatsoever in the proceedings.

Let us take a moment to review what it means in practical terms when a defense attorney plays no role in court proceedings. The judicial process uses an adversarial model to make sure that justice prevails and due process protections guaranteed by the US Constitution are met. This model provides that two opposing parties—the prosecutor, who brings the charges to the court's attention, and the defense attorney—engage in a contest. The defense attorney serves as a critical check against errors made by the prosecutor and other state government agents like law enforcement agents who collect the evidence to support the prosecutor's case. The judge's role is to oversee the contest by hearing each party's "story," to ensure the proceedings comport with the US Constitution's due process guidelines, and to make a final determination of the contest's winner—in other words, determine if the respondent is or is not legally responsible (guilty). For a defense attorney to play no role whatsoever in a process in which he or she is a necessary half is a strong indicator that due process has failed.

Grindall and Puritz also found that not all North Carolina juvenile defenders saw their role as an *expressed*-interests, as opposed to a *best*-interests, advocate. Recall that juvenile defenders are tasked with treating their juvenile clients the same as their adult clients for whom they are duty-bound to provide expressed-interests advocacy. Some admitted that they hesitated to engage in contentious adjudication in juvenile court cases, since they believed doing so would negatively affect their standing in other cases heard in the same court or by the same judge (Grindall & Puritz, 2003, pp. 6–7). Since many North Carolina judges hear both adult and juvenile cases, it is difficult to discern if Grindall and Puritz here refer to other juvenile cases or to adult cases or both. Any of these options is feasible in North Carolina, given its variable juvenile judge schedule. In fact, in North Carolina's counties it is common for judges to do "double duty" in juvenile *and* adult court (R. Waldrop Rugh, personal communication, February 2012).

The North Carolina assessment also revealed that juveniles frequently appeared to believe that the court counselors (North Carolina's version of juvenile probation officers) were their legal advocates without realizing that these counselors actually have, and could use, the power to testify "*against* [emphasis added] the juveniles' interests" (Grindall & Puritz, 2003, p. 39). There also appeared to be a lack of representation for juveniles for whom no placement, except detention, could be arranged (Grindall & Puritz, 2003). This is especially concerning given that detention is a restriction of liberty that, according to the spirit of *In re Gault* (1967), should trigger the right to effective assistance of a zealous (expressed-interests) advocate.

One of the most concerning of the assessment's findings was the extent to which juvenile defenders depended on "court counselors to plan and recommend disposition treatment plans" (Grindall & Puritz, 2003, p. 4). The assessment further stated that

> it was observed that judges, prosecutors and *defense attorneys* [emphasis added] routinely accept court counselor recommendations. In some counties, most cases (up to 70%) go to disposition immediately following adjudication, allowing no time for attorneys to develop alternative disposition treatment plans if they have not been completed prior to the court hearing. Even given a delay between adjudication and disposition, attorneys overwhelmingly failed to

adequately review or question disposition recommendations made by court counselors or present alternative plans. (p. 4)

The North Carolina assessment also acknowledged the existence of role confusion among juvenile defenders. In fact, one of its recommendations was to "clarify the appropriate role of defense counsel in various stages of the juvenile proceedings" (Grindall & Puritz, 2003, p. 46).

According to a recently released report by the North Carolina Office of the Juvenile Defender (NCOJD), the office responded to the state assessment by taking steps to improve the quality of representation for youth in delinquency court (NCOJD, 2013). More specifically, it explicitly identified the official juvenile defender role as an *expressed*-interests advocate. The NCOJD distributed an official role statement to juvenile defenders and "to all district court judges and chief court counselors" throughout the state in 2005 (p. 26). This statement reflects Guideline 2.1 of the *Performance Guidelines for Appointed Counsel in Juvenile Delinquency Proceedings at the Trial Level*, developed in 2005 and republished in 2007 by the North Carolina Commission on Indigent Defense Services (Newman et al., 2008, p. 1). The NCOJD also launched training workshops provided through the University of North Carolina's School of Government for juvenile defenders throughout the state. These training sessions were designed to address juvenile defenders' role definition and related issues (NCOJD, 2013). The NCOJD report was released to review these efforts and make recommendations for further improvements. It indicated that "representation was [still] uneven in some districts" but did not address the extent to which juvenile court functionaries appeared to have internalized the role statement (p. 10). The study on which this book focuses sought, in part, to investigate this internalization. Its data were collected in 2014, making it rather timely.

The study central to this book addressed the extent to which the NCOJD's role statement has been integrated into juvenile court practices in two of North Carolina's largest jurisdictions. Given the statement, its dissemination—to *all* juvenile court functionaries—and ancillary training, juvenile defenders should readily identify their role as *expressed*-interests advocates. Also, if the statement's message has been integrated into courtroom practices, juvenile defenders should report little role conflict and much support of their zealous advocate role from other courtroom functionaries. Finally, juvenile defenders should report little impact from role conflict.

As far as can be discerned, there has yet to be an empirical study that has engaged in a focused and purposeful empirical assessment of juvenile defenders' view of their role and the role conflict they experience. The state assessments discussed earlier sought to broadly capture factors affecting the effectiveness of, and access to, counsel. I was informed that as part of the assessments' interview processes, juvenile defenders were asked "about role confusion, conflict, and barriers to advocacy" (R. Banks, personal communication, April 17, 2014). However, my requests for further detail were unsuccessful. So, it is difficult to determine the extent to which juvenile defenders' views of their role and role conflict were examined.

To the best of my knowledge, no study like the one reported in this book has been conducted in North Carolina prior to or since the distribution of the NCOJD report in 2013. This assessment of juvenile defender role conflict in North Carolina is the next logical step after North Carolina's statewide assessment and the NCOJD report released in 2013. Not only would such a study provide for a direct examination of how juvenile defenders in North Carolina view their role, but it would expand our understanding of the nature and impact of the role conflict they experience. Even though it initially appears that such a study would be the first of its kind in North Carolina, or possibly anywhere, there has been empirical research that examines the juvenile defender role in less direct ways. In order to fully illustrate the contribution of the present study, it is critical to discuss these indirect investigations.

Empirical Examination of the Juvenile Defender Role

There is little social science scholarship on the juvenile defender role. One of the first empirical examinations of the juvenile defender role was published in 1972 (Stapleton & Teitelbaum). Stapleton and Teitelbaum used an experimental design to conduct a unique examination of juvenile court systems in two cities—"Zenith" (adversarial orientation like in adult court) and "Gotham" (cooperative, parens patriae orientation). The experimental variable was legal representation by "project attorneys" who had been provided with specialized training. This specialized training consisted of "orientation sessions . . . including visits to institutions, an introduction to police department procedures, a survey of available community facilities which worked with 'problem' youths, examination of relevant statutory and decisional law, and observation of juvenile court proceedings. In addition, the lawyers were enrolled in graduate law courses dealing with juvenile courts, delinquency, and unspecified related areas throughout their association with the project" (p. 59).

In Stapleton and Teitelbaum's study, youths facing delinquency charges were randomly assigned to project attorneys (experimental group) or left to such legal services as were available in the jurisdiction (control group). Using court records and case reports provided by the project attorneys, these scholars found that representation by a project attorney (i.e., one who zealously advocated for his or her client's *expressed* interests) had a slightly positive impact in one jurisdiction (Zenith—adversarial court) but no impact or a slightly negative (though not statistically significant) impact in the other (Gotham— cooperative, parens patriae court) (Stapleton & Teitelbaum, 1972).

Stapleton and Teitelbaum concluded that one of the most powerful factors affecting the role of counsel was the judge. They noted that while Zenith's court appeared relatively open to defense lawyers' adversarial tactics, Gotham's court impeded such efforts. Gotham's judges were willing not only to proceed with a case without a defense lawyer present but also to conclude the adjudication without the lawyer. Furthermore, Gotham's defense attorneys did not have the time necessary for careful determination of the plea, and they could not rely on the court to allow them that time (1972, p. 127).

Because the 1967 US Supreme Court decision in *In re Gault* endorsed the use of adversarial defense tactics for juvenile clients, explained Stapleton and Teitelbaum, courts cannot disregard them entirely. However, their study found that when these tactics were pursued, it created "severe *role strain* [emphasis added] for all parties" (1972, p. 146). Stapleton and Teitelbaum also asserted that traditional juvenile courts like Gotham arranged their procedures in a way that was incompatible with the presence of an adversarial role and failed to ameliorate role strain. However, in *both* the Gotham and Zenith courts, attorneys found themselves co-opted into the juvenile system's orientation: lawyers in Gotham reported a "higher incidence of pressure by the court to cooperate" (p. 147), while lawyers in Zenith reported "exertions of judicial pressure for cooperation," although this occurred half "as frequently [as] in Gotham" (p. 131). It is critical to recognize that *both* courts reflected some of this pressure (that is, role conflict).

Stapleton and Teitelbaum pointed out that traditional juvenile courts, like Gotham's, essentially rejected the adversarial function of the juvenile defender and expected defense lawyers to shift their function from adversary to "*ad hoc* social worker," depending on whether the charge was denied (juvenile pleads not guilty or not responsible) or the petition was sustained (juvenile is found guilty or responsible) (1972, p. 146). This would place defense attorneys in conflict with their ethical mandate to serve as zealous advocates for their clients' expressed interests. In addition, it would deprive the juvenile of the representation guaranteed in *In re Gault* (1967). Stapleton and Teitelbaum warned that tasking attorneys with such conflicting expectations would "sorely press the most adroit of actors" (1972, p. 146).

That such powerful influences could impede juvenile defenders' attempts to carry out their role is disturbing. As Stapleton and Teitelbaum pointed out, although criminal defense attorneys are officers of the court (as are any attorneys), their duty is to serve as an "aggressive representative of . . . [their] client" (1972, p. 157). They also pointed out that while defenders must serve the institution of the court by being fair and honest, their duties to society and the court are of secondary importance to their duty to their clients (1972).

Stapleton and Teitelbaum's 1972 study, while certainly informative and foundational, has several limitations, the most important of which is that it was conducted so soon after the 1967 *In re Gault* decision. The juvenile courts might not have had enough time to adapt to and implement *Gault*. Modern-day juvenile courts might demonstrate better adherence to the spirit of *Gault*. In addition, Stapleton and Teitelbaum's study did not involve in-depth qualitative interviews with the juvenile defenders (1972). Although their results provided an important indication that pressure from the court for juvenile defenders to depart from their adversarial role exists, they did not provide an in-depth examination of attorneys' experiences with these dynamics or of the impact of those experiences.

In other words, the existing scientific research on the juvenile defender role focused on two major role-related topics: whether the role was filled or not, and if it was, whether the role accommodated the court's best interest (rehabilitative) mission or assumed the adversarial, expressed-interests advocate role. Naturally, this leaves a major gap in several areas of importance regarding the role, including, but not limited to, its impact and effectiveness. However, trying to find answers to complex questions like the juvenile defender role's effectiveness in a complex and dynamic system is very difficult without first understanding exactly what the role is and if it is functioning the way it should. The assessments described earlier in this chapter strongly suggest the role is not working the way it is intended and that there is a fair amount of confusion about the role. Additionally, there appear to be particular obstacles to the role, including mixed messages about what the role should be. The nature and impact of these mixed messages, referred to as *role conflict* when they are about a person's role, are at the heart of the study on which this book focuses.

3. Juvenile Defender Role Conflict
An Empirical Study

R*ecall the questions* presented at the beginning of chapter 2. It is likely safe to say that many people have encountered a situation where their expectations of a role they inhabited were different from or even contradictory to what someone else expected of the role. For the most part, these differences or contradictions usually result in minor misunderstandings that are quickly cleared up with some communication or experience. In the meantime, perhaps nothing disastrous comes of the situation except for a possible missed deadline or task. But what if the role involves transplanting a heart? Or the constitutional protections, and possibly future, of a vulnerable young man from a struggling family? Role conflict might sound innocuous at first but can have very real consequences, at the very least, to the person attempting to carry out the role.

Role Conflict

Role conflict refers to "a situation that results when role expectations are inconsistent, as when a supervisor sends employees mixed messages about their roles" (Levy, 2010, p. 292). Role conflict is also referred to as "the simultaneous occurrence of two (or more) role sendings [i.e., communications about the role or role expectations] such that compliance with one would make more difficult compliance with the other" (Katz & Kahn, 1966, p. 184). These mixed messages need not come from a role incumbent's superiors; they can come from other *role senders*—that is, anyone who communicates messages about what is expected of the role incumbent (Cordes & Dougherty, 1993). In the juvenile court context, role senders may include the juvenile defender's client, the client's parent, a court counselor (juvenile probation officer), the judge, or the prosecutor. Role conflict is especially likely when there is also role *ambiguity*, or uncertainty about what the role incumbent is supposed to do. Recall that role ambiguity can be distinguished from role conflict in that it refers to insufficient information or clarity about the role's parameters and/ or requirements, while role conflict involves clear but conflicting information about the role. In light of the history of confusion about the juvenile defense attorney role, it is likely that juvenile defense attorneys experience both role ambiguity and role conflict.

Role conflict was largely a theoretical concept until 1954 when Getzels and Guba conducted the first field study firmly establishing role conflict as a measurable construct. Since then, role conflict has been studied for various professions, producing an abundant body of literature, a small set of instruments, and a relatively consistent set of correlates. For instance, empirical research has confirmed that "role conflict is associated with decreased satisfaction, coping behavior that would be dysfunctional for the organization, and experiences of stress and anxiety" (Rizzo, House, & Lirtzman, 1970, p. 154).

There has been some empirical attention to role conflict for law professionals, including juvenile prosecutors (Laub & Mac Murray, 1987; Sagatun & Edwards, 1979; Sanborn, 1995; Shine & Price, 1992), public service lawyers (Jackson, Turner, & Brief, 1987), and public defenders (Lynch, 1997). Role conflict, however, has yet to be studied in a systematic way among *juvenile* defenders. That there have been so many state assessments on juvenile defense implies that scholars have a strong interest in role meaning and conflict-related issues for juvenile defenders. However, inadequate information about the methodology used to procure assessment data makes forming firm conclusions about the validity of their findings very difficult.

Katz and Kahn offer a theoretical framework of role conflict that shows promise for studying role conflict among juvenile defenders (1966). Katz and Kahn's notion of *role behavior* focuses on the impact that individuals' role in an organization has on their behavior. They define an individual's role behavior as

> the recurring actions of an individual appropriately interrelated with the repetitive activities of others so as to yield a predictable outcome. The set of interdependent behaviours comprise a social system or subsystem, a stable collective pattern in which people play their parts. (p. 174)

This definition provides an appropriate framework for examining role conflict among juvenile defenders for three reasons. First, there are clear indicators that the juvenile defender role is burdened with inconsistent expectations. Second, this inconsistency stems, in part, from the "repetitive activities of others [juvenile courtroom stakeholders]" (p. 174), reflecting resistance to the official juvenile defender role: zealous, expressed-interests advocate. Third, state assessments of juvenile defense systems indicate that defenders' departure from the official role is partially in response to pressures from organizational stakeholders (see, generally, the state assessments found in the references).

Katz and Kahn identify at least four major sources of role conflict in an organization (1966). These are *intrasender* conflict, where the role taker receives contradictory expectations from a single source; *intersender* conflict, where the role taker receives different expectations from different role senders; *interrole* conflict, where the role taker occupies two contradictory roles, one of which is unrelated to his or her occupation (e.g., juvenile defender versus spouse); and *person-role* conflict, which occurs "when role requirements violate the needs, values or capacities of the individual" (p. 185).

For juvenile defenders, these four sources of conflict could be applied as follows:

1. *Intrasender*—a juvenile defender perceives the *Model Rules of Professional Conduct* as requiring her to represent both the expressed *and* best interests of her client.
2. *Intersender*—a juvenile defender understands that the *Model Rules* requires him to engage in zealous advocacy of his client's expressed interests, but he is pressed by the judge to not be *too* adversarial (that is, he should tone down his zealous advocacy) or he will be removed from the courtroom or the appointed counsel list of attorneys.
3. *Interrole*—a juvenile defender faces conflict because the time required by her family responsibilities interferes with her ability to effectively represent her clients.
4. *Person-role* (internal conflict)—a juvenile defender who is himself the parent of a young daughter finds that, when he is called upon to represent a very young girl who has difficulty articulating her interests, he tends to yield to his sense of paternalism (like the court's parens patriae orientation) and puts pressure on her to agree to what he believes is in her best interests instead of advocating for her expressed interests.

The severity of the role conflict depends on how incompatible the role expectations are and how the individual adjusts to or copes with the incompatibility (Getzels & Guba, 1954). How incompatible the expressed- and best-interests roles are for juvenile defenders is difficult to discern based on the existing literature. The answer might depend on how juvenile defenders define their zealous advocacy role and how they cope with the unique needs of juvenile clients, as well as on other stressors. These other stressors could be internal (for example, the defender's own definitions of the role, capacities, needs, and values) or external, including demands of the courtroom workgroup and logistical pressures (for example, time constraints, excessive caseloads, and the like).

Until Rizzo and his colleagues' seminal work in 1970, role conflict does not appear to have been empirically tested or systematically measured. After noting an association between role conflict and lower job satisfaction, anxiety, stress, and "coping behavior that would be dysfunctional for the organization," Rizzo and his colleagues developed and validated two instruments: one measures role conflict, and the other measures role ambiguity (p. 154). The role conflict instrument has been the hallmark measure of role conflict in subsequent relevant scholarship. However, because its items could be construed as too generic and do not allow for qualitative responses, the instrument was deemed unsuitable for the present study. For example, responses to a prompt by Rizzo and his coauthors such as *I receive incompatible requests from two or more people* might be artificially high given the adversarial nature of the juvenile defender role. Katz and Kahn's four sources of role conflict provide a more easily tailored rubric for this study's measures (1966).

As of this writing, a systematic empirical assessment of juvenile defenders' role conflict experiences has yet to be published. The study briefly outlined in the rest of this chapter is among the first. It employed Katz and Kahn's conceptual framework to examine role conflict using interviews with modern-day juvenile defenders (1966). The focus of this book is on the outcomes of an empirical examination of the nature, extent, and impact of role conflict for juvenile defenders who served in a jurisdiction that clearly defined the juvenile defender role as an expressed-interests advocate. A brief explanation of some of the methods engaged to accomplish this goal is helpful to set the stage.

The Study

The study on which this book focuses sought to close a major gap in the empirical literature regarding the juvenile defender role. Part of its primary purpose was to establish a foundation on which future research addressing the problems of the juvenile defender role could be built. Toward that end, it appropriately involved a qualitative examination of the role experiences of juvenile defenders from one of the jurisdictions that had undergone a state assessment, North Carolina. While a more detailed description of its analysis and validity is available in appendix A, the remainder of this chapter offers the reader a description of the study sample and key research questions to provide context.

Site Selection

The target population for this study was juvenile defenders who provide services as either public defenders or appointed defense counsel at juvenile courts in North Carolina counties. North Carolina was chosen as the study site for two reasons. First, as discussed previously, in 2003 it had been the subject of a statewide assessment of juvenile defense. Again, the assessment reported a "misapprehension of the *role* [emphasis added] of defense counsel in juvenile proceedings" (Grindall & Puritz, 2003, p. 2). The assessment even went so far as to recommend clarification of "the appropriate role of defense counsel in various stages of the juvenile proceedings" (p. 46). Second, North Carolina was selected because it had responded to the state assessment by officially endorsing expressed-interests advocacy for juvenile clients and instituting corresponding training for its juvenile defenders.

The two counties selected for the study were chosen because of their accessibility and for the comparability of their juvenile defense systems to others in the nation. As of 2014, "Alpha" County was roughly the same size as seventeen other counties in the United States (with populations between 900,000 and 1 million), and "Beta" County was roughly the same size as thirty-two other counties (with populations between 450,000 and 550,000) (US Census Bureau, 2014). Indigent defense systems are typically one of three types: contract, assigned or appointed, and public defender (Spangenberg & Beeman, 1995). At the time of the study, all states except for one (Maine) based their juvenile defense services on a state- or county-funded public defense scheme similar to North Carolina's (National Juvenile Defender Center [NJDC], 2014). Thirty-six of those states (73 percent) utilized some combination of systems, and thirteen (27 percent), including North Carolina, used all three systems of indigent defense. Seventeen states (35 percent) utilized the same system used by Alpha and Beta Counties, a public defender office supplemented by an appointed counsel list (NJDC, 2014). The prevalence of public defense, office-based representation with supplemental representation from the legal community (often referred to as the *local bar*) made Alpha and Beta Counties' juvenile defense systems comparable to most others in the United States.

The study's counties utilized the same blended system of juvenile defense: an attorney from the county's public defender office was primarily responsible for representing juveniles charged with acts of delinquency. Juvenile cases that the chief juvenile defender could not cover were either assigned to other attorneys in the office or were appointed on a case-by-case basis by judges from a private attorneys list that was populated and managed by the public defender. These appointed attorneys were selected, trained, and supervised by the chief juvenile defender.

Participants

The North Carolina counties chosen for this study graciously granted me permission to conduct research among their juvenile defense attorneys. The total number of juvenile defenders eligible for interviews, including all public defender office staff attorneys and their appointed attorneys, was sixty-five. I identified myself as having a background in law and industrial/organizational psychology and an interest in studying the professional development of work-group members in the juvenile courts, particularly defense attorneys. I made clear that interviews would be completely voluntary and confidential and that no identifying information for any individual mentioned in participants' responses (e.g., a named defendant) would be recorded at any time. Each attorney was invited twice using two methods of contact—electronic mail and telephone. If no response was received after the fourth contact, the attorney was removed from the list. If an attorney asked for further information about the study, I provided additional details from the waiver of consent form and offered to email it to him or her. I began inviting participants on May 30, 2014, and ceased after reaching the four-invitations-per-participant limit on November 13, 2014. All sixty-five attorneys were extended the four invitations to participate in the study unless they accepted before all four invitations were delivered. Interviews began on June 2, 2014, and concluded on November 13, 2014.

A total of twenty-four attorneys participated in the study. Ten of the participants completed the interviews in person, while the remaining fourteen were interviewed via telephone. I made every effort to make participation as convenient as possible. Interviews typically ran between one and one-and-a-half hours. Fourteen participants worked in Alpha County and ten in Beta. Two of the Alpha County participants were full-time employees of the public defender's office, and the remaining twelve were from the appointed list. One participant from Beta County was with the public defender's office, while the remaining nine were from the appointed list.

The response rate for this study was twenty-four out of sixty-five, or 37 percent; this translates into a 63 percent nonresponse rate. Most of the nonresponders did not reply to any of the four invitations. Three declined, offering no reason, and two indicated they no longer represented juveniles. One commented that he was nervous about participating in a study where he felt he would have to justify his decisions. Three initially agreed to participate but did not follow through with their interviews.

The sample, as seen in table 3.1, included seventeen males and seven females. The average age of respondents was nearly forty-six years. The average tenure of experience as a juvenile defender was nearly twelve years, with a range of one to forty-five years and a mode of four years. The majority of participants (twenty, or 83 percent) had completed some sort of juvenile defense–related training (e.g., continuing legal education; self-study—referring to an attorney's informal, self-directed examination of resources relevant to his or her role; or the like) and had some other relevant background (such as experience as a juvenile prosecutor or counselor).

Pilot Test

In preparing to validate the interview protocols, I conducted a set of pilot interviews with a group of five juvenile defenders who worked in nontarget North Carolina counties. The pilot interview findings suggested that, while juvenile defenders recognized and expected to carry out their official mandate to advocate for their clients' expressed interests, they also faced intense pressure from members of the courtroom workgroup to advocate "less zealously" than they had planned and to join the court in its efforts to determine what was *best* for the client. Some pilot participants reported experiencing emotional stress due to these pressures and discussed a variety of techniques they employed to resolve or adapt to incompatible role expectations.

The pilot interviews were helpful, then, in confirming that role conflict was a real issue for some, in identifying some of the sources of that conflict, and in suggesting ways that defense attorneys attempted to manage the problem. Pilot interviewees' responses about substantive issues such as these contributed to the development of the final interview protocol. Pilot interviews were also helpful in making modifications to questions that needed clarification and in suggesting appropriate follow-up questions, which were incorporated into the final interviews.

Research Questions

This study sought to establish two major pillars upon which future research could be built. The first involved the role of juvenile defenders and attendant role conflict. More specifically, this study sought to reveal juvenile defender–

Table 3.1. Demographic and Professional Characteristics of Participants

Characteristic	n = 24	Percentage
Age		
Average: 45.63		
Range: 28–74		
Sex		
Male	17	70.8
Female	7	29.2
Race		
Caucasian/white	17	70.8
African American/black	5	20.8
Other	2	8.3
Marital status		
Married/partnered	17	70.8
Single	5	20.8
Divorced/separated	2	8.3
Income		
$0–25,000	2	8.3
$35,001–45,000	3	12.5
$45,001–55,000	6	25.0
$65,001+	9	37.5
NA	4	16.7
Years in juvenile defense		
Average: 11.92		
Range: 1–45		
"Least" experienced = 0–9 years	11	45.8
"Most" experienced = 10+ years	13	54.2
Training experience	20	83.3
Other relevant background (e.g., school teacher, coach, juvenile prosecutor)	17	70.8

derived definitions of their role and to elicit their lived experiences of role conflict as well as their perceived sources of role conflict.

The second pillar addressed the question of *So what?* It therefore involved the *consequences* of role conflict as perceived and experienced by juvenile defenders. For the scientific-minded reader, it should be pointed out that the social constructivist approach was taken for the study's design, data collection, and analysis. This orientation assumes that multiple realities exist and that different members in the same group will have diverse interpretations of similar events (Patton, 2002). It seeks to ascertain what individuals report as truths or constructed realities. It also focuses on how individuals make meaning of their experiences (Crotty, 1998). The social constructivist approach enabled me as investigator to explore the unique experiences of each respondent as valid and worthy of attention. This understanding is key to social constructivism and to fulfilling some of the foundational goals of this study. (See appendix A for additional methodology details.)

In order to establish these two major pillars, the investigation utilized pilot-tested qualitative interviews made up of operationalizations of Katz and Kahn's role conflict theoretical framework (1966). An operationalization is a term scientists use to describe the outcome of the process that makes an abstract phenomenon (such as attitude or intelligence) measurable through observable behavior. The verb "operationalize" roughly translates into *make measurable* (e.g., *the justice policy analyst* operationalized *the trial judge's job performance by examining how many of his cases the appeals court overturned*). Examples of role conflict operationalizations are provided in the discussion of each major research question, below. Additionally, the focus of Katz and Kahn's theoretical framework was the general notion that role conflict emerges from the conflicting expectations others have of role incumbents. Therefore, some questions were designed to elicit responses about conflicting expectations from various sources.

The interview questions were designed using three additional sources of information. First was the invaluable expertise of Eric Zogry of the North Carolina Office of the Juvenile Defender. Zogry oversees the quality of juvenile counsel for the entire state of North Carolina. He served as a sounding board for interview question wording, provided me with copies of his office's reports, and offered expertise on North Carolina's juvenile justice system and process. Second were the findings of the pilot study. Third was the North Carolina state assessment, discussed previously. The finalized interview protocols included items that were structured around the following six major research questions. (See appendixes C and D for protocol items.)

1. HOW DO JUVENILE DEFENDERS IN DELINQUENCY COURT VIEW THEIR ROLE?

The first portion of the interview focused on juvenile defenders' meaning of their role and experience with role conflict. (See also appendix C.) The role meaning questions included these:

> *What does zealous advocacy mean to you in terms of advocating for your client's interests?*
>
> *In your opinion, should a defense attorney ever depart from advocating for the expressed interests of a client?*

These questions are the most foundational of the group. It stands to reason that in order to capture the clearest picture of role conflict, as experienced by role incumbents, one must first identify how exactly they view their own role. For instance, if juvenile defenders all view their role as best-interests advocates and the juvenile court espouses its mission to be serving the best interests of juveniles, then one might reasonably predict that juvenile defenders will not report experiencing any role conflict. This prediction would be based on two major components: (1) the information addressed in previous chapters indicating that the best-interests mission is promoted, even in the face of professional rules requiring lawyers to advocate for their clients' expressed interests, and (2) the definition of role conflict, which tells us that in order for it to occur, role information must be perceived by the role incumbent as inconsistent.

If juvenile defenders themselves believe that their role is to serve as their clients' best-interests advocate, then they might not perceive or experience inconsistent role messages from other juvenile court stakeholders who believe the same thing, despite the fact that both perspectives conflict with the professional rules. At the same time, juvenile defenders might still experience *internal* (person-role) role conflict because they understand their professional duty, as defined by the professional rules, is to advocate for their clients' expressed interests but believe personally that they should advocate for their best interests instead. This scenario could also reflect inconsistencies that present juvenile defenders with role conflict, though they might recognize it less often because their own view of their role aligns with the court's. Therefore, getting a sense for how juvenile defenders themselves view their role is a critical first step in any examination of the role. Once we understand how juvenile defenders view their role, we can identify whether, and the extent to which, they experience role conflict.

2. TO WHAT EXTENT DO JUVENILE DEFENDERS IN DELINQUENCY COURT EXPERIENCE ROLE CONFLICT?

This construct posed some difficulty in terms of making it measurable because participants might not have realized they were facing role conflict as defined in the literature. In order to work around this inevitability, questions were created out of role conflict's basic components, as provided by Katz and Kahn (1966). For example, *intrasender* and *intersender* sources of role conflict were tapped using the following question:

> Do you ever feel like there are conflicting expectations of you in your role as a zealous advocate for juveniles? How so?

Person-role sources of role conflict were tapped using this question:

> Do you ever feel like you, personally, are conflicted about your role as a zealous advocate for juveniles, or what it requires you to do? How so?

Interrole conflict was not directly investigated because it did not implicate factors in the juvenile justice system that might be responsible for juvenile defenders' experiences of role conflict. However, it was indirectly investigated by examining responses to other questions where participants might have volunteered that other roles they have, such as mother or father, presented them with a conflict about their role. However, when participants volunteered these situations, they implicated *person-role* conflict, since the conflict was often internal and involved conflicting values as opposed to conflicting roles. An example of true interrole conflict for a juvenile defender would be where the juvenile defender was also an employee at the Department of Social Services and the two roles disagreed. Such investigation goes beyond the theoretical framework of this study.

In many ways, role conflict prevalence was the most difficult to make measureable. If juvenile defenders do not always recognize when they are facing role conflict, they certainly cannot recognize the extent to which they face it. For this reason, I carefully applied follow-up techniques using participants' own language (e.g., *pushback* or *pressure to depart*) to inquire about circumstances that fit the definition of role conflict but were not defined literally as such. In fact, follow-up questions proved to be, as they often do, a rich source of information that addressed the third major research question, which concerns the sources of role conflict.

3. WHEN THERE IS ROLE CONFLICT, WHAT ARE ITS SOURCES? FROM WHOM, OR WHERE, DO PRESSURES TO DEPART FROM A ZEALOUS, EXPRESSED-INTEREST ADVOCATE ROLE EMANATE?

The interview items were open and general by design in order to encourage elaboration and promote authenticity and validity. This sometimes made it unnecessary to ask a direct question on a topic or even to make follow-up inquiries. This was often the case with the issue of sources of role conflict. Participants often mentioned sources when describing their experiences with role conflict, pushback, or pressure to depart from their expressed-interests advocate role. To maintain consistency, when participants did not volunteer information about role conflict sources, direct questions were used. Specifically, participants were directly asked about sources implicated in the literature, such as the judge, caseload, time, financial resources, and other courtroom functionaries.

For example, participants were asked the following questions:

> *What do you think is the source or sources of these conflicting expectations?*
> *Who or what do you think is responsible for any pressure you experience to depart from the zealous advocate role? Can you make a list?*
> *In your experience, do you think judges support your role as a zealous advocate of the expressed interests of your juvenile client? Why or why not?*
> *In your experience, do you think other courtroom workgroup members support your role as a zealous advocate of the expressed interests of your juvenile client? Why or why not?*

The questions, designed to tap into juvenile defenders' views of their role, role conflict experiences, and views on role conflict sources, supplied a great deal of rich information. This information confirmed the problems initially identified by the state assessments addressed in previous chapters but, despite its importance, tells only part of the story. The other, equally critical, part of the story is the *impact* that juvenile defenders perceive that role conflict has on them and their work. Therefore, the remaining three questions addressed the study's second foundational pillar.

4. DOES THE NATURE AND QUALITY OF DEFENSE REPRESENTATION VARY ACROSS THE DIFFERENT STAGES OF THE DELINQUENCY CASE PROCESS?

As part of this study, participants were invited to share their views regarding the extent to which pressure to depart from their zealous advocate role varies by juvenile process stage. This area of inquiry proved to be one of the study's most provocative, controversial, and fertile and served as an interesting bridge connecting the study's two pillars: role conflict and role conflict impact. The interviewees revealed that they experienced the most intrasender role conflict (shifting their definition of their role and/or viewing departures from the role as acceptable) at the disposition stage.

The obligation of the defense attorney to zealously advocate on behalf of his or her client's expressed interests is likely to be least ambiguous at adjudication, where the issues involve pleading responsible—or accepting a plea offer—and/or determining how to best defend the client at trial. The juvenile defender's role at this stage is identical to that of a defense attorney in adult criminal court. However, the disposition stage of the juvenile process is different from the sentencing stage of a criminal proceeding in that the court is meant to emphasize rehabilitation over punishment for the respondent. For instance, at disposition, the juvenile could be sentenced to any of a variety of outcomes—theoretically some kind of treatment, detention, placement, or other directive (e.g., avoid certain friends, maintain good grades, and the like). If juvenile defenders perceive of the disposition as punishment, then they might try to lessen that punishment as they would in a criminal case with an adult client. If attorneys perceive of the disposition as treatment, however, their role becomes more ambiguous. Do they advocate for whatever treatment the client prefers? Make and present an independent analysis of what treatment they believe to be in the client's best interests? Advocate for the least intrusive treatment? Or simply defer to the judgment of the court counselor and the judge and take no position at all?

The ABA's *Model Rules* (2013) provides little guidance on this matter except to indicate that decision-making authority for these kinds of decisions is entirely in the *client's* hands, and those decisions are binding on his or her lawyer. Rule 1.2 states, "A lawyer shall abide by a client's decisions concerning the objectives of representation and, as required by Rule 1.4, shall *consult* [emphasis added] with the client as to the means by which they are to be pursued." However, it also states that "in a criminal case, the lawyer shall abide by the client's decision, after consultation with the lawyer, as to a plea to be entered, whether to waive jury trial and whether the client will testify," indicating that when it comes to *outcomes*, the client's expressed interests rule. In the matter of a role shift at the disposition phase, a juvenile defender would therefore likely find it difficult to justify a departure from the expressed-interests advocate role under this rule.

In addition, the *National Juvenile Defense Standards* provides guidelines in Standard 1.2, where juvenile defenders are disallowed from substituting their own view of the client's best interests for those their clients express (NJDC,

2012, p. 18). Additionally, these standards direct juvenile defenders to proceed in an expressed-interests advocate role if they are unable to convince their clients to change their expressed interests "throughout the course of the case" (p. 18).

Finally, North Carolina has implemented explicit guidance for its juvenile defenders on the matter of expressed-interests advocacy at the disposition stage. The North Carolina Office of the Juvenile Defender released a work in 2005 specifically stating that expressed-interests advocacy is to be used for juvenile clients at all stages (NCOJD, 2005, *Role Statement*; see also Newman et al., 2008). And North Carolina has provided training materials recognizing that juvenile defenders must fill an expressed-interests advocate role at *all stages* of the juvenile process (NCOIDS, 2006).

The remaining two questions more fully fit into the role conflict *consequences* of the study. They were specifically designed to address consequences for the role incumbent and his or her clients while also inviting participants to share how they handled the consequences of role conflict.

5. HOW DO JUVENILE DEFENDERS COPE WITH ROLE CONFLICT?

Participants in this study were asked about the coping strategies they utilize to manage the role conflict they experience. Coping has been defined as a response that is intended to change the objective nature of a stressful situation (French, Rodgers, & Cobb, 1974). It also refers to behavior that "protects people from being psychologically harmed by problematic social experience" (Pearlin & Schooler, 1978, p. 2).

The second portion of the interview included questions designed to elicit information about how juvenile defenders cope with role conflict (see appendix D). These questions were adapted from Burke and Belcourt's seminal empirical examination of coping responses to role conflict in the workplace (1974). Participants were invited to consider the experiences they had shared in the previous interview exercise and then were asked several questions about their reactions.

> *Would you please describe if those experiences caused you any tension or stress?*
> *Would you please describe what you have done that you found particularly effective at reducing that tension or stress?*
> *Would you please describe a specific example of those kinds of experiences?*
> *Would you please describe specifically how you coped with that experience?*

The use of interviews allowed participants to provide rich, textual information about their experiences of role conflict and the ways they are affected by it that neither a survey nor courtroom observations would have revealed. The exclusive use of surveys for this study would have limited the study due to the lack of opportunity to follow up on participant responses and the lack of space to provide the thick description so valuable in qualitative research (Geertz, 1973). It might also have failed to engender the type of focus from the participant that a live interview encourages. In addition, courtroom observations not only would have been limited to what I could observe but also would have required too much inference to justify their use for this type of study.

A vignette exercise, which gave participants an opportunity to demonstrate how they cope with role conflict dilemmas, was presented in the third and final portion of the interview (see appendix E). Participants were presented with eight brief scenarios highlighting obstacles to juvenile defenders' legitimate efforts to zealously advocate for their clients. I selected the dilemma vignettes from input or materials provided by Eric Zogry, North Carolina juvenile defender; Tamar Birckhead, associate professor of law and interim director of clinical programs at the University of North Carolina at Chapel Hill; Barry C. Feld, Centennial Professor of Law at the University of Minnesota; and training materials provided by the North Carolina Office of Indigent Defense Services (NCOIDS, 2006). The scenarios were selected to reflect a variety of relatable role conflict dilemmas that subject matter experts and pilot participants indicated were commonplace in North Carolina's juvenile courts.

6. HOW DOES ROLE CONFLICT AFFECT THE QUALITY OF DEFENSE REPRESENTATION?

Finally, the study's participants were invited to discuss the ways in which role conflict experiences affect their case outcomes, the general quality of their work, and themselves as incumbents of the juvenile defender role (e.g., whether they experience tension or stress as a result of role conflict). According to role conflict scholars, the tension or stress that role incumbents experience as a result of role conflict can lead to deleterious effects on the job, such as turnover (role withdrawal), burnout (emotional exhaustion; see Cordes & Dougherty, 1993; and Jackson et al., 1987), and lower productivity (Van Sell, Brief, & Schuler, 1981). Participants were therefore asked the following:

> When there are pressures that prevent you from being as zealous an advocate as you would like to be, how does that affect case outcomes?
> What is your impression of how these kinds of experiences have affected the quality of your work?

Participants were also asked:

> *What is your impression of how these kinds of experiences have impacted you
> as a juvenile defender generally?*

Again, the complete lists of interview protocol items can be found in appendixes C and D. Additionally, more methodology details are presented in appendix A, one of two places that directly address the study's validity and limitations; the second is chapter 8. The remaining chapters present the study's findings and examine their meaning relevant to the overarching problems of role conflict and its impact on juvenile defenders and implications for their clients and the juvenile justice system at large. Finally, the book discusses the extent to which the study achieves its goal of establishing a foundation upon which future research can be built. The extremely controversial nature of juvenile defense work in practice—the protection of the due process rights of our most vulnerable citizens—demands the systemic and organizational support worthy of its duties. As the remaining chapters reveal, such support is not as much a reality as one might expect.

Method Limitations

A critical limitation to the study's methodology was that it was restricted to juvenile defenders in two counties in a single state and included only twenty-four participants. The jurisdictions studied could have had unique cultural factors that reduced their representative value. Additionally, the organization of the public defender system, the legal rules, and the legal culture of the juvenile court in the sites where the study took place were likely to be unique in some ways.

Another limitation involved the interpretive nature of qualitative research. Although I have never served as a juvenile defender, I was the sole data collector and analyst for this study. I might have missed nuances and inferences as a result of my lack of experience in the role. A juvenile defender conducting this study might have interpreted response meanings more accurately and understood implications more readily than I did.

Notwithstanding these limitations, the findings detailed in the chapters that follow provide great insight into the dilemmas that North Carolina's juvenile defenders face. They also offer an excellent foundation upon which future research can be built.

4. Zealous Advocate for Whom?

Think back to when you were in elementary or junior high school. Try to remember any number of misunderstandings you might have had with a classmate or friend or that time you wanted to be part of the "cool club" that managed to convince you they would accept you if you did a particular act you knew could get you into trouble but thought, in your preteen brain, was worth the risk. So, remember our fourteen-year-old boy, Max, who gets caught shoplifting DVDs from Walmart as a rite of passage for entry into the aforementioned "cool club." Walmart's security caught him on video putting the DVDs inside his coat. Walmart has chosen to file charges, and the police are now involved. They have contacted his mother, who, since the divorce, has to work two jobs to make ends meet. Max is embarrassed; he is crying and mad at himself for getting caught, and now he has to do something he has never done before: go to court. Let's assume diversion is not an option for him—maybe his jurisdiction does not have enough resources or the latest juvenile justice policies do not provide for them. Either way, he has now been brought to the attention of, and is under the scrutiny of, the justice system.

Everyone is telling Max what to do—his mom, the police, and the court counselor, who has had Max (outside the presence of counsel) answer a whole lot of what he feels are nosy questions about his home life, schoolwork, and private thoughts. Max has even started to suspect that one of the "cool kids" has ratted him out because of whispers in the school halls. Stealing the DVDs was *not* his idea, but he does not want to look like a jerk by blaming the other kids. He had always heard that you are supposed to keep your mouth shut if the police ever try to talk to you. Everyone knows that, right? But, Max also feels pretty angry about his situation and thinks that he got into trouble for something he feels he was duped into doing. He knew it was wrong. But, he was always getting teased by these kids for his clothes, food, old cell phone. He thought if he could show them that he could be slick and cool, like them, they would accept him. Max does not want anyone to know how stupid he feels for getting caught, and no one seems to care about what he is thinking or feeling, just that he be made an example of or get help for problems he did not even realize he had.

One grown-up says she wants to help him. She says he's her boss and she has to do what he tells her to in terms of telling the judge what happened and what Max wants. It is confusing, though, because she tells Max that she's his lawyer and has to do what he says, but when he tells her to get rid of the court counselor's requirement that he stay away from the so-called cool kids, she argues that the judge will probably not accept that. Max struggles with how to view his lawyer. Should he trust her? He sees her talking in a friendly manner with the prosecutor and the other people in the courtroom. How can Max believe she really cares about what he has to say?

Role Meaning

The importance of juveniles' authentic participation in their cases by placing trust in their attorneys cannot be overstated and has been addressed by Puritz and Majd (2007). They argue that juvenile defenders must advocate for their clients' expressed interests, despite the obstacles blocking these efforts, in order to ensure the protection of juveniles' due process rights. The study at the center of this book asked juvenile defenders about how they define their zealous advocate role in a number of different ways. Their responses provide us with some insight into the ways they see themselves as advocates for their juvenile clients.

Recall that the *Model Rules of Professional Conduct* (ABA, 2013) defines the lawyer role as having two functions: *adviser* (or counselor) and *advocate* (pmbl. § 2). The *Model Rules* further states that, in the adviser/counselor function, the attorney "provides . . . an informed understanding of the client's legal rights and obligations and explains their practical implication" and, in the advocate function, "zealously asserts the *client's position* [emphasis added] under the rules of the adversary system" (pmbl. § 2). Participants in this study readily made the distinction between the adviser/counselor and advocate functions, which is rather encouraging and helps to allay some of the concerns raised by the North Carolina state assessment that juvenile defenders experience a great deal of confusion about their role. If nothing else, this study's findings confirmed that juvenile defenders are clear about this two-part role. The details of their responses provide us with an excellent picture of where the line between counselor and advocate sits.

Legal Counselor Role: Educate and Advise

One of the best ways to clarify attorneys' advocate role is to identify what the role is *not*. The counselor role can be seen as mutually exclusive from the advocate role. This distinction is critical because one of the overarching goals of this book is to highlight the problems inherent in juvenile defenders' advocate role only, namely the dilemma presented by conflicting role expectations.

The distinction between the adviser/counselor role and the advocate role was recognized by several participants in this study who acknowledged that the counseling functions of their role, including legal strategizing, do *not* require them to prioritize their clients' expressed interests. They also pointed out that advisers provide expert legal advice about their clients' circumstances, rights, and responsibilities and counsel them about strategies and possible case outcomes. Participant 005, one of the most reputable participants with twenty-three years of experience, concisely explained, "Your client gets to make the ultimate decision as to where you go with the case. As I tell a lot of my clients: you get to decide practical, I get to decide the tactical." (See table 3.1 for experience parameters.)

Participants indicated they would not expect their juvenile clients, individuals of tender years who lack the legal education of attorneys, to provide their own legal advice. Many also recognized that children make unique clients because of their lack of life experience and less-developed decision-making capacity. Therefore, juvenile defenders are not expected to prioritize their juvenile clients' expressed interests when performing their counselor function. Juvenile defenders' unique position as counselors of children is addressed to some extent in North Carolina's *Performance Guidelines for Appointed Counsel in Juvenile Delinquency Proceedings at the Trial Level* (North Carolina Commission on Indigent Defense Services [NCCIDS], 2007). Guideline 9.1(a) indicates that if there is an "absolute impasse as to tactical decisions [at adjudication], the juvenile's wishes *may* [emphasis added] control" (p. 17). The guidelines do not address this conflict at other stages of the process except to say that such "tactical disagreements ... do not justify withdrawal from a case" (p. 2). The guidelines might be written this way to provide some protection to defenders who choose to defer to their clients' expressed interests when it comes to tactical decisions (i.e., *how* to achieve an interest expressed by the client).

The guidelines specify that defense attorneys must treat their juvenile clients just as they would their adult clients (NCCIDS, 2007, p. 1). Since attorneys would not defer to their adult clients when it comes to legal strategy and advice, their reluctance to defer to their child clients in these matters is understandable. However, participants did recognize the importance of effectively communicating strategy and advice to their child clients, as explained by Participant 022, an expressed-interests attorney from the least-experienced group:

> At every point I feel that you should be explaining the law to your clients. . . . There will certainly be points where in my experience [clients] will almost always defer to your judgment because we're attorneys and because they don't really know what a motion means or they may not understand what precedents there are when it comes to a specific legal aspect of their case.

Participant 022 makes an important point about the need to *explain* the law to clients, but the legal counselor function does not end with providing information. Participants commonly extend their counselor function to attempts to persuade clients to change their interests when, in the attorney's view, doing so would be beneficial.

The persuasion task might be construed as a link between the counselor and advocate functions. For example, if, despite the attorney's advice, a juvenile client expresses desired outcomes that, in the experienced eyes of the attorney, are not feasible or sensible, the attorney might try to *persuade* the client to change those desired outcomes. This situation can be referred to as a *conflicting-client-interests* dilemma. The client expressly wants specific things, but the attorney views those wishes as undesirable for whatever reason and thus faces a dilemma about how to proceed. Arguably, if attorneys are successfully persuasive, they will not face the ethical dilemma of advocating for clients' expressed desires with which they disagree. They will also not face the ethical dilemma of departing from the zealous advocate role, since it requires that they advocate for their clients' *expressed* interests.

Legal Advocate Role

When one *counsels* another, one is presumably more expert at the topic at hand than the individual being counseled. That is primarily a difference in knowledge but not necessarily in skill. When one serves as an *advocate* for another or serves as another's *voice*, the advocate is presumably in a better position to serve in this way and in the context (such as the courtroom) than is the client. This arrangement reflects a difference in both knowledge and skill. In other words, lawyers have more knowledge about the rules and procedures of a courtroom than do their clients and are definitely more skilled at navigating them than their clients. This is particularly true if the client is a juvenile. At the same time, these advocates' job is to stand in the place of clients using their unique knowledge, skill, and position to promote the interests that their clients—who lack the unique knowledge, skill, and position to speak on their own behalf—have expressed to them. Even though some people choose to represent themselves in the court system (referred to as pro se defendants or respondents), it would not make sense to require all who come under the scrutiny of the justice system to school themselves in the rules and procedures related to their cases in order to be heard. In fact, proceeding pro se in court is considered a bad idea even for a law professional; as goes the old adage, "He who represents himself has a fool for a client." Let us take into consideration a more formalized definition of advocate.

An advocate is "a person who assists, defends, pleads, or prosecutes for another" (Garner & Black, 2006, p. 23). This definition implies that advocates stand in and use their voice to speak on behalf of another, a view that was prevalent among participants in this study. As noted above, an advocate "zealously asserts the *client's position* [emphasis added] under the rules of the adversary system" (ABA, 2013, pmbl. § 2). Participants involved in this study, though, had a more varied view of their role with juvenile clients.

In general, participants expressed a clear understanding of their role as zealous (i.e., expressed-interests) advocates of juveniles. Some acknowledged the official expressed-interests advocate mandate. However, they also pointed out some factors that seemed to contribute to role ambiguity, and a small number of participants suggested the expressed-interests/best-interests dichotomy might be an oversimplification.

Participants were asked two questions about their role meaning. The first was the opening question of the interview and was indirect. The second was the very last item on the interview and was far more direct. The direct question will be discussed first.

Participants were asked to complete this statement: *I view myself as an advocate for my client's _____ interests.* Interestingly, their responses did not fall *only* into the two categories of expressed interests and best interests, even though over half of them did. Participants who identified as other than expressed-interests or best-interests advocates declined to elaborate further on their answers, some pointing out that they had already done so earlier in the interview. A contributing factor to this reluctance might have been that interviews often went over the predicted one-hour length, and this question was the very last item of the interview process. Participants who declined were very clear that they did not want to answer the question. In order to adhere to the promise that all participation was voluntary, I did not push these participants to elaborate further.

An important point to make about those who identified as expressed-versus best-interests advocates relates to their tenure as attorneys. Participants were split into two groups: most experienced attorneys and least experienced. Participants were categorized by tenure in the following way: most

Table 4.1. Advocate Type and Zealous Advocacy Meaning

Advocate type	n = 24	Percentage
Expressed interests (44.4% most experienced; 55.6% least experienced)	9	37.5
Best interests (80% most experienced; 20% least experienced)	5	20.8
Legal interests (66.7% most experienced; 33.3% least experienced)	3	12.5
Personal/best-personal-desired interests (100% least experienced)	2	8.3
Other ("true interests," "best-defense interests") (100% most experienced)	2	8.3
Declined to answer (66.7% most experienced; 33.3% least experienced)	3	12.5
Zealous advocacy meaning question ("expressed interest")		
Mentioned	21	87.5
Did not mention (66.7% most experienced; 66.7% best-interests advocates)	3	12.5

experienced participants had ten or more years of experience as attorneys, and least experienced participants had zero to nine years of experience (see table 3.1). The divide between the groups roughly follows the timeline of the NCOJD's first role statement dissemination in 2005 (NCOJD, 2013).

Interestingly, less than a third (four out of thirteen) of the most experienced participants identified as expressed-interests advocates, while a little under half (five out of eleven) of the least experienced participants identified as expressed-interests advocates. Looking at these dynamics in another way, the most experienced attorneys were almost twice as likely to identify as best-interests advocates than as expressed-interests advocates. Four of the five (80 percent) of the best-interests advocates were in the most experienced category, with ten or more years of experience as attorneys, but only four of the nine (44 percent) of the expressed-interests advocates were in the most experienced category. Even though it is difficult to ascertain why more experienced attorneys would more often identify with a role alternative to the one they are ethically mandated to fill, one might consider that the NCOJD's *Role*

Statement (2005) and the NCCIDS's *Performance Guidelines for Appointed Counsel* (2007) were published only nine and seven years, respectively, before these data were collected. The *Role Statement* was distributed in 2005, so perhaps the newer, less experienced attorneys have been able to better internalize the new paradigm. In addition, this finding does not take into account the alternative, or declined, responses provided by 55 percent of participants who were among the least experienced attorneys. Perhaps their responses support the oft-cited argument that advocating for juveniles charged with crimes is far more nuanced than the expressed-/best-interests dichotomy implies. For the remainder of the book, information regarding participants' self-identified *advocate type* (best or expressed interests) and level of experience (most or least) will be provided alongside their quotes to assist the reader with considering the connections between advocate type/experience level and other phenomena targeted by the interviews. These connections and their implications are addressed throughout the discussion of each phenomenon.

The variation of these responses is important to discuss. Since the jurisdiction in which these participants practiced juvenile defense was officially, and unequivocally, *expressed* interests at the time of the interviews, it should not be a surprise that the most common response to this question was "expressed interests." What *is* a surprise is that the percentage, despite being the highest of all the categories, was still so low and not much higher than the percentage of participants who identified as their clients' *best*-interests advocate (20.8 percent, as opposed to the nine, or 37.5 percent, identifying as expressed-interests advocates).

The alternative responses were not included in the percentage analysis because doing so would have involved too much inference. However, that there are so many alternative responses is meaningful in and of itself. An explanation might be revealed through an examination of the alternative answers that participants provided. It would not be difficult to imagine that participants who defined themselves as their clients' *personal-*, *best-personal-*, or *true*-interests advocates recognized their duty to prioritize their clients' expressed interests but chose to use a different term. However, this would have required a level of inference I was not comfortable making and presumes a potentially oversimplified dichotomy between expressed and best interests. In fact, the participant who identified as supporting his clients' *true* interests, Participant 008, one of the most experienced attorneys, cautioned me against treating expressed and best interests as so mutually exclusive. Perhaps it is not much of a stretch to imagine that the participants who identified as their clients' *legal-*interests advocates were focusing on the counseling or strategizing aspects of their role, aspects that will be briefly addressed later in this book. One could also imagine that Participant 007, who identified as his clients' *best-defense* advocate and was among the most experienced attorneys, could have been considering the strategist part of the juvenile defender role.

Such speculation does not allow the reader to assess the extent to which these participants would substitute their own opinion of the clients' interests for the clients' expressed interests. This is especially true because even the participants who identified as *best*-interests advocates (012, 015, 016, 017, and 019, all of whom, except 015, were among the most-experienced attorneys) were very clear in other parts of the interview that they recognized the importance of prioritizing the *expressed* wishes of their juvenile clients. Also, the participants who declined to answer this question suggested that zealous advocacy requires considering clients' best *and* expressed interests (Participants 005, 006, and 009, only 005 of whom was among the most-experienced attorneys). In fact, Participant 006 admitted that while she pushed for the clients' best interests, she told her clients that they are the ultimate decision-makers. Participant 009 said that he advocated for his clients' best interests but not in a way that involves *not* taking a "zealous defense role." It is critical to mention at this point that all but one participant, including most of those who identified as their clients' best-interests advocates, discussed or alluded to (Participants 007 and 015) the importance of expressed-interests advocacy as part of their definition of zealous advocacy of their juvenile clients in response to the open-ended question on zealous advocacy meaning. The exception was Participant 019, who is one of the most-experienced attorneys and identified himself as a best-interests advocate. However, his recognition of the importance of expressed interests to the zealous-advocate-for-juveniles role came out in his answers to other questions. Perhaps an examination of their responses to the indirect question will help elucidate some of the ambiguity presented by their responses to the direct *I view myself as an advocate for my client's* _____ *interests* statement.

Participants were asked an indirect question about their role definition in the very first item on the interview protocol: *What does zealous advocacy mean to you in terms of advocating for your client's interests?* Their responses revealed a little more cohesiveness in terms of expressed interests. All but three (87.5 percent) participants volunteered that their definition of zealous advocacy involved a focus on the expressed interests of their clients. Interestingly, of those who did *not* volunteer this focus, two identified as best-interests advocates (015, 019) and one as best-defense (007). It is important to note that despite not volunteering this focus in response to this particular interview question, all three of these participants acknowledged the importance of expressed-interests advocacy in their responses to other interview questions or in the vignette exercises. Nevertheless, the majority of participants reported viewing zealous advocacy as involving an expressed-interests focus (see table 4.1).

Three participants (005, 006, and 009) declined to identify themselves as a particular advocate yet still acknowledged the mandated expressed-interests advocacy facet of their role. Even though they represented the full tenure-length spectrum, with 005 having decades of experience and the other two having only a few years, all three appeared to understand this requirement. Participant 009, with only three years of experience, acknowledged, "We're so ingrained that as a zealous advocate you have to do what your client wants," and Participant 005, one of the most respected and experienced attorneys in the sample, stated, "I believe we are ethically bound to do what our client wants us to do."

Participant 008, also one of the more reputable and experienced juvenile defenders with a tenure of twenty-four years, cautioned me against making so sharp a distinction between expressed and best interests. At the same time, he stated, "Okay, here's the thing: you have to advocate what your *client's position* [emphasis added] is. And your client can have a stupid position or have a wrong position or have a dumb position." Even though he identified himself as his client's true-interest advocate, these comments suggest that Participant 008 might equate true interests with expressed interests.

Interestingly, Participant 016 (most-experienced) identified herself as a best-interests advocate and provided one of the most illustrative explanations of the expressed-interests advocate focus in terms of zealous advocacy meaning:

> I think zealous advocacy first of all starts with finding out what it is that they are hoping to accomplish and then presenting that position and presenting it in the best way possible, whether that's gathering information [or] providing resources for the client—for example, if the client wants to do probation, you want to make sure to set them up for success and of course advocate on their behalf in a way that promotes *their interests* [emphasis added].

Participant 016's comments certainly reflect a perspective that prioritizes her clients' expressed interests, as do comments from almost all the other participants in response to the role-meaning question. Again, only three participants (007, 015, and 019) did *not* explicitly refer to clients' expressed interests when asked about their zealous advocacy meaning. Participants 015 and 019 discussed the importance of pursuing the *best outcome* or *results* for their clients as a major part of their zealous advocacy definition, which some, like Participant 007, might view as "minimizing as much damage as possible to my clients." However, they did not specifically mention advocating for their clients' expressed interests as part of that endeavor. The following excerpts illustrate.

> I think for me what [zealous advocacy] means is getting the *best outcome* [emphasis added] that they can possibly get and [doing] whatever I need to do within the parameters of my job or ethics . . . to get the best outcome they can get. (015)

> Well, in this case, juvenile clients, [zealous advocacy] means particularly fully defending them against criminal charges that they've been charged with and making sure that we get the *best results* [emphasis added] for their particular case. (019)

That both 015 and 019 identified as their clients' best-interests advocates and 007 identified himself as his clients' best-defense advocate suggests that these particular defenders might view their role differently from the way others do who did not identify as these types of advocate and for whom expressed-interests advocacy is at the forefront of their zealous advocacy definition. It is also important to note that all three of these participants mentioned the importance of expressed-interests advocacy to their role in their responses to other questions. However, one might imagine that it was not at the forefront of their zealous advocacy definition at the time they were asked about it, especially since this question was the very first of the interview.

Even though these participants did not explicitly prioritize clients' expressed interests, their responses did not necessarily indicate a dismissal of expressed-interests advocacy. For instance, Participant 015 recognized that he must advocate within the parameters of his *job* or *ethics*. He is presumably aware of his ethical responsibility to advocate for his child clients' expressed interests since he not only has taken an oath to represent *all* his clients in this way, pursuant to the *Model Rules of Professional Conduct* (ABA, 2013), but also has doubtless been made aware of his jurisdiction's explicit rules on expressed-interests advocacy. Additionally, it is clear that Participant 019 viewed his role as one that "fully defend[s]" his clients "against criminal charges." What is not clear is whether or not he was willing to disregard his clients' expressed interests to do so, a topic addressed later in this chapter.

In practical terms, one might expect these three attorneys to be more accepting of departures of the zealous advocacy role; experience more support from others in the best-interests court culture; and experience less role conflict, internally and externally, because their view of their role appeared to align more with one of the major forces thought to create role conflict, the best-interests court culture and the court's functionaries. Even though this did not turn out to be the case, these are still critical topics to consider for future research.

That more than half of participants failed to identify themselves as expressed-interests advocates after participating in, at minimum, an hour-long interview in which the expressed-/best-interests dichotomy was a focus is interesting. That so many participants identified as alternate types of advocate might reflect the complex nature of the juvenile defender role. However, whether it indicates role confusion requires further consideration.

Juvenile defenders who identify themselves as their clients' *personal-*, *best-personal-*, or *true*-interests advocates could still recognize their duty to prioritize their clients' expressed interests, even if they choose to refer to it differently. Even though this assumption would require too high a level of inference for this study's purposes, again, it could indicate the oversimplification of the dichotomy between expressed and best interests instead of the existence of role confusion. Recall Participant 008's specific caution against treating expressed and best interests as mutually exclusive, not to mention Birckhead's similar suggestion (2010). In addition, participants' identification as their clients' *legal*-interests advocates might indicate they are more focused on the counseling or strategizing function of their role than confused about the advocate function. The same could be said for Participant 007, who identified as his clients' best-defense advocate. Even though a deep examination of the potential oversimplification of the expressed-/best-interests dichotomy is beyond the scope of this study, it is an important topic for future consideration and a critical question in any discussion of the juvenile defender role.

Notwithstanding the aforementioned, participants who identified as their clients' best-interests advocates (012, 015, 016, 017, 019) presented a conundrum. In other parts of the interview they clearly recognized that their zealous advocate role requires their prioritization of their juvenile clients' *expressed* wishes. The same could be said for the participants (005, 006, and 009) who declined to identify as a particular advocate type, but their responses to the open-ended question were more nuanced, suggesting they believe that zealous advocacy requires considering clients' best *and* expressed interests. For example, Participant 006 admitted that while she pushes for the clients' best interests, she tells them that they are the ultimate decision-makers. In addition, Participant 009 indicated that he advocated for his clients' best interests but not in a way that he believes fully violates his zealous defense role. This is the explanation he provided:

In terms of advocating for the expressed interests of the client, again, I take a step back and . . . with the exception of mental health or drug abuse . . . I would always advocate exactly what the client wished. But I do think I am the representative of the child and, at the same time, look after his best interests, and so I would say that if the client had an expressed interest which I thought was very much in conflict with a holistic treatment or something that was going to better him in some sort of way, I might . . . sidestep a little bit and say, "But you know, historically, I'm not sure that's the best course of action." [I would] not completely . . . contradict the client but point out alternatives that I think might be helpful, and that's not something I would do in the adult system, so I wouldn't say that's necessarily departing from advocating [for the client's expressed interests]. . . . Well, it's slightly departing from advocating for [them].

The more nuanced responses of these three participants could indicate that they balk at the expressed-/best-interests dichotomy. Like Participant 008, they might view such a dichotomy as overly simplistic. This view might have been responsible for their reluctance to identify with a particular type of advocate for the completion task, and it might be responsible for others' identification with alternative types of advocate. A larger future study on this topic would be useful in teasing out these relationships; this is a possibility discussed more thoroughly in chapter 8.

Notwithstanding the variation demonstrated by participants' responses to questions about their views on the zealous advocate role, particularly the completion task, they appeared to show consistency in their identification of expressed-interests advocacy as central to the role. These findings did not seem to mirror the level of role confusion or conflict suggested by Grindall and Puritz's 2003 report. This makes sense since they are based on data collected more than a decade after the report and nearly a decade after North Carolina's *Role Statement*, clarifying juvenile defenders' role as emphasizing *expressed*-interests advocacy (NCOJD, 2005). These findings might suggest the *Role Statement*'s successful integration, to some extent. At the same time, participants' responses to the completion task indicated some remaining confusion about the role, or reluctance to restrict one's role definition to expressed interests. This variation might also suggest that the expressed-/best-interests dichotomy is an oversimplification, North Carolina's mandate has not been completely internalized among its juvenile defenders, or there could be meaningful differences between self-identified expressed- and best-interests advocates. A deeper examination of participants' views of their role meaning, starting with the advocate role itself, might shed light on these speculations.

Other Zealous Advocate Definitions

Recall that an advocate is "a person who assists, defends, pleads, or prosecutes for another" (Garner & Black, 2006, p. 23). Included in their responses to the open-ended (indirect) role question, participants provided two other major definitions of their advocate role, namely a *voice* for their clients and a *temper, check,* or *balance* against a powerful government.

Several (eight out of twenty-four, or 33.3 percent) likened their advocate role to serving as their clients' *voice.* Participant 003, who identified as an expressed-interests attorney and who was among the most experienced, explained, "It's my job to be that juvenile's voice." Participant 001, also a most experienced and expressed-interests advocate, noted, "My role in the court system is to be the voice of the juvenile . . . not to be what's the best interests of the juvenile." Participant 011, yet another most experienced and expressed-interests advocate, described an analogy she used to communicate this notion of her role to her clients in the following way:

> Zealous advocacy means . . . you try and figure out what your kid really wants. You try and be their voice. . . . And I explain to them, "You're my boss, I am your voice to the judge. I'll filter it so you can cuss all you want to me and I won't [cuss] to the judge." . . . To me zealous advocacy means really trying to get what that kid wants and make them feel heard even when you know you're going to go down in flames in front of a judge.

Participant 011's "boss" analogy, shared by other participants, reflected her belief that her child clients have the capacity to form and articulate their own interests, even if she has to make some effort to discern what those are. She also appeared to believe her advocate role entailed accepting the consequences of that advocacy as long as her clients felt they had been heard.

Participants' recognition of their role as lending their clients' voice and essentially serving as their employee reflects awareness of the learning opportunity the juvenile court experience can provide respondents. As suggested in chapter 2, juveniles' experience with the court system is rich with opportunities for them to practice making empowered and informed decisions. It is also full of opportunities for them to learn to trust the one adult who is constitutionally tasked with serving juveniles' expressed interests and giving them a voice in the courtroom. These opportunities are extremely critical, given that poor decision-making, feelings of invisibility and voicelessness, and the unavailability of seemingly interested and trustworthy adults might play a significant role in how some juveniles come to be in front of the judge to begin with. This reality was clearly recognized by the study's participants.

Another way to illustrate the importance of juvenile defenders' role as their clients' voice is to acknowledge what happens when juveniles' voices are absent from their own cases. Some participants pointed out the potential consequences of *not* serving as their clients' voice because of their special role among other justice system functionaries. For example, Participant 004, an expressed-interests advocate who was among the least experienced attorneys, argued, "If I don't give voice to what they want, then nobody else does. . . . If I don't speak up for my kid, nobody hears his or her voice." Several participants openly recognized that a key function of their role is to serve as a check against other, arguably more powerful figures in the courtroom. For example, Participant 004 noted,

> I've come to realize that my job as a zealous advocate and as a defense counsel is sometimes to be the thorn in the side [of the court's authority]. And I'm willing to do that, and so my role . . . is sometimes for me to hold up my hand and say, "Stop." And if they stop, fine, and if they don't, then [I] try to do whatever I can to slow things down and say, "Take another look at this; consider this alternative."

If juvenile defenders have fully internalized their role as expressed-interest advocates, one of the ways they might define their zealous advocate role is as a check against misuse of state authority toward their clients, despite the court's best-interests orientation. While all participants likely recognized that their role serves to *temper* other figures in the courtroom, not all of them might have considered it a central part of their zealous advocate role.

Other participants argued that they *balance* the predominantly best-interests forces (e.g., the court counselor and judge) in the courtroom. In other words, the juvenile already has the court counselor, the judge, the prosecutor (to some extent), and the system at large serving his or her best interests, making the defense attorney's advocate role all the more critical. Eleven (45.8 percent) participants made this type of argument, one of whom stated,

> I think that there are enough people in the courtroom to make sure that the best interests of the juvenile [are] observed, so I think that, yeah, just generally it's a[n] uphill battle, and everybody thinks they know what the juvenile should be doing or what's in the juvenile's best interests versus what the juvenile might want, and even from a personal standpoint [as opposed to a legal professional's

standpoint] sometimes I know that a fourteen-year-old doesn't need certain things, but if that's what they're asking for, my job is to make sure that their voice is heard and that I'm representing them and asking for what they want. (018, least experienced, expressed-interests advocate)

Interestingly, none of the seven participants who raised the temper aspect of their role identified themselves as a best-interests advocate. The majority identified as expressed-interests advocates, and two identified as either true- or legal-interests advocates. As for the participants who noted their balancing role, only one (Participant 16) identified as a best-interests advocate, and again, despite this identification, she clearly recognized expressed-interests advocacy as central to her zealous advocacy definition. The others were predominantly expressed-interests advocates with one being a legal- and another being a best-personal-desired-interests advocate. In addition, all participants in the three groups (voice, temper, and balance) volunteered expressed-interests advocacy as central to their zealous advocacy definitions. Thus, the same convergence can be seen among the participants who made up the three groups, even though only four participants (004, 013, 018, and 022) are members of all three.

Another interesting note to make about the participants who volunteered these perspectives is that there seems to be a pattern among them determined by their tenure as attorneys. Even though there was an even split of the voice analogy participants between the most and least experienced, those who raised the temper function of the role were likelier to be less experienced (57.1 percent), as were those who raised the balance function of the role (63.6 percent). An explanation for this finding could be that the less-experienced attorneys retained some idealism about the role they play in the larger context of the courtroom. It could be that they had not yet experienced enough occasions where their balancing function was mitigated by other forces in the courtroom, dampening their belief in the efficacy of that function. On the other hand, their shorter tenure might have placed them in a timely position to benefit from North Carolina's tremendous efforts to firmly establish expressed-interests advocacy among juvenile defenders.

These perspectives—that the defender serves as the client's voice and balances courtroom power and viewpoints—reflect the juvenile defender values set out in the NCOJD's 2005 *Role Statement* (reiterated in 2013), the *Performance Guidelines for Appointed Counsel* (NCCIDS, 2007), and the National Juvenile Defender Center's *National Juvenile Defense Standards* (2012). That participants' views showed consistency within themselves and with these guidelines suggests there might be less role confusion among North Carolina's juvenile defenders in 2014 than when the state assessment was conducted in 2003. However, as demonstrated earlier in this chapter, participants' interpretations of their advocate role still reflected some inconsistencies, even when it came to the expressed-interests component. Clearly, not all twenty-four participants identified themselves as expressed-interests advocates, and three did not focus on expressed-interests advocacy in their zealous advocacy definitions, a finding indicative of some role ambiguity or confusion among North Carolina's juvenile defenders. The responses from which the voice, temper, and balance themes emerged reflect convergence among apparently similarly minded participants, indicating a pattern that could be examined in future research. However, since there is still a healthy amount of inconsistency among juvenile defenders about their definition of the role, it raises the question of whether the *In re Gault* (1967) promise of assistance of counsel is truly realized. Merely asking juvenile defenders about how they define their role is insufficient to elicit a meaningful answer, but examining the extent to which they view role departures as acceptable might provide a deeper understanding.

Role Departures

It is reasonable to think that anyone in a professional role might find cause to depart from the role's requirements occasionally if the reasons were compelling enough. The consequences for role departures naturally vary. The nature of the responsibilities of the role also determine how potentially harmful a departure is. Juvenile defenders not only are responsible for guarding juveniles' due process rights but also serve as educators to juveniles for how the system works and what their rights are and could be among the first adults to convey to some juveniles that they are worthwhile. Despite that fact that participants demonstrated some inconsistency with their role definitions, they all recognized the importance of the expressed-interests component to their zealous advocate role. Participants were therefore asked, *In your opinion, should a defense attorney ever depart from advocating for the expressed interests of a client?* As seen in table 4.2, most participants (sixteen or 66.7 percent) identified departures from expressed-interests advocacy as *not* acceptable. Many referred to the legal profession's ethical mandate or struggled to imagine a scenario where such a departure would be acceptable. Eight of the twenty-four respondents (33.3 percent) believed such a departure was at least sometimes acceptable and provided explanations that will be addressed in the remainder of this chapter.

Table 4.2. Role Departures

Zealous advocacy departure acceptable	n = 24	Percentage
No (56.3% of most experienced; 43.8% of expressed-interests advocates)	16	66.7
Yes/sometimes (62.5% of most experienced)	8	33.3

At first blush, these findings could be seen as encouraging *and* discouraging. They are encouraging in that they might reflect the extent to which juvenile defenders have internalized the NCOJD's *Role Statement* since its first dissemination in 2005. This is a difficult conclusion to reach, however, because there are no data from the 2003 state assessment to indicate if the present findings reflect an increase or decrease in the extent to which juvenile defenders view role departures as justifiable (Grindall & Puritz, 2003). However, it is not unreasonable to assume that the percentage might have been lower than 66.7 percent, since the assessment indicated that North Carolina's juvenile defenders were regularly co-opted into the juvenile court's best-interests orientation. The state then went to great lengths to counteract this practice. It is therefore reasonable to believe that participants' responses reflect a *decrease* in the extent to which departures are seen as justifiable (Grindall & Puritz, 2003).

Additional analysis revealed that there was only a slight difference between the most and least experienced attorneys, where 28.6 percent of the most experienced and 20 percent of the least experienced viewed zealous advocacy departures as acceptable. This difference is small but is possibly one that could be explored in future research with a larger sample. Less experienced attorneys might not yet feel confident enough with their skills to imagine departing, might not feel confident enough in their professional standing to explicitly state that they would find departure acceptable, or, as already suggested in this chapter, might have internalized the expressed-interests advocate mandate more because their entry into the role coincided with the *Role Statement*'s first dissemination and accompanying trainings.

A closer look at advocate type provides more divergent results. Only 22.2 percent of the expressed-interests advocates reported they thought such a departure was acceptable, but 40 percent of the best-interests advocates reported the same. This particular finding makes sense because one would expect juvenile defenders who identify as best-interests advocates to feel more comfortable with departures from the expressed-interests advocate role. What is more interesting is the fact that three of the five best-interests advocates stated they did not think such a departure was acceptable. As could be the case for many of the percentages provided throughout this book, the percentage discrepancy could be explained by the difference in group size given that there were almost twice as many expressed-interests advocates than best-interests advocates, suggesting the need for additional research with a larger sample.

Of the three participants who did not volunteer that they believed expressed-interests advocacy was central to their meaning of zealous advocacy, two (007 and 015) indicated that they viewed such departures as acceptable. This makes sense because the omission of expressed-interests advocacy from their zealous advocacy meaning might indicate it was not a priority for them; after all, they see their role as best-interests advocates. However, Participant 019, the third, stated he did not believe such a departure was acceptable despite having identified himself as a best-interests advocate *and* not having volunteered expressed-interests advocacy as central to his view of zealous advocacy. Confusingly, Participant 019 reported only one instance of internal role conflict. But, as will be discussed in chapter 5, he is one of the six participants who indicated that role conflict happened often for him, so the conflict he experiences might have come primarily from external sources. Or, the discrepancy could reflect the role ambiguity that scholars have identified.

This study's findings could also be viewed as somewhat discouraging because they indicate that many juvenile defenders in North Carolina believe role departures are justifiable *despite* nearly a decade of the role being officially and clearly defined as one of expressed interests. One must also take into account the numerous trainings addressing this matter that had been provided to juvenile defenders during that same time period. A decade might not have been sufficient time for the policy to sink in, but these findings also make it seem as though there were still powerful pressures encouraging juvenile defenders to depart from the role. These pressures likely originated in the court system and its stakeholders, as suggested by the North Carolina state assessment (Grindall & Puritz, 2003) and confirmed by this study's findings.

On the other hand, the persistent view that departures are justifiable could reflect role confusion or critical points of disparity between perspectives on representing juvenile and adult defendants. In other words, this view could reflect factors that are unique to juvenile defense that make a strictly expressed-interests advocacy unpalatable to or impracticable for some juvenile defenders. Again, some legal scholars suggest juvenile defense might be a unique type of practice that does not lend itself to the traditional expressed-/best-interests dichotomy (Birckhead, 2010; Henning, 2005). Nevertheless, participants were quick to point out the factors they believe create motivations, and possibly justifications, for zealous advocate role departures, and they mostly related to some form of compromised client.

All twenty-four participants identified clients, or clients' condition (e.g., status as children with less capacity and autonomy than adults), as a source of role conflict in some way. However, that does not mean all participants believed any role conflict originating with their clients created a justification to depart from the zealous advocate role. Such justification appeared to largely depend on the following factors: (1) the client's age (004); (2) the client's capacity/mental health (004, 005, 007, 009, 014, 015, 022); (3) the client's substance use status (005, 007, 009); and (4) the client's living/health conditions (002, 006, 016). The parenthetical participant numbers are provided to indicate which participants explicitly volunteered these circumstances in response to the question about whether they thought a defense attorney should ever depart from advocating for the expressed interests of a juvenile client. These participants replied "yes" or "sometimes" to that question and followed up with descriptions of circumstances under which they found such departure acceptable.

Client Age

Birckhead astutely points out that "in any attorney-client relationship, assumptions, biases, and feelings of resignation might arise, but when the client is a child, this dynamic is magnified as such factors as paternalism, *role confusion* [emphasis added], and culture clash enter into the mix" (2010, p. 986). Juvenile defenders' views on children's ability to understand what is best for them and to articulate their own interests clearly had an impact on the way these attorneys viewed their role, ethical duties, and the extent to which they saw role departures as acceptable. In fact, participants were specifically asked if having a very young client ever affected their zealous advocacy role. Their responses reflected Birckhead's assertions.

Participants reported that limits to expressed-interest advocacy sometimes involved the extent to which they believed child clients, as a result of their age, could form or articulate their own interests. For example, Participant 020 (least experienced, legal-interests advocate) remarked that when "the client is fourteen, fifteen years old, . . . they're generally idiots." And Participant 019 answered "their age" when asked what he thought contributed to juvenile clients' lack of understanding of what might be best for them.

Participant 020 articulated very well the tendency for some juvenile defenders to feel more compelled to depart from the expressed-interests advocate role due to their clients' age. The following excerpt illustrates.

> I think the younger they are, [I'm] absolutely . . . going to fall into that best-interests analysis more and more so. . . . I think . . . they're going to have a hard time even understanding what's going on, much less expressing what they want to happen with the case, so absolutely, maybe I can imagine in those cases thinking much more along the lines of best interests.

Participant 009—one of the least experienced attorneys but one who declined to identify with any particular type of advocate—clearly recognized how easy it was for a juvenile defender to be so compelled:

> Young children just don't often fully appreciate what's going on, and . . . I feel like there's . . . a little bit of a knee-jerk reaction when it's not clear what the kid wants, or what the kid understands [about your doing] . . . what you think is the right thing. I would say that can affect the zealous advocacy role . . . that you are really snapping much more towards the "let's help the kid" as opposed to defending the kid when there are attributes [for instance, inculpatory evidence] in place.

As these excerpts indicate, some juvenile defenders struggled with the boundaries of their role as a result of their clients' age and the decision-making implications thereof. Juvenile clients' age presents a complicated pressure because it calls into question the underlying reason for their lack of understanding. For example, is a juvenile's lack of capacity solely due to his or her age? Or is it caused by a mental illness or neurological deficit that might or might not be amenable to diagnosis or treatment? If the former, what are the implications for the client's ability to articulate an interest at this particular point in his or her development? If the latter, will there be internal or external pressure on the defender to depart from the expressed-interests advocate role so that the client can receive services, even if the child did not commit the act of which he or she is accused? Some scholars have suggested a client's young age could be viewed as a *cognitive deficit*, similar to the way mental illness is viewed by defense attorneys of their adult defendants (see Cohen, 1965). These are critical questions for future research on the challenges juvenile defenders face in their role and have implications for juvenile defense practice and policy, not to mention the credibility of the juvenile justice system as a whole.

These questions also raise concerns about the extent to which juveniles' status as individuals lacking experience, maturity, and capacity to make complex decisions should be considered in the courtroom. Given the US Supreme Court's growing recognition of the need to account for age in justice system decisions (see, e.g., *Roper v. Simmons*, 2005; and *J. D. B. v. North Carolina*,

2011), the time might be ripe for addressing the implications of juveniles' age-related mental status for juvenile defense. This issue is beyond the scope of this study, but its relationship to the present topics and worthiness of future empirical attention is undeniable.

Suffice it to say that juvenile defenders often face pressure to depart from their expressed-interests advocate role by mere virtue of their clients' status as juveniles. One can imagine that juvenile defenders face internal conflict about their role because of juvenile justice practices and policies that could bring children as young as age six (R. Waldrop Rugh, personal communication, July 27, 2016) in front of an increasingly punitive court (Birckhead, 2010). Participants clearly recognized this reality and found themselves motivated to depart from the expressed-interests advocate role as a result. Some felt justified departing from the role. This was particularly true for those who have had very young clients. It was also true for participants whose clients lacked capacity for non-age-related reasons or had special needs.

Client Special Needs

Participants were directly asked the following: *Does having a very young, or special-needs, client ever affect your zealous advocacy role? How so?* Even though not all participants had had the opportunity to work with these types of clients, virtually all (twenty-three or 95.8 percent) agreed that having a special-needs or very young client would, or could, affect a defense attorney's zealous advocacy in some way, though not necessarily causing a departure. Only one participant (021, a legal-interests advocate who was among the most experienced participants) answered "no" without providing any further comment. However, Participant 021 also demonstrated that he recognized the unique dilemma having such a client might present when he provided answers to the vignette exercises (see "John" vignette in appendix E).

Participants' justifications for role departure often centered on the client's *capacity* to assist in his or her own case—specifically, to know and articulate his or her wants:

> If I have issues about my juvenile's capacity to proceed or to understand the process, then my role might switch to a best-interests advocacy because I can't get to their expressed interest or I can't trust that they [understand], as much as a juvenile can understand, that their expressed interests may be against their best interests. (014, least experienced, expressed-interests advocate)

More specifically, participants justified departures from the expressed-interests component of their zealous advocate role when it came to clients who lacked capacity or suffered from a mental illness. The following demonstrates one participant's rationale:

> I can think of a scenario ... where you might have to [depart from the zealous advocacy role], and that's where your client's severely mentally ill. ... If I've got a client that I think is incompetent from mental illness ... I'm cautious about [departing from the zealous advocacy role], but yeah, I'll kind of step out of that role. ... I think there's a few times where you've got to step outside that, and that's when they're mentally ill or incompetent to stand trial. (007, most experienced, best-defense advocate)

Participant 007 recognized the implications that severe mental illness can have for a client's competence or capacity. As explained previously in the age discussion, individuals' capacity determines the extent to which they can understand the charges against them and assist in their own defense. Participant 007 appeared to view mentally ill clients whose competence was compromised as lacking in capacity. He therefore justified departing from the zealous advocate role with this type of client.

To be sure, clients who lack the capacity to understand the charges against them or to assist in their own defense make it very difficult for juvenile defenders to adhere to the expressed-interests advocate role. How can clients with special needs, particularly the kind that affect their cognitive and decision-making ability, form or articulate a wish clearly enough for their juvenile defender to advocate for it?

> If there were a mental illness problem on the part of my client where I really don't feel my client fully understands what's going on, and their view of the world due to their mental illness is skewed ... and that's really the most difficult clients to represent ... sometimes you just don't know the truth. And you don't feel confident that your client is either giving you the truth or is capable of giving you the truth. ... And they just weren't in touch with reality, so ... now I really have a question about whether it's true, so to the extent of representing the child's expressed interests, you don't feel like the child's expressed interests are based upon reality, [and] then it's a little difficult to represent, strictly, their expressed interests. (003, most experienced, expressed-interests advocate)

Participants' approaches to their special-needs clients did not appear to contravene the *Performance Guidelines for Appointed Counsel* (NCCIDS, 2007). The guidelines encourage defenders to follow an outlined procedure when they have a "good faith doubt" as to their client's capacity (p. 8). Beyond delineating the procedure, the guidelines say very little about how counsel is to respond to such a situation. However, they do state that "although the juvenile's expressed interests ordinarily control, counsel might question capacity to proceed without the juvenile's assent or over the juvenile's objection, if necessary" (Guideline 5.2b, p. 8). This allows juvenile defenders some formal justification for departures from the role that are based on client capacity issues. Their role with clients who lack capacity or struggle with mental illness might be somewhat like the role of those who represent adults with mental illnesses (Cohen, 1965). Even though it is beyond the scope of this study, this analogy might be a useful one to explore in future research.

A client's mental state is a critical factor in the attorney-client relationship, regardless of the client's age. Participants unanimously recognized that situations involving mentally deficient clients not only require them to view their clients' expressed interests with caution but also make it likelier that they will depart from their expressed-interests advocate role. As they explained in their responses to the vignette involving a mentally deficient client scenario (see "John" vignette in appendix E), participants had a systematic way of handling these clients. The process typically would begin with a client competence assessment, if the client's capacity were in question, and then the defender would proceed with great care in terms of responsibly communicating with the client. This approach appears to indicate that North Carolina's guidelines for juvenile defenders have been internalized.

The consistent way participants approached special-needs clients raises the question of whether the approach truly constitutes a departure, given the established procedures for handling clients with special needs. Perhaps the expressed-interests element of the zealous advocate role presumes a competent client who has full use of his or her faculties. Under this presumption, when juvenile defenders take a best-interests approach with special-needs clients, they neither depart from their role nor violate their ethical mandate.

Juvenile defenders appeared to believe that when a client's mental capacity made the expressed-interests component of the zealous advocate role almost impossible, a departure from the role was justified. Some participants raised an extreme, and rare, type of scenario in which they would likely depart from the role even if the client's capacity were *not* compromised. These situations were referred to as mandatory reporting scenarios.

Mandatory Reporting

In response to the role-departure question, a small number of participants referred to their obligation to depart from their expressed-interests advocate role in a mandatory reporting situation (e.g., client is a danger to self, is in a dangerous home situation, is a danger to others, and so on). Eric Zogry, the juvenile defender of North Carolina, explained that there is no concrete law on the matter of mandatory reporting for juvenile defenders. He added that he believed the North Carolina bar would support attorneys who maintained their clients' confidence instead of reporting a dangerous situation, and it would be unlikely for an attorney to get prosecuted for *not* complying with the mandatory reporting laws (personal communication, July 29, 2015).

Participant 006, who declined to identify as an advocate type and had been an attorney for only three years, stated that departure from the role would be justified "if someone is going to do self-harm or harm to others." And Participant 002, an expressed-interests advocate with thirteen years of experience as an attorney, explained the same justification in the following way:

> I will give you an example.... You know you have to keep [your client's] confidences, but in the situation where you think there might be abuse or neglect of your client, you have the authority to report that irrespective of what your client wants. In other words, this client didn't want me to tell the part about his dad beating him because that was the social services aspect of the case. He didn't want to be removed from his mom. His mom was allowing his stepdad to beat him.

Mandatory reporting situations are of considerable and unique concern to juvenile defenders because they involve two areas of ethical consideration for attorneys and one area of consideration for them as North Carolina citizens. First, of course, is the defender's ethical duty to adhere to the expressed-interests advocate role. Second is the defender's duty to maintain his or her client's confidence. Attorneys are required to maintain their clients' confidence with very few exceptions (such as when they might be a danger to themselves or others or in danger from others). For instance, if a juvenile respondent were to share information with his defense attorney indicating that he threatened his stepfather with a knife because his stepfather was beating him, the attorney might feel compelled to use this information to defend her client against charges of criminal threatening. However, if the client did not want the attorney to use the information in the defense strategy, the attorney would have to comply, according to her duties as a zealous advocate. A third area of consideration for juvenile defenders is that under North Carolina law, all North Carolina citizens are mandatory reporters for child abuse incidents (NC Gen. Stat. § 7B-301). This law could place juvenile defenders at odds with their confidentiality duty to their clients.

Domestic abuse can frequently be a part of some juveniles' lives. In extreme situations, it could be the reason a juvenile has been charged with a crime. This was the case in the "Steven" vignette (see appendix E). In the vignette, Steven has been charged with simple assault against his mother and expressly desired placement back in the home; this was an unlikely outcome given that his mother is the victim in Steven's charges. Steven had claimed he was being abused at the time and was acting in self-defense.

Steven's request to be placed back in the home with the mother he had allegedly victimized would become a problem only if Steven did not want his attorney to report the abuse he claimed he has suffered. Again, since attorneys are mandatory reporters in the state of North Carolina, a juvenile defender might seek to involve the Department of Social Services in a case like Steven's, as six of twenty-two (27.3 percent) participants indicated when responding to the vignette. (Only twenty-two of the twenty-four participants in the study provided responses to the vignette scenarios.) Five (83.3 percent) of these particular participants were among the most experienced attorneys, and all six were either expressed-interests (66.7 percent) or legal-interests (33.3 percent) advocates.

This could mean that more seasoned attorneys recognized the importance of reaching out for service providers that are appropriately designated to assist with families in order to promote children's best interests. The participants who identified themselves as best-interests advocates might not have raised the mandatory reporting issue because their approach to juvenile defense might incorporate enough of a best-interests component, with cooperation from other courtroom functionaries like the court counselors, that reaching out is unnecessary. This conclusion is difficult to draw with so few participants; further examination of this dynamic might be suitable for a future study.

To be clear, involving the Department of Social Services would be a zealous advocate role departure because Steven had not given his consent to his attorney to share this privileged information. Recall that the head juvenile defender for all of North Carolina, the attorney who oversees all things juvenile defender in that state, indicated that it is unlikely for juvenile defenders to be sanctioned for prioritizing their clients' confidences over the mandatory reporting rule. This might be due to the nearly sacrosanct status of attorney-client privilege, something attorneys are heavily discouraged from violating. And, there is another juvenile court workgroup member, the court counselor, who works for the court and whose primary goal is to inquire after the juvenile's *best* interests, including familiarizing himself or herself with the juvenile's home life. If defense attorneys, being the only justice system workgroup members designated to work only for the juvenile and serve as his or her voice, betray their client's trust, they could arguably destroy the last chance of convincing the juvenile that society's rules and values are worth his or her commitment.

Participants who viewed role departures in mandatory reporting situations as justifiable, notwithstanding the strict rules about attorney-client confidentiality, represented a modest consensus. Even though Participant 002 (most experienced, expressed-interests advocate) noted that the "Steven" scenario is "very similar to a lot of cases that [he's] had over the years," the fact that so few participants volunteered this specific type of pressure to depart from the role could indicate that the dilemma is not very prevalent. Nevertheless, this is an issue that would benefit from future examination, particularly in jurisdictions with mandatory reporting laws like North Carolina's.

As made clear in the preceding paragraphs, participants identified a small number of situations in which they viewed zealous advocate role departures as either not *true* departures (e.g., when clients suffered from severe mental illness) or otherwise justifiable. Participants who raised the issues of mental capacity and mandatory reporting situations appeared to form a consensus that an alternative approach under those circumstances is acceptable. However, there was no such consensus for client substance use problems.

Client Substance Use and Abuse

Even though North Carolina's guidelines are silent on this issue, juvenile defenders identified client substance use or abuse as a circumstance where they *might* consider departing from the expressed-interests advocate role. Participants noted that they might consider a role departure in these situations because of the client's potential for compromised cognitive functioning as a result of drug use. Participant 009, a least-experienced attorney and one who declined to identify as an advocate type, explained this perspective in the following way:

> If there is a substance abuse or mental health issue, obviously that's something that has to be brought up with the court, and just [like] if you have someone who's crazy, you don't go and then run and do exactly what they want. That needs to be dealt with beforehand.

Participants seemed to have a pretty cohesive idea of how to handle this type of scenario. They typically would directly address the matter with clients, explaining to them their options and encouraging them to accept assistance, despite the implications of a responsible (that is, guilty) plea. Some participants reported getting creative with the circumstance, as Participant 007, one of the more experienced attorneys and a best-defense-interests advocate, explained:

> On one occasion . . . the juvenile was facing a lot of time, and we had some issues to fight with, but he had a really bad drug problem too, and so I negotiated with the prosecutor and the court counselor to reduce the charges but get him in drug treatment. And so, that's kind of stepping, I guess, outside of the role because he has something to fight with. . . . He could've been adjudicated [responsible] and then had all the problems that go with that . . . as far as the . . . heavy charges he was facing, so I guess that's kind of how you step outside [the zealous advocate role] sometimes.

Participant 007 described how he stepped outside of his zealous advocate role, reflecting the challenge a client's substance abuse situation might present a juvenile defender. That he identified as a best-interests advocate provides a critical link between the type of advocate defenders might view themselves as and how such identification manifests itself into defender behavior. In this particular case, the juvenile had "something to fight with," but it is not clear that Participant 007 failed to advocate for his client's *expressed* interests. However, his acknowledgment that he stepped outside his role in this particular situation implies that he believed he did.

Other times, participants reported prioritizing the client's expressed interests in order to comply with their zealous advocate role, but not without some internal conflict. Participant 014, a least-experienced, expressed-interests advocate, explained his thought process when wrestling with this situation:

> Oftentimes I may get a case where my client is telling me that they are addicted to drugs, using drugs. And so when the case gets resolved they want to go back and get high. And then I have to determine whether or not what they're telling me is, well, are they telling me information such that I feel that they're a danger to themselves, that would raise an ethical obligation for me to disclose that? Or, are they giving me information that I don't feel . . . creates an issue where they pose a danger to themselves or others? I don't have a duty to disclose it. And so now I have to push aside the tendency to lessen the zealousness of my advocacy in hopes that the juvenile is found responsible so that they can get services as opposed to continuing to advocate zealously using every tool available to me to get the juvenile's expressed wishes, which is normally to walk away, even though I know that they may be walking away to get high.

Even though participants viewed substance use as posing a similar problem to mental deficiency, they did not seem to view actual departure under this circumstance as justifiable. In other words, they seemed to make a distinction between these circumstances in terms of how they would proceed. Clearly, there could be some question as to the client's capacity in the case of drug or alcohol abuse, but participants seemed to view it as a less serious matter than a capacity question that involved age or mental illness. In fact, Participant 006 (least experienced, declined to identify advocate type) argued, "I don't think being an addict affects making decisions for yourself unless you're high right there." Some of the reasoning behind this perspective might have to do with two critical distinctions between organic or trauma-induced mental deficiency and mental deficiency due to drug or substance use. One is that an organic or trauma-based mental deficiency is presumably chronic (at least from the time of the trauma), whereas a substance-based mental deficiency is presumably acute or episodic—as Participant 006 stated, "unless you're high right there." The second is that clients who consume substances do so voluntarily, while an individual suffering from trauma-based mental deficiency does not choose to do so. Thus, the presumption with clients who present with substance use behavior could be that they are otherwise competent but make poor decisions, much like any juvenile. These presumptions could explain participants' reluctance to justify expressed-interests role departures in substance use situations.

The details of the "James" vignette follow.

> James is fourteen years old and has been arrested for possession of heroin. In the course of preparing his case, you learn he is an addict. You also come across evidence that the search leading to his arrest may have been illegal. Do you file a motion to suppress knowing James won't get treatment for his addiction? His mother doesn't have insurance and the only way for him to get treatment is for him to be adjudicated delinquent. What is the main dilemma and how would you cope with it? (appendix E)

Clearly, the vignette involves a client who presents with drug abuse behavior, but participants were not told what James has expressed he wants. Instead, they were asked how they would cope with the scenario based on the information presented. Twenty-one of the twenty-two participants who responded to this vignette recognized the expressed-/best-interests dilemma and either explicitly stated (fifteen participants) or implied (six participants) that they would defer to their client's expressed interests. Participant 010 indicated she would either go to trial or try to get James services because James's record would be fine since it was only juvenile court.

As participants explained during their interviews and in their responses to the "James" vignette, this type of dilemma presented them with pressure to depart from the expressed-interests advocate role because of their desire to get the client help. Recall that this kind of role conflict is referred to as *internal* or person-role conflict and originates from within the attorney. Despite the pressure to depart from the role, participants' responses indicated that, after having failed to persuade their clients to change their interests, they would ultimately advocate for their clients' expressed interests. So, participants did not seem to view client substance use or abuse as justification for zealous advocate role departure.

Participants' responses to questions about the meaning of their zealous advocate role indicate a rather cohesive definition, inclusive of an emphasis on their clients' expressed interests. They clearly recognized that, in terms of their duties, they are meant to serve their juvenile clients as if they were serving adult clients. Even still, participants openly recognized that there were some obstacles to their ability to fully inhabit the zealous advocate role that are unique to representing juveniles. There is no doubt about juvenile defenders' recognition that juveniles might lack capacity due to their youth, have home life challenges well outside their control, and face substance abuse issues. At the same time, these attorneys are human beings and in a position to help clients steer their lives in a better direction. However, they also recognized that they must prioritize their role as a zealous *advocate* for the juveniles' expressed interests in order to effectively fulfill their ethical duties as attorneys, particularly given the state's formalized expressed-interests advocacy requirement. So, the variation in their interpretations of their role as advocates for juveniles facing criminal charges suggests the influence of forces—such as pressure from other courtroom workgroup members, particularly the judge—the power of which is difficult to determine.

It makes sense that juvenile defenders, like anyone inhabiting a complex professional role, would exhibit variation in their interpretation of the role's requirements. The question then becomes, What does the variation mean, if anything? Some of the variation could be a mere matter of semantics (e.g., legal-interests advocate), and some of it could indicate powerful forces that affect how the role is carried out (e.g., internal or intersender role conflict). Again, it is very curious that so many participants (specifically, fifteen out of twenty-four, or 62.5 percent) did *not* say they were their clients' expressed-interests advocate in the completion task. Recall that this task was the very *last* item in what was often an hour-and-a-half interview addressing the importance of the expressed-interests approach to the zealous advocate role.

Also recall that *all* participants recognized the importance of the expressed-interests component of the zealous advocate role. To be sure, the interview items targeting participants' role meaning and advocate type barely scratch the surface of juvenile defenders' experience of their role. The same cannot be said for the items targeting whether, how, and from what sources participants experienced role conflict. Their responses to these items provided some insight into why their role definitions were so varied.

5. Land Mines
Role Conflict Prevalence and Sources

*R*ecall *the playground* analogy from the book's introduction. Thus far, our jungle gym supervisors have provided us with a solid sense of what they believe their role entails as well as some reasons they would justify role departures. We already know from the 2003 state assessment that our jungle gym supervisors encounter "land mines" in the form of role conflict, but the report does not go into much detail about what such conflict could look like or from what sources it stems (Grindall & Puritz). This study sought to suss out these kinds of details. Toward that end, role conflict prevalence and nature were measured directly and indirectly. Participants were asked, *Have you ever faced obstacles or pressures to depart from the zealous advocate role? What were they?* Another question was, *Do you ever feel like there are conflicting expectations of you in your role as a zealous advocate for juveniles? How so?* Finally, they were asked about pressures that prevented them *from being the kind of advocate [they] would like to be.*

Role Conflict Prevalence

As seen in table 5.1, most participants answered "yes" to the obstacles question. Very few answered "no," even though the majority of those who said "no" also reported experiencing conflicting expectations of them in their role, indicating that they had experienced role conflict in that particular manner. Most participants specifically reported they felt there were conflicting expectations of them in their role. And the only participant to answer "no" to both questions, Participant 024 (most experienced, legal-interests advocate), was still able to describe role conflict she had experienced, even if she had not recognized it as "obstacles," "pressures," or "conflicting expectations." Only about half the participants who said "yes" to the obstacles question were among the most experienced attorneys, but most of those who said "no" were among the most experienced. As with other conclusions based on such small numbers, it is difficult to extrapolate a great deal of predictive value from these findings. However, it is prudent to briefly discuss their potential meaning for the purposes of future research.

Table 5.1. *Role Conflict Prevalence*

	n	Percentage
Experienced pressure to depart from zealous advocate role (n = 24)		
Yes (45% were most experienced; 45% were expressed-interests advocates)	20	83.3
No (75% were most experienced; 100% were expressed-interests advocates)	4	16.7
Experienced conflicting expectations of role (n = 24)		
Yes (66.7% were most experienced; 38.9% were expressed-interests advocates)	18	75.0
No (66.7% were least experienced; 33.3% were expressed-interests advocates)	6	25.0
Role conflict prevalence (n = 17)		
Never (75% were most experienced; 25% were best-interests advocates)	4	23.5
Rarely (50% were most experienced; 66.7% were expressed-interests advocates)	6	35.3
Sometimes (100% were least experienced; 100% were expressed-interests advocates)	1	5.9
Often (66.7% were most experienced; 50% were expressed-interests advocates)	6	35.3
Did not indicate (57.1% of most experienced; 14.3% were best-interests advocates)	7	41.2

It makes sense that participants with more experience would indicate they had not faced obstacles or pressures to depart from the zealous advocacy role. It stands to reason that more seasoned attorneys might have become immune to such forces, as indicated by Participant 012, a best-interests advocate from the most experienced group, who stated, "I don't succumb to pressure easily, so if there is pressure I don't recognize it because I just push back."

The only pattern that could be discerned among the "no obstacle" participants was that they included two of the three legal-interests advocates but none of the expressed-interests advocates. It is a surprise that only one of these four participants (Participant 012) was a best-interests advocate. One might imagine if a juvenile defender were such an advocate, he or she would not experience pushback or pressure to depart from the expressed-interests advocate role because he or she might already be departing from it. On the other hand, it could be that the defender is a best-interests advocate because of role conflict he or she had experienced but did not refer to as an "obstacle." In fact, Participant 012 was so adamant about having experienced conflicting expectations of her in her role that she answered the following question in a sarcastic but illustrative way:

> INTERVIEWER: Are there people, either other courtroom functionaries or parents . . . who ever give you the impression they don't think that you should be doing [expressed-interests advocacy] and they think that you should be doing something else as a juvenile defense attorney?
>
> 012: [Sarcastically] You mean except for defending them and protecting their rights and interests, that I should be doing something else like getting them to submit to the charges and moving them out through the system, is that what you're saying basically? . . . Well, I would say everybody was.

Participant 012, like seventeen other participants (for a total of 75 percent), reported experiencing conflicting expectations in her role as a juvenile defender. Six participants (25 percent) reported that they had not experienced conflicting expectations of them in this role. Only two of these six (019 and 024) were among the most experienced, and the group of six represented two different types of advocate, in addition to one (Participant 006) who declined to identify as any type of advocate. So, even though both the obstacle and conflicting-expectations questions targeted role conflict, they clearly did not completely cover the same facets of it. Most of those who said "no" to the obstacle question were among the most experienced attorneys. Quite the opposite, most of those (four out of six, or 66.7 percent) who said "no" to the conflicting-expectations question were among the least experienced attorneys. And only one of them, Participant 024, a legal-interests advocate from the most experienced group, also said "no" to the obstacle question.

Perhaps the less experienced attorneys had not been practicing long enough to encounter conflicting expectations. Or perhaps their entry into practice in North Carolina coincided enough with the shift in official juvenile defender policy to have made it less likely that they would encounter these manifestation of role conflict. This encourages one to believe that the new policy, including the attendant *Role Statement* (NCOJD, 2005) dissemination and trainings, had met with some success. With regard to both direct questions, it could also be that participants did not recognize role conflict experiences as obstacles or conflicting expectations but as something else altogether.

As can be seen from the earlier discussion, role conflict was referred to in a number of different ways using the definitions provided in the literature (e.g., Rizzo et al., 1970). As just described, the interview questions referred to role conflict as "pressure to depart" from the expressed-interests advocate role and "conflicting expectations" of participants in their role. However, throughout the interviews participants also referred to "pressure to depart" as "pushback." Therefore, "pushback," "pressure to depart," and "conflicting expectations" were all viewed as "role conflict" manifestations.

A critical point to make about reducing the need for inference with regard to participants' responses relates to the placement of the questions in the interview protocol. Participants had already been asked to consider their zealous (expressed-interests) advocate role, its meaning for them, and the extent to which they viewed departure from that role as justifiable before being asked about the extent to which others held conflicting expectations of them in their role. It is therefore reasonable to infer that participants' responses related to their experiences of role conflict as distinguished from the normal pressures and pushback they would expect to experience as part of the adversarial process. This is particularly true because these questions specifically directed participants to consider their zealous advocate or advocate (as opposed to counselor) role.

As a reminder for readers, the nature of court systems in the United States is adversarial. This means that there is a process of determining guilt that involves a contest between two opposing parties: the prosecuting attorney, who brings charges against the defendant, and the defendant, who is typically represented by a defense attorney. The two attorneys present evidence to a disinterested third-party fact-finder—for example, a judge for the juvenile system—who ultimately determines if the evidence supports the conclusion that the defendant should be held responsible for violating the law. This contest is adversarial, so it naturally involves conflict. However, this type of conflict can be distinguished from the *role* conflict that is the focus of this study in that role conflict can be presented to the juvenile defender by anyone involved in the juvenile court, not just the prosecutor or judge. In addition, the prosecutor and judge are both formally educated as to the proper role of the defense attorney, and even though they play different roles in the court system, they should still be able to demonstrate respect, understanding, and even support for the defender role as a necessary part of the judicial process. At the same time, there might be some circumstances where it is difficult to distinguish adversarial conflict from role conflict, but only for the prosecutor and judge (to some extent), whose job it is to push back against the defense attorney in a professionally suitable fashion. Participants seemed to be able to identify when pushback was outside the scope of the adversarial process. Nevertheless, some overlap could exist, making it important to tease the two apart, if possible, in future research.

All participants reported experiencing some form of role conflict, either as conflicting expectations or as pushback/pressure to depart from the role, though not all of them provided examples in response to the *direct* questions. In other words, participants might have said "no" to the direct questions but in the course of answering other questions—for instance, if they felt judges in general supported their role—revealed that they had had an experience where a judge pushed back against them in their role that seemed outside the normal course of the adversarial contest. In other words, even though participants might have said they had not experienced role conflict when asked directly, their description of a scenario where they experienced pushback from the judge would count as role conflict.

Additionally, not all participants could articulate *how often* they had experienced role conflict. Of those who were able to estimate role conflict prevalence (seventeen out of twenty-four, or 70.8 percent), only four (23.5 percent) reported that they *never* experienced pushback. Six (35.3 percent) reported they *rarely* experienced pushback. Only one (5.9 percent) participant indicated he sometimes experienced pushback, and six (35.3 percent) indicated they *often* experienced pushback.

So, participants unanimously (directly or indirectly) reported facing some form of role conflict as either conflicting expectations or pushback/pressure to depart from their role. As analytic themes emerged from the data, particular categories of situations, sources, and effects became evident. Recall that Katz and Kahn's (1966) rubric for organizing role conflict sources provided the following coding categories: intrasender (inconsistent expectations from the same role sender); intersender (inconsistent expectations from different role senders); interrole (the role incumbent occupies two conflicting roles); and person-role or internal (the role's requirements conflict with the individual's values, needs, or capacities). Interrole and intrasender conflict were not supported as categories after data analysis. Person-role conflict is referred to as *internal* role conflict and is addressed later in a discussion about internal forces that create role conflict. However, emerging themes followed the final category, intersender role conflict, fairly well. In fact, most of the role conflict experiences that participants reported fit easily into this category and were further categorized by source.

To reiterate, intersender role conflict occurs when the role incumbent experiences conflicting role expectations from different role senders (sources of role information). For juvenile defenders, an example would involve discrepant messages about the juvenile defender role from the *Model Rules of Professional Conduct* (ABA, 2013) and judges. In other words, both the *Model Rules* and judges wield authority over juvenile defenders, but they might send these attorneys different messages about how juvenile defenders are expected to perform the role. For instance, the *Model Rules* requires these attorneys to advocate for their clients' expressed interests, while some judges might expect that defenders will advocate for their juvenile clients' best interests.

Naturally, all of the intersender role conflict originates with forces *external* to defenders and results in pressure for them to depart from their expressed-interests advocate role, regardless of whether they accommodate, or succumb to, the pressure. Participants reported facing these pressures mostly from individuals (parents, prosecutors, and the like) and from the system itself. To be clear, participants seemed to view these role conflict sources as forces they were unlikely to accommodate, unlike those circumstances addressed in the "Role Departures" section of chapter 4. Participants also seemed to view role departures due to these sources as unjustifiable (see table 4.2).

Participants also offered explanations for the role conflict they experienced. They reported the belief that others pressured juvenile defenders to depart from their zealous advocacy role because they did not adequately understand, or respect, the juvenile defender role. Interestingly, participants used this same explanation for role conflict originating with courtroom functionaries who are trained in due process rights and who should be knowledgeable about the critical role that defense attorneys play in safeguarding those rights. As will be discussed later in this chapter, role conflict from law-educated courtroom functionaries might result more from a lack of respect for the role than from a lack of understanding. It is important to remind the reader that participants mostly believed that a juvenile defender's departure from his or her role would *not* be justified because of these role conflict sources, unlike those addressed in the "Role Departures" section of chapter 4. Nevertheless, participants reported experiencing most of their role conflict from nonfunctionaries, namely clients and parents.

Role Conflict Sources

Participants were asked about conflicting expectations they experienced and were also asked, *What do you think is the source or sources of these conflicting expectations?* Additionally, participants were asked directly if they thought judges and other courtroom workgroup members supported their expressed-interests advocate role. And they were asked generally, *Who or what do you think is responsible for any pressure you experience to depart from the zealous advocate role? Can you make a list?*

Participants identified a plethora of sources of the role conflict they experienced. They also offered explanations for what they perceived as the main reasons for this role conflict. Sources were varied in nature and spanned multiple levels. The most widely cited sources of role conflict, as evidenced in table 5.2, were other individuals (in descending order of frequency, clients and parents, prosecutors, court counselors, and judges) and the system itself (particularly, the pressure to process cases efficiently).

Participants reported that others exerted pressure on them to depart from their expressed-interest advocacy role or had conflicting expectations of them in their role because they did not adequately understand or respect the juvenile defender role. Interestingly, participants described experiences where inadequate understanding or respect did not come solely from those courtroom functionaries who lacked legal training. In fact, several reported that they had also experienced this kind of pressure from prosecutors and judges. Since all lawyers are trained in due process rights, it is likely safe to assume that prosecutors and judges are aware of due process protections and of the critical role defense attorneys play in safeguarding them. It therefore stands to reason that the role conflict that prosecutors and judges pose reflects, at least at some level, a lack of respect for, not a lack of understanding of, the juvenile defender role. However, it is from those individuals who are nonfunctionaries in the juvenile court that participants unanimously reported the most pushback.

Clients

It is important to clarify that juvenile clients as sources of role conflict generally are distinguished from client-based justifications for role departures as discussed in chapter 4 (e.g., client age, capacity, special needs). Participants unanimously identified clients as a source of role conflict in a number of different ways. For instance, participants' responses to the general role conflict questions and to the vignettes indicate that they experienced pressure to depart from the zealous advocate role because of a client's inability or unwillingness to share information that was particularly relevant to outcomes the client might have desired. Participant 015, from among the least experienced participants, explained this type of pushback in the following way:

Table 5.2. Role Conflict Sources

Source	n	Percentage
Micro-level (individual) (n = 24)		
Parent/guardian	24	100.0
Client	24	100.0
Very young or special needs client*	23	95.8
Prosecutors (81.8% of least experienced; 88.9% of expressed-interests advocates)	18	75.0
Court counselors (80% of best-interests advocates)	17	70.8
Judges (76.9% of most experienced)	15	62.5
Other defense attorneys (38.5% of most experienced)	7	29.2
Self (person-role conflict)* (best-interests advocates averaged 2.8 examples vs. 1.92 from expressed-interests advocates)	24	100.0
Meso-level (organizational/contextual) (n = 24)		
Resources		
Time* (an attorney's time) (81.8% of least experienced; 77.8% of expressed-interests advocates)	18	75.0
Caseload* (intertwined with time)	9	37.5
Service providers (access to)* (61.5% of most experienced; 66.7% of expressed-interests advocates) (exclusive of other resources)	8	33.3
Pay/money* (38.4% of most experienced; 33.3% of expressed-interests advocates)	8	33.3
Access to sufficient information	6	25.0
Macro-level (institutional/societal) (n = 22–24)		
System		
Process stage—disposition	22/24	91.7
Stage departure justified (85.7% were most experienced; 28.6% were best-interests advocates)	7/22	31.8
Stage departure *not* justified (53.3% were most experienced; 53.3% were expressed-interests advocates)	15/22	68.2
System efficiency (81.8% of least experienced; 80% of best-interests advocates)	19/24	79.2

Note: All of these sources were volunteered by participants except where indicated by an asterisk (*). Asterisked sources were part of a direct question about the source.

When a client doesn't tell me something, it always turns out bad for them. And so, . . . I'm thinking of times when the clients didn't tell me everything I needed to know and I went in ready to go down swinging and I had information that was very different. And so then . . . I kind of lose my ability in some ways to get a good outcome, at least as good as maybe if I had had that information.

Participant 015 identified as a best-interests advocate and viewed departures from the expressed-interests advocate role as justifiable. What he considered a "good outcome" for his client might have been inconsistent with his client's desires. This attorney noted that if he believed his client "just [didn't] understand" the decision the client must make, he would "actually make a decision contrary to [his] client's . . . wishes that would be what [he thought was] better for their interests." Participant 015's comments illustrate a dilemma many other participants raised about representing very young children with limited capacity to understand their situation.

Participant 016, also a best-interests advocate but from the most experienced group, also noted clients' tendency to "get in their own way," and in hers, by not returning phone calls, failing to meet with the attorney, and failing to appear in court. She explained that "sometimes they just don't show up, so that can totally be an obstacle, because then you either have to delay your zealous advocacy, or sometimes you're just not able to present it at all." The logistical concerns Participant 016 raised are quite logical. Sometimes clients fail to meet with attorneys because they have no means of transportation. In other instances, the failure reflects a lack of trust. Participants' responses left the general impression that attorneys recognized the reality that more time and effort are required to build trust with juvenile clients than with their adult counterparts. Their responses also suggested that caseloads are high and time is often in short supply, leaving them struggling to afford the necessary time and effort.

Like Participant 015, Participant 016 identified as a best-interests advocate and viewed role departures as justifiable. She also recognized the impact clients' young age (such as their youth and inexperience) could have on their ability to understand their legal situation. Participants reported the view that clients' youth and inexperience were partially responsible for their conflicting expectations and pushback against their defense attorneys' efforts. Even still, participants mostly attributed this client-based role conflict to their clients' inadequate and incorrect understanding, and mistrust, of the juvenile defender role.

Participants reported that quite frequently clients did not understand the defense attorney role, some clients did not seem to care, and some had hidden motives for resisting their defenders' efforts. Participant 002 (expressed-interests advocate, most experienced group) provided an excellent example of a situation where his hands were tied because his client had, perhaps detrimentally, declined to use a valid defense:

> I had a kid come in one time, thirteen years old. He was charged with assaulting his stepfather with a knife he had gotten from the kitchen, and he and I went into the little room to talk about it. He said, "I just want to go ahead and admit this charge." And I said, "Why?" He said, "Because Social Services is involved and I don't want to be taken away from my mom." And I said, "What [do] you mean Social Services is involved?" He said, "Well, the reason I pulled a knife on my stepdad is because he beats me real bad and I just finally got tired of it, so I went and got a knife from the kitchen and I attacked him." And I said, "Well, it sounds to me like you have a self-defense argument." And he said, "I don't care, I don't want to talk about any defenses, I just want to go ahead and admit this because I don't want Social Services to take me away from my mom."

Participant 002, despite identifying himself as an expressed-interests advocate, viewed role departures as justifiable. He provided this scenario as an example of when he saw it as acceptable to depart from advocating for a youth's expressed interests. He ultimately did involve Social Services, departing from his expressed-interests advocate role, because he believed the client's family circumstances placed him in danger—recall the mandatory reporting justification discussed in chapter 4.

Participant 002's scenario is also an excellent example of the client's lacking understanding of, or trust in, the juvenile defender role. This lack of trust has been associated with juveniles' misunderstanding of their lawyers' role in the social science literature (Pierce & Brodsky, 2002). If defenders do not have their clients' trust, they are unlikely to be able to obtain accurate or adequate information from the clients. As a result, clients are unlikely to get an outcome that serves either their expressed *or* best interests. The implications of clients' lack of respect, trust, or understanding of the defender role go beyond defenders' interactions with their clients. It could also be a reflection of their perceptions of other courtroom functionaries' openly demonstrated lack of respect and understanding of the defender role.

Participants explained that the role conflict they experience from clients oftentimes results from clients' desire to get their court experience over with—so commonplace among youths—or from intimidation by the system or by their parents. Overall, clients seemed to misunderstand that juvenile defenders are there to help them navigate the system and to serve as their voice. Participant 003, an expressed-interests advocate from the most experienced group, explained the type of situation that presents him with the most difficulty. In fact, the situation illustrates circumstances with which even some adult defendants might struggle.

> I think that one of my most difficult times is when I have to tell our client he has to admit to something he didn't do when it's a kid between the ages of eight to fourteen.... You hear people all the time, "Well, if he didn't do it, why did he admit to it?" Well, because he didn't want to go to prison for twenty years [the prosecutor was threatening transfer to criminal court] as opposed to being on probation. [I] think it's difficult for a kid to wrap his head around, especially when he's not really going to go to prison.

This excerpt is poignant because it reflects the client's inadequate understanding of the attorney's duties *to his client*, the client's mistrust of the attorney, and the attorney's status as an expert of the juvenile justice system. Juvenile defenders must advocate for their clients' expressed interests but only after discussing all of their options and making recommendations about what they think is the best course of action. Participants indicated that the best course of action sometimes differs from the client's expressed interests. This seemed to be especially true if the client was very young or had overbearing parents.

If an attorney is concerned that taking a case to trial creates a risk of greater potential punishment for the client than the client would face if he or she admitted responsibility, then the attorney might advise the client to admit responsibility. In the state of North Carolina, juveniles under the age of thirteen cannot be transferred to adult court, according to the North Carolina General Assembly General Statutes, Article 22, "Probable Cause Hearing and Transfer Hearing," § 7B-2200. So, it would be possible for Participant 003's clients of ages thirteen and up to be transferred to adult court if he were not successful at convincing his clients to accept a plea and admit responsibility. Transfer of children at that age is considered rare, but it does happen (R. Waldrop Rugh, personal communication, July 25, 2015). However, once the client chooses an outcome to pursue, the attorney is required to pursue that outcome unless it violates another of his or her duties. So, if the client disagrees with the attorney's recommendation, as explained previously, the attorney must honor that and advocate for the client's expressed wishes (ABA, 2013, Rule 1.2a). If the client does not understand or trust in the attorney's role or familiarity with the juvenile justice system, he or she is less likely to cooperate in ways that allow the attorney to bring about the expressed outcome for that client. The juvenile is also less likely to be persuaded by the attorney when the expressed outcome is not what is best for the client, legally or personally. Therefore, mistrust of the attorney can be seen as an obstacle not only to the juvenile defender's advocate function but to his or her counselor function as well.

Another poignant aspect of Participant 003's comment about "not really going to go to prison" relates to the fact that juvenile courts have become more punitive in the modern day (Birckhead, 2010). The child might not be facing adult prison, though many do, but he or she still faces a loss of liberty. This loss of liberty could easily include incarceration in an institution that provides the kind of socialization that in reality defeats the espoused rehabilitative purpose of the juvenile justice system.

Parents

All twenty-four participants reported that parents were responsible for most of the pressure they experience to depart from their expressed-interests advocate role. They also reported that much of the parent-based role conflict came in the form of their reluctance to allow juvenile defenders to have one-on-one time with clients. Participant 001, a most experienced, expressed-interests advocate, indicated that he rarely experienced role conflict. Nevertheless, he reported, "I think the biggest pressure I have faced in juvenile court is being able to separate the juvenile respondent from the parents. Lots of parents do not like to have me meet with their child separately."

This type of obstacle can have ethical implications for juvenile defenders because it makes confidential communication and protecting attorney-client privilege a challenge. When it comes to speaking with one's client, attorneys are trained to be extremely mindful of their duty of confidentiality. This means they cannot discuss their clients' cases with anyone, even a child's parents, without the express permission of their clients. In addition, in order to be most effective and ethical, attorneys must be very careful about communicating with their clients indirectly, or through third parties, like parents.

Another ethical challenge with parent-based role conflict occurs when parents attempt to supplant their child as the lawyer's client or to take the place of the defender as the attorney. Participant 001 further explained:

> Lots of times there is an issue with being able to meet with the client confidentially without the parents present and the parents not understanding that

and then the respondent getting outside pressure from the parent or guardian to do something with the case. . . . So, basically the parent[s] tried to make decisions for the juvenile or have already talked to the juvenile and sort of told that juvenile, "We're going in this direction."

Pushback from parents in such forms was a common experience for participants. Participant 005 (most experienced, declined to identify advocate type) explained how intense some of these attempts can be:

You get a lot of pushback from parents, and that's probably the bigger area where you get pushback. The parents many times say, "Well, I am the parent and this needs to happen," and I have to explain, "They're my client and you're not," to the point . . . [that] sometimes it becomes a semi-heated exchange.

Again, Participant 005 was one of the study's most experienced juvenile defenders. He declined to identify as an advocate type, making it somewhat challenging to assess the extent to which he had internalized North Carolina's *Role Statement* (NCOJD, 2005). At the same time, his willingness to engage in a "semi-heated exchange" in order to assert his role as his client's, not the parents', attorney indicated he has fully internalized his zealous advocate role, including its expressed-interests component. His frequent references to advocating for clients' expressed interests while explaining his interpretation of zealous advocacy validated this conclusion.

Participants also commonly reported parents' attempts to inappropriately commandeer the court's authority. In other words, some parents attempted to utilize the court and juvenile justice system to achieve ends that were not within the court's authority. Participant 011 (most experienced, expressed-interests advocate) recognized the punitive realities of the juvenile court system, despite its espoused rehabilitative mission. She explained how one of her client's parents attempted to misuse the court system. Her explanation also addressed a myth she has encountered about her work.

Usually [I get pushback] from parents. I've had parents really pissed off at me saying . . . that I wasn't doing their child right and that . . . they were going to hire a real lawyer to represent their child, which meant represent what *they* wanted for their child. The real obstacles are from the parents. I've actually been fired. Some rich [local town name] dad went and hired a lawyer, an outside lawyer, because I wouldn't do what he wanted for his kid (i.e., make him be locked up for another week just to learn his lesson) and stuff like that. . . . [So,] parents would be at the top the list [of sources of role conflict]. Particularly the parents that want to lock their kids up and throw away the key.

Parent-based role conflict is likely unique to defense attorneys for children. The juvenile court is a relatively recent development in the American legal system, and the expressed-interests advocacy requirement is even more recent. As a result, parents might naively expect the court, due to its parens patriae orientation, to prioritize parental authority over due process, namely the defense attorney's duty. In addition, parents are unlikely to be familiar with the nature of the defender role, including defenders' ethical obligation of confidentiality to their juvenile clients. This might lead parents to misunderstand who has legal authority in their child's case; they likely do not realize it is their child who has this authority, not them. Participant 020 (least experienced, legal-interests advocate) described his experience with this phenomenon in the following way:

> I think the absolute most common situation [of role conflict] is going to be butting heads with parents, and the conversations tend to be pretty similar. . . . I'm pretty open with the parents from the very beginning about what my role is; a lot of times they'll be frustrated. Sometimes they then will go on to ask how they can get a new attorney, which brings us full circle right back to "Well, you don't get to fire me. It's actually the juvenile who gets to decide whether they want to fire me."

Another participant, 015 (least experienced, best-interests advocate), indicated that some parents actually make things worse for their children:

> Parents are the worst thing that ever happened to the defendant in a criminal case because they always talk their child into doing something that they probably shouldn't do and . . . they don't often listen to the attorney. . . . You know, parents are often the reason that their children get a worse outcome because they convinced their child to do something they shouldn't do against their attorney's advice.

Participant 015 explained that parents are "not gonna understand the way the system works, but they don't understand that it would be better if you did it one way or another, and so they're pushing their child to do one thing."

Other participants' comments reflected the belief that parents' misunderstanding of or lack of respect for the juvenile defender role was responsible for their pushback. Participant 014 (least experienced, expressed-interests advocate) noted,

> [Parents do] not fully understand my role as a juvenile defense attorney or . . . the juvenile legal system. . . . [And] because they don't fully understand I

have a specific ethical duty to represent my juvenile client in a particular way
. . . I think it's difficult for them.

He recognized this failing even though he admitted that as a father "it'd be difficult for me to have somebody tell me, 'No, I can't be in that room when you're talking to my child about the case.'" Participant 014 viewed role departures as largely unjustifiable. His recognition of parents' unique position likely allowed him to empathize with their concerns, but he did not appear to compromise his dedication to the expressed-interests advocate role as a result.

Participants explained that parents also seemed to misunderstand the role of the court and of the juvenile justice system at large. In support of this belief, Participant 003 (most experienced, expressed-interests advocate) pointed out that even well-intentioned parents could misunderstand the juvenile system's due process function:

Quite often you are at odds with the parents. The parents are the one[s] that told them, "Go to the police department and tell the truth." And you're sitting here saying, "Well, you should've kept your mouth shut." And the parents said, "No, I told you to tell the truth." And to some extent the courts are recognizing that the parent can't waive the juvenile's right to silence.

Participant 020 (least experienced, legal-interests advocate) reflected some of the same sentiment raised by Participants 003 and 011: parents often wanted the juvenile court to perform a function outside its authority and expected the defender to fall in line with this mistaken expectation. He explained that parents

want help from the court system to discipline the juvenile, so typically they want . . . some type of punishment. They want more than a slap on the wrist. They want . . . the court to do something that's going to shape up the juvenile.

As Participant 020 pointed out, some parents pushed for more punitive outcomes than were reasonable in an apparent effort to use the juvenile justice system as a dumping ground for their unwanted children or to otherwise relieve themselves of their parental obligations. Participant 001 (most experienced, expressed-interests advocate) noted this tendency as well when he remarked that the pushback he gets from parents typically occurs when

the parents come to court and want the juvenile court system to punish the child more than they can be under the statute. . . . [I get] pressure from them to lock the child up when [that's not my role].

This seemingly prevalent parental expectation is very interesting. Do parents take the juvenile court's parens patriae orientation too literally? In other words, does this rehabilitative culture give parents the impression that the court's role is to *completely* substitute itself for the parents of juveniles in the fashion some parents appear to expect? That some parents have such unreasonable expectations of the court is unsettling. Equally concerning, though not surprising, is some parents' expectation that juvenile defenders defer to parents' wishes over the child client's. As indicated by participants' comments, parents tended to give the impression that their own expectations of their children's court experience trump attorneys' ethical obligations, specifically, to maintain confidentiality with their clients and to give voice to the expressed interests of their child clients.

As suggested earlier, parent-based role conflict might be unique to juvenile justice. This type of role conflict presents a problem that might not be easily resolved with policy changes like North Carolina's *Role Statement*, since parents have a legal duty to protect their children. Additionally, it is not unreasonable for parents to bristle at a stranger's insistence on meeting with their minor child in private without their presence, regardless of that stranger's official role. At the same time, a failure to protect the attorney-client privilege can have severe ramifications for the juvenile, the case outcome, and the attorney's professional standing and career. For instance, if a juvenile client does not wish his parents to be involved with his attorney meetings but does not have the courage to ask them to leave, not only might he feel unable to communicate freely with his attorney, but the attorney's confidentiality duty could be jeopardized. A client could always waive the privilege and allow his parents to be in the room when he speaks with his attorney. However, that decision could trigger additional dilemmas, placing the client at the center of role conflict, and as discussed earlier in this chapter, clients themselves already present juvenile defenders with enough role conflict. In fact, a number of the vignette scenarios participants considered for this study involved situations where clients' parents attempted to interfere with the attorney-client relationship. Participants predominantly remarked that they would cope with the situation by asking the parents to leave, and if that failed, they would seek assistance from the judge to force the parents to refrain from interfering. Participants indicated they expected this support from the judge in this kind of situation (see table 5.3).

Thus far, participants' views on role conflict originating with juvenile court stakeholders who were not members of the court workgroup have been discussed. That all participants identified clients and their parents as primary

Table 5.3. Role Support

Support for role	n = 24	Percentage
Judges	24	100.0
Prosecutors (20% of least experienced; 11.1% of expressed-interests advocates)	3	12.5
Court counselors (50% of most experienced; 55.6% of expressed-interests advocates)	8	33.3
Other defense attorneys	7	29.2

Note: Participants were directly asked only about *judges* as sources of role conflict; participants volunteered other juvenile court stakeholders as sources.

sources of pushback comes as no surprise, given these stakeholders' lack of familiarity with the court system and with the due process protections the juvenile defender role is meant to guard. Naturally, most parents and children are unlikely to be as familiar with the courtroom functionaries' official roles as the functionaries are themselves. However, these stakeholders' lack of familiarity with the court system does not explain why participants reported experiencing role conflict from other courtroom functionaries, particularly those with legal training.

Courtroom Functionaries

At varying rates, participants identified multiple courtroom functionaries as sources of role conflict. Participants reported that they experienced pressure to depart from their zealous advocate role from functionaries in the following descending order: prosecutors, court counselors, judges, and other defense attorneys (see table 5.2). In addition, five participants noted that they felt such pressure from other court functionaries in general. Participants were also asked whether, based on their experience, they thought *judges* supported their role as zealous advocates of the expressed interests of juvenile clients. Additionally, they were asked, *In your experience, do you think other courtroom workgroup members support your role as a zealous advocate of the expressed interests of your juvenile client? Why or why not?*

JUDGES

Participants were asked, *In your experience, do you think judges support your role as a zealous advocate of the expressed interests of your juvenile client? Why or why not?* All twenty-four participants expressed the belief that judges were supportive of their role as zealous advocates of their clients' expressed interests (see table 5.3). This is an interesting result, given that fifteen participants identified judges as sources of role conflict. There seemed to be very little difference between the expressed-interests (five out of nine participants, or 55.6 percent) and best-interests (three out of five participants, or 60 percent) advocates in terms of identifying judges as a source of role conflict. However, a sizable difference appeared between the most experienced (ten out of thirteen participants, or 76.9 percent) and least experienced (four out of eleven, or 36.4 percent). In other words, the most experienced participants were likelier to identify judges as a source of role conflict than were the least experienced participants. A closer look at the advocate type groups reveals that among the eight participants who identified judges as sources of role conflict, six (75 percent) of them were from the most experienced group, indicating that experience could play a larger role in determining who faces role conflict from judges. This result could be explained by more experienced attorneys' greater confidence in the role and willingness to take risks with, or stand up to, judges.

Understandably, judges were viewed as the most powerful juvenile courtroom functionary. Judges are also theoretically experts in the due process rights that form the foundation of the juvenile defender role, should be aware of the Supreme Court's decision in *In re Gault* (1967), and should be aware of the NCOJD's guidelines and its *Role Statement* (2005). Therefore, they should be supportive of the juvenile defender as an expressed-interests advocate despite the juvenile court's best-interests approach. It is thus surprising that so many participants identified judges as sources of role conflict.

One explanation of the discrepancy involves the politics of the courtroom and the culture of the legal profession. The judge inhabits the most powerful role in the juvenile court; a critical component to any attorney's professional success is his or her ability to avoid showing disrespect to judges or getting on their bad side. Thus, juvenile defenders might be reluctant to openly acknowledge judges' failings, even in a confidential interview. However, that might not be the case for all juvenile defenders. Participant 018 (least experienced, expressed-interests advocate) appeared to have had the confidence to remind an inquiring judge of his "actual role." When sharing a role conflict scenario he had experienced, he reflected, "It was a little bit concerning because my job is to act in the expressed interest of the juvenile, and I had to refresh the judge's memory that it wasn't best interests but it was expressed interest." Participant 018 indicated he experienced role conflict "all the time." Such frequency might not be surprising, since he appeared to have been a stalwart expressed-interests advocate who viewed role departures as unjustifiable. He was also new to ju-venile defense, having practiced only one year, so he might have received more pushback as other courtroom functionaries tested his boundaries.

At the same time, when asked about whether he ever felt personally con-flicted about his role, Participant 018 offered more examples of internal role conflict than other participants. This might also reflect his growing pains as he adjusted to his new role as a juvenile defender. Internal role conflict will be addressed later in this chapter; however, it is important to recognize its presence here since it might be the distinguishing factor between participants like 018 and others who provided fewer examples of internal conflict and reported experiencing less role conflict overall. For example, Participants 001 and 014 were also expressed-interests advocates who viewed role departures as unjustifiable, but they reported experiencing role conflict rarely. At the time of their interviews, Participant 001 had practiced juvenile defense for nine years and 014 had practiced for only two, so years of experience might not account for this difference. Age, however, might. Participant 018 was only twenty-eight at the time of his interview, while 001 and 014 were forty-two and thirty-six, respectively. Perhaps with age came confidence or de facto blinders to role conflict manifestations.

For some participants, judicial support was mixed with pushback. For example, Participant 006 (least experienced, declined to identify advocate type) explained, "In the trials I've had . . . I feel like I've had equal time. I feel like equal weight was given to what I say." She then followed up with, "There's one judge . . . who is very likely to rule against your client. You just know that. If you have a trial before the judge, it will be hard to convince them." Since Participant 006 declined to identify as an advocate type, it is difficult to determine if her dedication to the expressed-interests role makes her more vulnerable to pushback. However, in her definition of the "zealous advocate" role, she emphasized her ultimate commitment to her clients' expressed wishes but still viewed role departures as justifiable.

Participant 003 (most experienced, expressed-interests advocate) remarked that judges were generally supportive of him in his role; "in fact, I had a district court judge regularly serve in juvenile court who constantly would compliment me to my clients about [how] I would represent them zealously." However, this participant quickly noted that this praise came only after a number of occasions where he had stood his ground against the judge, who had been pressuring him to depart from his zealous advocate role and almost held him in contempt for not accommodating that pressure. He added,

I think that judges should recognize that that's what the attorney does. And most of the . . . judges that I've dealt with understood that's what I was doing. Do they support it? Ninety-five percent of the time [they do]. Does it have a lot of effect on [judges]? No. . . . It would probably just come in the form of you just don't feel like the judge is listening to you. . . . And when I see it, them not liking it, what I mean is they may have something in their mind that they think is appropriate and best for the child, and I'm putting up roadblocks and saying, "Your Honor, you can't legally do that," or, "You know the statute doesn't provide for that." And so it frustrates them and their purpose.

Participant 003's comments suggest that perhaps experience allows defenders the opportunity to pick up on nuances from judges that less experienced attorneys might not notice. This explanation makes sense given that Participant 003 had been practicing juvenile defense for nearly two decades at the time of his interview. This might also be what Participant 011, also an experienced, expressed-interests advocate, referred to when she described pushback from one particular judge: "Although I do love him, [he] gets this real angry look, and sometimes I'm worried that because he's angry at me, he's going to take it out on my kid."

These more experienced participants' ability to pick up on judges' preferences or idiosyncrasies was reflected in responses of other participants, more often those with more experience. This ability might be considered akin to something referred to in the social science literature as *social capital*, a topic loosely defined as a network of social connections and acumen that will be discussed more thoroughly in chapter 8 (Fukuyama, 1997; Putnam, 1995). These responses might also indicate that some judges experience role confusion about the defender role. Additionally, they could indicate role *denial* on the part of judges who might be so distracted with other concerns (e.g., courtroom efficiency) that they overlook the purpose of the defender role and its importance to due process. Judges could be attempting to create boundaries to zealous advocacy by demonstrating that they have different degrees of tolerance for zealousness. For example, some judges appeared to punish defenders who took their expressed-interests advocate role too seriously. Participant 024, a most experienced, legal-interests advocate who views role departures as unjustifiable, explained:

There's been a couple of attorneys that have received consistent complaints because they litigate to the nth degree everything. And they have no balance as to what's the really important thing to fight for and what's not, and a couple of judges have gotten to the point where they said . . . they won't allow them to be appointed to any cases coming on their list because they find them so detrimental to their clients and disruptive of the court process.

Participant 024's comment about judges not assigning new cases to defenders who litigate everything "to the nth degree" raises a number of questions. Is this an example of mismatched expectations of juvenile defenders in their role? Or, is it part of an informal but otherwise legitimate process undertaken by judges who are tasked with weeding out attorneys who gum up the works with frivolous objections and motions? What constitutes a "frivolous" motion, and does that differ by advocate type or respect for the juvenile defender role? To what extent does it become unfair that defense attorneys' zealous advocacy, despite slowing down the court process, might lead to a loss of appointments for them? Could fighting for one's client "to the nth degree" be detrimental to the client, even though fighting hard for the clients is what attorneys are supposed to do, according to their rules of professional conduct?

If it is the case that juvenile defenders who fight hard for their clients find that their zealous advocacy counts *against* their clients, perhaps a more creative, or integrated, approach to juvenile defense, as suggested by Birckhead (2010), would be more appropriate for juvenile clients. Could it be that, practically speaking, an integrated approach to juvenile defense, such as one that incorporates clients' expressed *and* best interests, is more suitable given the unique status of the clients and the orientation of the court? This suggestion, and others, will be addressed to a greater extent in chapter 8.

Given North Carolina's efforts to inform juvenile court functionaries of its *Role Statement*'s (NCOJD, 2005) emphasis on expressed-interests advocacy for juvenile respondents, it is surprising that so many participants identified judges as sources of pressure to depart from their designated role. Participants provided some explanations.

Most participants believed that judges did not respect their role, even though judges are the courtroom functionaries who should *most* understand the juvenile defender role, given that they are due process experts. However, judges are also managers of an organization and its stakeholders. They are also human beings. Even individuals in so respected a role as a judgeship could lose their perspective to the pressure they feel from the court's organizational needs and thus place a higher priority on efficiently processing the day's docket. Or, they might simply have too little respect for the juvenile defender role. Participant 017 (most experienced, best-interests advocate) explained this perspective in the following way:

Sometimes what court judges will do is they'll bring you up to the bench and tell you what they are leaning towards or what they would want to do. So, in that way they may be supporting what you want for your client, or they may be telling you exactly what they think is best for your client.

When I asked Participant 017 why he thought judges do that, he replied, "I think sometimes it's respect or lack thereof."

Participant 017's recognition that this behavior was disrespectful is interesting. He identified as a best-interests advocate, but he also viewed departures from the zealous advocate role as unjustifiable. So, from what role did he view departures as unacceptable? If he saw his role as a best-interests advocate, would that not also mean he was, de facto, more accepting of role departures from the standard zealous (expressed-interests) advocate role? He viewed judges telling juvenile defenders how they planned to decide cases before cases had been presented as disrespectful, so does that mean he did not allow himself to be co-opted into judges' pre-hearing plans? When asked what "zealous advocacy" meant to him, he replied that it meant "doing what's necessary to reach the end that my client feels I need to reach. In other words, if my client says he's innocent, then I zealously defend him from the beginning to the end." Participant 017 also indicated that he rarely experienced role conflict, so perhaps in his three decades of experience he had learned to navigate judges' attempts to co-opt him without feeling like he had departed from his zealous advocate role (i.e., he had built and exercised social capital). A juvenile defender's experience and skills are critical to negotiating the power relationships that exist in juvenile court.

Regardless of how Participant 017 handled judges who gave him a "heads-up," the importance of the judge—the functionary with the most due process expertise and the most power in the courtroom—in respecting and supporting the juvenile defender role cannot be overemphasized. The judge serves as a referee not just to the adversarial contest between the prosecutor and defense attorney but also to the contest between individual citizens and a powerful government. Additionally, the judge serves as a role model of how to behave, and to whom respect should be shown, in the courtroom. A judge's lack of respect for the only check on government power over individual citizens diminishes the check's impact and sends an important message about the strength, or lack thereof, of due process guarantees. Even if there were a question about how appropriate a strictly expressed-interests advocacy approach is for juvenile respondents, there clearly is still a need for power balance in the courtroom. Recall that in the adversarial model, the judge is meant to be a disinterested third party who weighs the evidence presented by the prosecutor and defense attorney, who each present a story line of events, one of which the judge must choose as "truth." So, for the judge to push back against the juvenile defender role makes little sense and is a bit surprising. On the other hand, pushback from prosecutors seems more expected to some extent.

PROSECUTORS

The job of the prosecutor is to present evidence that the respondent (recall that juveniles charged with crime are not referred to as "defendants") is responsible for committing acts that violated a criminal code. Toward that end, he or she must inevitably be at odds with the juvenile defender, if there is one involved in the case. At the same time, the prosecutor has received essentially the same legal education as the defender and passed essentially the same bar exam required for licensure. An important note to make here about legal education is that law students do not "major" in particular areas of law, even though they might have a few electives during law school that focus on a specific area. Much like medical school, law school provides law students with essentially the same curriculum. In addition, *all* law students are required to take a course on the US Constitution and criminal procedure, and licensed attorneys must pass a licensure exam (the "bar exam") that includes questions on these topics. So, prosecutors are fully aware of the necessary role that juvenile defenders play, and it would be no surprise if participants in this study reported experiencing pushback from them, as several did.

Only three of the twenty-four participants (12.5 percent) volunteered that prosecutors were supportive of their role as zealous advocates of their clients' expressed interests (see table 5.3). Even though these responses were volunteered (that is, they were not elicited through a direct question), this low number is concerning because of the immense power that prosecutors have in the juvenile courtroom. Participant 004 (least experienced, expressed-interests advocate) shared that he felt prosecutors were supportive but were still a source of role conflict for him because of their position of imbalanced power. He explained, "The district attorney representing the state basically owns the adjudication proceedings from . . . the state side and will be very involved in things like producing discovery [and] scheduling probable [cause] hearings and trials." Participant 004's comments on prosecutor-based role conflict are not surprising given that he was an expressed-interests advocate and viewed role departures as only sometimes justifiable. Interestingly, he reported that he experienced role conflict "every day!" Since so few participants mentioned prosecutors as supportive of their role, it is difficult to discern what makes these three stand out from the rest. This is especially true since all three identified as different types of advocate, and two were among the least experienced.

Most participants described prosecutor-based role conflict situations where the prosecutor would leverage his or her power in order to move things along more quickly or steer the case a certain way. For example, Participant 009 (least experienced, declined to identify advocate type) stated, "I do see the [district attorney and judge] sometimes pressuring departation [*sic*] from [the] zealous advocacy model. . . . I think there's pressure to expedite cases." Participant 009 viewed role departures as only sometimes justifiable but indicated that while he had been the target of pressures to depart from zealous advocacy, he did not "see that they hinder me representing the juvenile's interests at all." Further discussion of the impact that role conflict has on juvenile defenders is presented in chapter 7.

Participant 005 revealed the power that prosecutors have to beset juvenile defenders with role conflict when he commented that

> there are pressures from the other side . . . from the district attorney's office. . . . "Well, we want to get this done, and if you don't do it a certain way then you know we're going to load him up with everything he can possibly do." And you have to deal with that pressure. . . . Understanding that you are going to deal with this DA . . . repeatedly, you have to walk a thin line of trying to get along but also do the right thing.

There being so few participants who volunteered prosecutors as supportive of their role makes sense because most participants (eighteen, or 75 percent) voluntarily identified prosecutors as a source of pressure to depart from their zealous advocate role. Understandably, a higher percentage (eight out of nine participants, or 88.9 percent) of expressed-interests advocates volunteered prosecutors as a source of role conflict than did best-interests advocates (three out of five, or 60 percent). It would then seem that if defense attorneys "play along" with the best-interests orientation of the court, it is likelier that they will avoid pushback from the prosecutor. On the other hand, if they are expressed-interests advocates, defenders' chances of getting pushback from the prosecutor are likely to be greater, as is reflected in these results.

Another interesting, and logical, pattern can be seen between the most and least experienced participant groups. The most experienced participants proffered that prosecutors were supportive of them at a lower rate (one out of thirteen, or 7.7 percent) than did the least experienced participants (two out of eleven, or 18.1 percent). In addition, the least experienced participants were more likely (81.8 percent) to volunteer prosecutors as a source of role conflict than were the most experienced participants (69.2 percent). In other words, the most experienced participants might not have viewed prosecutors as very supportive of what they did, but they did not seem to experience as much pushback from them as did the least experienced participants.

Participant 011 (most experienced, expressed-interests advocate) described her experiences with prosecutors' push for efficiency in the following way:

> We've had some DAs come through juvenile court that really have no desire to be there. In our system in the [Alpha] County Public . . . DA's office system, juvenile court is the way you get moved up to superior court because you're doing felonies that nobody's looking at. And so a lot of them that move through there have the goal of moving up as fast as they can by getting felony convictions so they can prove they can do felonies . . . but that's not the kid's best interests. And I'm like, yeah, that's your standard, not mine.

Other participants, for example 010, reflected Participant 011's impressions about prosecutors. Participant 010 (least experienced) identified as an advocate of her clients' personal interests and viewed role departures as unjustifiable. She also indicated that she did not face any pressures to depart from her zealous advocate role. Nevertheless, she pointed out the following about prosecutors' focus on procuring convictions and how it affected her role:

> It's still conviction-based for them [district attorneys]. You know, "How can I get a conviction?" rather than "How can we assist the juvenile moving forward?" . . . I'll say this: there are times when you have . . . the district attorney . . . in the courtroom. . . . They want a conviction, so it's kind of hard to negotiate and advocate [for] your client when they're looking at the conviction instead of "How can we assist this client?" and . . . "Let's do a deferral instead of a guilty." So those pressures are real because I'm thinking a deferral is probably better, but you're [referring to the DA] trying to make sure that you get a conviction. So those are pressures that we see a lot. . . . They do affect how you can advocate for your client.

These findings make sense because less experienced attorneys might still be building their confidence, skills, and reputations, so prosecutors might be testing these newer attorneys' boundaries. This boundary testing might not occur as much with the more seasoned defenders who have already successfully demonstrated resistance to such pressure or have developed reputations for their ability to do so.

At the same time, these descriptions paint a less-than-encouraging picture of a key figure in the courtroom workgroup. Prosecutors, as law professionals with essentially the same legal education as defense attorneys, *should* understand the defense role. Consequently, their reported level of pushback is troubling. Perhaps North Carolina reflects some of what the Georgia state assessment reported: that prosecutors and judges seemed to prefer a less adversarial juvenile court (Puritz & Sun, 2001). The assessment indicated that this preference was a result of the belief that a best-interests orientation ultimately poses no risk of negative consequences to juveniles, making the defender role altogether unnecessary. While it is important to recognize that the prosecutor serves the state's interests and is the official adversary of the defense attorney, this should not preclude prosecutors, presumably as well-trained in due process requirements as defense attorneys, from recognizing and respecting the need for a check against their power in the courtroom.

Participants' responses made it clear that prosecutors felt pressure to obtain convictions and move cases expeditiously through the court process. However, participants also suggested other reasons for prosecutor-based role conflict, such as their belief that prosecutors either misunderstood or lacked respect for the defender role. The parens patriae orientation of the juvenile court might encourage prosecutors to loosen the boundaries normally placed on their roles and defenders' roles in the adversarial system, causing them to pressure defense attorneys to depart from their expressed-interests advocate role. This might reflect a lack of respect instead of a lack of understanding, as it would were the pressure to come from a parent or client.

Participant 008 was one of the study's most experienced juvenile defenders and identified as an advocate of his clients' true interests. He viewed role departures as justifiable. He also indicated that he saw the expressed-/best-interests dichotomy as an oversimplification such that juvenile court is more "everybody get on the same page, let's fix this kid, let's not let this kid fall into the hole of becoming a criminal." He also indicated that this approach does not interfere with his expressed-interests advocacy. Even though he did not volunteer that prosecutors were unsupportive of his role, he reported that they were a source of role conflict: "We do get pressure in some situations where . . . well, always the DAs think we're supposed to be helping them, which is completely insane." When I asked if these were experiences he had had in Alpha County, he replied, incredulously, "Oh all the time. . . . Constantly. The DAs think we're supposed to help them!"

The pushback described by Participant 008 reflects conflict that was clearly not a normal part of the adversarial process. However, that does not mean that the role conflict that participants experience is never confounded with the kind of conflict that typically accompanies the adversarial process. Again, prosecutors and defense attorneys represent opposite sides in an adversarial system. Prosecutors are *supposed* to create pressure or pushback for the defense. It is an inescapable requirement of the prosecutorial role, a reality to which some participants alluded. As a result, it could be difficult to tease out where the prosecutor's own zealous advocacy ends and role conflict manifestations begin. Perhaps the answer might be found in an examination of situations where the prosecutor encourages defense attorneys to "play along." This is a nuance that could be the focus of future investigations. However, it is not a nuance that explains role conflict from courtroom functionaries who are *not* trained in law.

COURT COUNSELORS

The court counselor (also known as the juvenile probation officer), unlike the prosecutor, is *not* the official adversary of the defense attorney. So, juvenile defenders' experiences of pushback from court counselors might be easier to distinguish from other role behaviors. The court counselor's role up to adjudication (i.e., the fact-finding stage) is to work closely with the juvenile and his or her family to understand what the child's life is like and what factors might be contributing to his or her poor choices (R. Waldrop Rugh, personal communication, July 25, 2015). At some point, the court counselor might "diagnose" a problematic factor that could be addressed with services that he or she suggests in a report to the judge at the disposition (sentencing) stage.

The court counselor's role is definitely not legal but *informational* and *relational*. In other words, while a juvenile defender's role is to protect the juvenile's legal rights, the court counselor's role is to find ways to meet the juvenile's personal needs in recognition of the youth's tender years. At disposition, the court counselor's role is to make treatment and/or residence recommendations to the judge based on his or her understanding of the unique needs and circumstances of the juvenile (R. Waldrop Rugh, personal communication, July 25, 2015).

The juvenile defender and court counselor roles are, essentially, mutually exclusive in that they cover different turf—legal and personal, respectively—with regard to the juvenile's needs. However, they share a desire to improve the juvenile's life in some way. As a result, and due to the apparent lack of territory overlap, one might expect most juvenile defenders to report believing their role is supported by court counselors, but not many of the study's participants reported feeling this way.

About one-third of the participants (eight, or 33.3 percent) volunteered that court counselors generally supported the juvenile defender role (see table 5.3). A higher percentage of the participants who found court counselors supportive were expressed-interests (five out of nine, or 55.6 percent) rather than best-interests advocates (two out of five, or 40 percent). This is a somewhat confusing finding because one would have expected more of the best-interests advocates to view court counselors, whose shared goal is to serve the juvenile's best interests, as supportive. The answer might lie in the fact that both best-interests advocates who found court counselors to be supportive were also among the most experienced attorneys. More experienced attorneys (50 percent) were likelier to proffer court counselors as supportive than were less experienced attorneys (20 percent). This possibly indicates that the more experienced attorneys had demonstrated their confidence and boundaries, as might have also been the case with prosecutorial support. This could also indicate that they might have reputations that served to prevent or deflect pushback, or they might have developed good relationships with the court counselors throughout their years of service. So, for the purposes of this topic, attorney experience might have affected their perspectives on court counselor support more than their type of advocacy did.

Seventeen participants (70.8 percent) reported experiencing pressure from court counselors, nearly the same number who reported experiencing it from prosecutors (eighteen, or 75 percent). Participant 010 (least experienced, personal-interests advocate) indicated that pressure from a court counselor to depart from the expressed-interests advocate role was "one of the main things that sticks out that happens probably more often than not." Interestingly, best-interests advocates reported court counselors as a source of role conflict at a higher rate (80 percent) than did expressed-interests advocates (66.7 percent). As with the "support" topic, the answer to this surprising finding might lie in the power of participants' level of experience, because 75 percent of these best-interests advocates who cited court counselors as sources of role conflict were also among the most experienced. However, overall, roughly the same percentage of the most experienced (ten out of thirteen, or 76.9 percent) and least experienced attorneys (seven out of eleven, or 63.6 percent) reported court counselors as a source of role conflict. Clearly, the sample numbers are too low to infer any predictive value in these variables. However, it is critical to recognize the extent to which court counselors were identified as sources of role conflict to understand participants' experiences of these pressures.

Participant 023 (least experienced, "best-personal-desire"-interests advocate) noted that

> the ones that don't [support my zealous advocacy role] the most are the court counselors. Sometimes I butt heads with court counselors, and again that's

a tricky line because they're not lawyers, but . . . also . . . they get a lot more personal sort of connection to the client.

Participant 023 viewed role departures as unjustifiable, even at the disposition stage, where the court counselors have the most input to the judge.

Court counselors' considerable influence with the judge at the disposition phase might have also been responsible for the "tricky line" Participant 023 identified, but his point about their unique connection to the client is important. Perhaps some court counselors might feel territorial or protective of juvenile respondents because of their more intimate familiarity with the juvenile's life and personal needs. Perhaps because they lack legal training they fail to recognize the due process repercussions of inadequate assistance of counsel and therefore also fail to recognize the importance of the defender role. Participant 011 (most experienced, expressed-interests advocate) shared her frustration at having to repeatedly explain her role to court counselors who seemed unable to accept the reality of the defender's role:

> I've had court counselors tell me that I'm not really working in the kid's best interests. And I repeatedly say, "That's not my job; that's yours." I have to keep saying it over and over again. The same court counselor will come in and say— and I'm trying to get the kid out of detention—and they're saying he really needs to stay in until he goes to placement or he's gonna get more charges. And I go, "I know that. But my job is to say what he wants, not what you want."

I asked this participant if she still found that this was the situation in her county.

> Yes. Even now. And even with the same court counselors, over and over again, that are just surprised that I don't come in and rubber-stamp what they want in the best interest of the child. They can't believe that I will go into the courtroom and . . . really try hard to get them out. "Why you trying so hard?" Because it's my job. Because the kid needs to see me fighting for them. I will tell the kid behind closed doors, "We're gonna go down in a blaze of glory, but hey, it's gonna be a big blaze and I'm going to make it big; we're gonna fight hard." And I have gotten a few kids out . . . who I shouldn't have, but I told them I was gonna fight for them, and I did.

It seems logical that a juvenile courtroom functionary who has not received legal training would feel compelled to push back against the juvenile defender role. In other words, someone who is not familiar with the nuances of constitutional rights might struggle to justify actions that do not appear to prioritize a child's best interests. This could be especially true when court counselors see other courtroom functionaries, like judges, pushing back against juvenile defenders as well. In addition, court counselors might not have confidence in the adversarial system to achieve the rehabilitation goals that the court counselor role and the court itself are designed to accomplish. Participants offered their own ideas of why court counselors pressure them to depart from their expressed-interests advocate role.

For example, participants shared that court counselors were a source of role conflict because they lacked understanding of or respect for the juvenile defender role. Participant 010 (least experienced, personal-interests advocate) offered an excellent example of both inadequate understanding and respect for the juvenile defender role.

> I'll give you a specific case. I have a client who I think . . . may be charged with . . . assault, but speaking with the court counselor, they know and understand that the DA is not going to be able to prove their case because my client was not seen hitting the child, wasn't seen kicking the child, wasn't seen punching the child, she was just there and just got caught up with everybody who got arrested or got cited. So the . . . court counselor [comes to me and] says, "Look, I know this case should be dismissed, but the girl's father isn't in her life, the mother is an alcoholic, she lives with the grandmother, the mother's in and out of the home, so I want to be able to get the child services as well as the mother services, and the only way I can get the child services is if you allow her to plead guilty." . . .
>
> So those are pressures that we see a lot. . . . They do affect how you can advocate for your client. . . . [T]he court counselors . . . will [also] kind of push you towards . . . "I want to get this kid the services, so if you can get him to plead, you know, just so we can get the services that we need, so . . ." I do run into those situations.

Participant 010's experience of a court counselor pressuring her to advocate a certain way reflects a lack of respect for the juvenile defender role. The court counselor in the excerpt seemed to understand the way the justice system works because he said, "I know this case should be dismissed." The court counselor must have understood the defender role to some extent because otherwise he would not have known to ask the juvenile defender to "allow [her client] to plead guilty." At the same time, the fact that he asked her to do this reflects too little true understanding of the defender role and its ethical duty to zealously advocate for the expressed interests of the client. In addition, it is easy to see how this juvenile defender might feel her role is disrespected when a court counselor admits the case against her client should fail but still presses her to allow her client to admit guilt. Even though the court counselor's intentions for the juvenile might be benevolent, his having pushed the defense attorney to depart from her role indicates that he lacked respect for the role.

The court counselor, or juvenile probation officer, is the functionary who is the most responsible for advocating for the juvenile's best interests. This functionary distinguishes the juvenile justice system from the adult system and, theoretically, makes the juvenile system unique and effective. It is therefore understandable that court counselors might feel toward their juvenile respondents a certain level of territoriality, protectiveness, and authority over them. However, the necessary existence of a best-interests role in a court system that, in reality, doles out punishment and utilizes an adversarial model exemplifies Birckhead's "culture clash" (2010, p. 959) and can have serious implications for the expressed-interests advocate and his or her client.

Another factor that might contribute to court counselors' apparent sense of territoriality is the greater extent to which court counselors are familiar with the juveniles. Their familiarity begins at an earlier stage and occurs at a deeper, more personal level. Finally, court counselors' recommendations are accorded a great deal of deference, even to the point that judges are viewed as merely rubber-stamping them (Participant 011). This could lead to court counselors feeling a false sense of authority over juvenile respondents, or defenders, emboldening them to push back against defenders' expressed-interests advocacy efforts.

Whatever their motivations, court counselors were viewed by many participants as lacking understanding of or respect for the juvenile defender role. This could have serious implications for the expressed-interests advocate's efficacy. The most practical solution to this particular problem is likely to educate court counselors and raise their awareness about different functionaries' roles instead of changing the roles or their parameters. Another solution could be to discourage pushback from other courtroom functionaries, particularly when it comes to the defense attorneys themselves.

OTHER DEFENSE ATTORNEYS

Surprisingly, some participants identified other defense attorneys as responsible for pressure to depart from the zealous advocate role. This courtroom functionary was least likely to be held responsible by the participants (seven out of twenty-four, or 29.2 percent) for such pressure. While there was virtually no difference between the expressed-interests (two out of nine, or 22.2

percent) and best-interests (one out of five, or 20 percent) groups for this topic, there was something of a difference between the most experienced groups (five out of thirteen, or 38.5 percent) and least experienced (two out of eleven, or 18.2 percent). So, more experienced attorneys were likelier to get pushback from one another than less experienced attorneys, possibly in response to the experienced attorneys' greater confidence in asserting their zealous advocate role or in resisting pushback from sources of role conflict.

Multiple responses indicated this has typically been an issue in group (or multiple) respondent cases or when some of the involved juvenile defenders were either new to juvenile defense practice or unclear about their role. Participant 003 (most experienced, expressed-interests advocate) explained his views on this particular source of role conflict.

> I probably [get pushback] more so . . . from other defenders. . . . I think what's been most troubling is running into other attorneys who may not have the same view of zealous advocacy as I do. . . . I've run into several situations where I might have arrived at the courtroom later than the other attorney [in a multiple defendant scenario] and they've already made their decision to roll without having talked to me. "You don't know what our position is." . . . There's lots of reasons that attorneys do and don't do what they're supposed to. I mean, . . . a good defense attorney . . . really is interested in representing his clients, but unfortunately there's some attorneys where it's a job and the easiest way they can get it done is the way they get it done. So, I mean, that's why you have good attorneys and you have bad attorneys. . . . I can't say what their reason is for what they do. . . . I think there's some attorneys who don't necessarily like to fight and they see juvenile court as an easy place to . . . you know, "Let's just all work it out" as opposed to . . . [fighting].

Participants tended to view pushback from other defense attorneys as partly the result of confusion about the meaning of their role; this would confirm some of the previously discussed findings of the 2003 state assessment (Grindall & Puritz). Additional explanations of role conflict from other defense attorneys imply a disinterest in juvenile defense or a view of the juvenile defender role as merely a stepping stone to another, presumably more desirable, role. Finally, the pushback seems to come from other defense attorneys internalizing the pressure they might feel from the court to "move things along." This explanation has been touched upon in prior sections discussing other sources of role conflict, such as judges or prosecutors. So, the efficiency, or expediency, pressure could constitute a role conflict source on its own.

System Push for Efficiency

The system itself was the second-most frequently identified source of role conflict for juvenile defenders; recall that parents and clients tied for first. Nineteen participants (79.2 percent) regarded the system itself as, in some way, a source of pressure for juvenile defenders to depart from their zealous advocacy role (see table 5.2). There appeared to be a negligible difference between advocate type groups on this source of role conflict. Best-interests advocates were only slightly (80 percent) more likely to identify the system as a source of role conflict than were expressed-interests advocates (77.8 percent). This difference is too small for commentary. However, the difference between experience groups was a quite a bit larger. Participants in the least experienced group were likelier (81.8 percent) to identify the system as a source of role conflict than were participants in the most experienced group (76.9 percent).

The logic behind this discrepancy could be that lack of experience makes efficiency more of a challenge. Along those same lines, the awkwardness of the learning curve consumes time that reduces defender efficiency, raising the defender's awareness of the system's pressure for efficiency. Finally, it could be that less experienced defenders are still building their confidence and reputations, leaving them vulnerable to other functionaries' exertion of pressure on them for more efficiency. Based on these reflections, it is no surprise that of the five participants who did *not* identify the system as a role conflict source, four (80 percent) were from the most experienced group; there was no meaningful pattern among the advocate type groups for these five participants.

So, while a number of participants praised the system for working well, most noted aspects of it that were problematic for them in their expressed-interests advocate role. For instance, some participants held the system responsible for being co-opted by parents to respond to child issues that parents were unable or unwilling to manage. And some held other system functionaries responsible for facilitating the system's push for efficiency. Participant 009 (least-experienced, declined to identify advocate type) explained his view on this pressure:

> I think there's pressure to expedite cases. There are a lot of people standing in the courtroom, there's an awful lot of money . . . and so I think there's some pressure to move cases along as opposed to really delving into the facts, particularly in the disposition stage. . . . I have had some issues with district attorneys who, when I intimate that a case might be triable, . . . they look through the file, and . . . there's some pressure from the DAs to have an efficient disposition.

The pragmatic considerations Participant 009 raised are likely a source of concern for all courtroom functionaries, regardless of their role. However, the pressure to expedite cases could be difficult to tease apart from pressures posed by other sources and for different reasons. For example, it might be difficult for juvenile defenders to distinguish between judge-based role conflict that stems from a desire for efficiency or from disrespect for the defender role. Ultimately, it might not matter if defenders believe they must accommodate the pressure in order to avoid harm to their clients. Participant 016 (most experienced, best-interests advocate) referred to this dynamic:

> I think for the most part [judges] understand that you're doing your job, but for whatever reason, whether it's the juvenile's history or the nature of the charges . . . if the judge is telling you what they're going to do already and you can kind of see the irritation or frustration again for the time constraints and the caseload, you may feel like you're just kind of treading on thin ice there. But I think there's a way to advocate zealously but at the same time respecting the court and the process and not just saying, "You're just not going to hear my argument and you're violating my client's constitutional rights." . . . It's not an incorrect statement, but . . . it does not always go over well, and I think that can hurt your zealous advocacy in the future for clients because sometimes attorneys get labeled as long-winded or what have you, and so it's almost like before you even start saying anything they've already kind of decided that you are going to say a whole bunch of nothing, and unfortunately that's not the case. . . . But, that's just the perception sometimes, so it's a fine balance between understanding your time constraints, the court's time constraints, the interests of the juvenile, and just kind of how to really put that out there fully without ending up having a negative impact on your client, which is not what you're trying to do.

Participant 016 makes a critical point. She clearly recognized that her role is to zealously advocate for the expressed interests of her client. However, she also understood that pressing the judge, when it was clear that he had already made up his mind, might have negative ramifications for her client. She suggested that pushing forward with expressed-interests advocacy might negatively affect other clients' future chances with the same judge.

As indicated previously, judges are not supposed to decide cases before hearing from both the prosecutor and the defense attorney. However, participants' responses made clear that some North Carolina judges regularly engaged in this practice and possibly did so in the interest of efficiency. Juvenile defenders were then left with having to decide just how far they wanted to push for their clients without incurring the wrath of certain judges. Successfully navigating this decision takes experience, finesse, and considerable interpersonal skills. The system efficiency pressure also raises several questions concerning the appropriateness of the zealous advocacy model for the juvenile process when it comes to the defender role. These topics will be discussed more thoroughly in chapter 8.

The role that the system's push for efficiency might play in juvenile defenders' role conflict presents a critical area for future research, given how widely reported it was in this study. The excerpts discussed here suggest that participants believed the system had a major internal inconsistency, specifically, a due process requirement (necessitating careful use of an adversarial structure and the expressed-interests advocate defender role) alongside immense pressure to process cases efficiently. While this inconsistency also exists in the adult court, the fact that it exists in the juvenile court, where the espoused mission is to take time and care with youths because of their tender years, calls the system's efficacy, credibility, and legitimacy into question. This inconsistency can lead to role confusion, raising the question, again, about how to balance the need for due process protections for juveniles with the possible inappropriateness of a strictly expressed-interests advocate role for juvenile clients facing criminal charges. Future research could certainly reveal critical factors and relationships and possibly lead to solutions.

Thus far the role conflict sources discussed have been external to the juvenile defender. However, the role conflict that juvenile defenders face might sometimes originate within themselves.

Internal Role Conflict

Individuals' personal values, perspectives, or goals might play a part in how they view their professional role, regardless of how well a governing authority defines it. The influence of these forces could lead to role confusion or what Katz and Kahn referred to as "person-role," or internal role, conflict, which occurs "when role requirements violate the needs, values or capacities of the individual" (Katz & Kahn, 1966, p. 185). It could also indicate role meaning conflict or role confusion. This study assessed internal role conflict by asking participants, *Do you ever feel like you, personally, are conflicted about your role as a zealous advocate for juveniles, or what it requires you to do? How so?* All twenty-four participants were able to provide examples of internal conflict they had experienced in response to this question, and over half provided more than one.

Ten participants provided only one example, while fourteen (58.3 percent) provided two or three. There did not appear to be any difference in the number of examples provided in terms of the most or least experienced participants. However, the best-interests participants provided a slightly higher average number of examples (2.8) than did the expressed-interests participants (1.92) (see table 5.2) This difference suggests that the best-interests advocates recognized a dissonance between the official need to prioritize their child clients' expressed interests and their desire to advocate for their clients' best interests. Perhaps they struggled with reconciling North Carolina's *Role Statement* mandate (NCOJD, 2005) with other roles they inhabit or with their other views, beliefs, or values. This would make sense given all of the efforts the North Carolina Office of the Juvenile Defender and Office of Indigent Defense Services had made to ensure its juvenile court functionaries recognize and internalize the expressed-interests nature of the juvenile defender role. In addition, the higher reports of internal conflict among best-interests advocates make sense given the fact that these same participants also explicitly recognized the centrality of expressed-interests advocacy to their zealous advocate role in the "zealous advocacy meaning" question, despite their prioritization of their clients' best interests. This was true with the exception of Participants 015 and 019, both of whom identified as best-interests advocates but indirectly recognized the importance of expressed-interests advocacy to their role in their responses to other questions.

As stated, all twenty-four participants offered at least one example of a situation where they experienced internal conflict about their zealous advocate role and what it required of them, whether or not they succumbed to the pressure. A very small number identified the rare situation where their role as parents presented them with conflicting feelings about their advocate role, but those situations invariably involved parental values, not the actual parental *role*. Others noted they felt personally conflicted about their role when the client was in need of services but might not be actually guilty of the charges filed against him or her.

Participant 018 (least experienced, expressed-interests advocate) described an example of this as a "dilemma [of] my personal concern for this kid versus my professional duty." Participant 015 (least experienced, best-interests advocate), explained internal role conflict in the following way:

> I'm probably one of the few defense attorneys around that—and I hate to say this, but it is what it is— . . . actually has a moral apprehension about doing defense work. It's funny. I do it and I think I do a good job at it, but at the same time . . . if my client's guilty . . . my loyalty is more to the system and making the system work than it is to "get your client out of it" or something

like that. So, when I'm representing someone that I know is guilty, it does impact me in some way.

Here, Participant 015 openly recognized that he put the system ahead of his client if the client was guilty. Recall that Participant 015 identified himself as a best-interests advocate and viewed role departures as acceptable, even at the disposition stage. He also identified the system's push for efficiency as a source of role conflict. This excerpt reflects how his "moral apprehension" about his role might shift his view of his role at the disposition stage.

Other examples of internal conflict listed by participants often reflected a friction between their values as attorneys and values as humans with compassion for children in need. For instance, the following excerpt shows how Participant 016 (most experienced, best-interests advocate) worked to compartmentalize these roles and maintain professionalism for her clients.

Oh yeah, you can get confused, absolutely . . . because sometimes personally, or in your own conscience, you're taking the side of the prosecutor, or you're taking the side of the parent or the court counselor or all of the above. . . . I think we all have opinions about clients and cases, and I think that you just have to really work hard to keep that opinion out of your advocacy, whether it's good or bad. Sometimes you've got a positive opinion about the client, sometimes you've got a negative opinion about the client, but that should not factor into how you advocate for them.

Participant 016 clearly struggled to separate her personal opinions from her professional duties. In fact, she provided more examples of internal role conflict than many participants. The extent of her internal role conflict might be partly responsible for her identifying as a best-interests advocate despite her recognition of the importance of clients' expressed interests to her zealous advocate role. Or, these opposing views could be responsible for her internal role conflict. Most important, Participant 016 recognized the reality of this struggle and acknowledged her need to conquer it in favor of her clients.

A very small number of participants identified the seemingly rare situation where their role as parents presented them with conflicting feelings about their advocate role. Others noted they felt personally conflicted about their role when the client was in need of services but might not be actually guilty of the charges filed against him or her.

For example, Participant 012 (most experienced, best-interests advocate) recognized her internal conflict but opted to prioritize her juvenile advocate role over her role as a compassionate human being. It is crucial to note here that Participant 012 was a best-interests advocate who viewed role departures as unjustifiable, even at the disposition stage. She also indicated that she did not experience role conflict but acknowledged that there was a balance that must be struck when dealing with whoever had custody of her clients. She explained that even when she had a client who really needed services, she still fulfilled her zealous advocacy responsibilities to that client. She was candid in admitting that while she was "only human," she would not feel good compelling her client to plead responsible in a case just to "get him all this treatment" when the "case [didn't] really warrant my client going in there and pleading responsible."

Like Participant 016, Participant 012 recognized the pressure but did not accommodate it. Their comments and others' regarding internal role conflict indicate that these types of dilemmas typically did *not* result in role departures. It would seem, then, that juvenile defenders did not view role departures due to internal conflicts as typically justifiable. At the same time, recall that participants identified situations in which they did view role departures as justifiable, possibly validating Birckhead's assertion that prioritizing a client's expressed interests over his or her best interests is often more difficult than it sounds (2010). This can depend on a number of factors, including the individual-level factors thus far discussed. It can also depend on the context within which juvenile defenders practice.

*F*rom *the study* that was the basis fsor this book, four major factors emerged from participants' descriptions of role conflict experiences as context-relevant: the disposition stage, the juvenile court culture, juvenile defenders' professional ethics, and resource availability.

Disposition Stage

One of this study's most compelling findings was participants' divergent views of their role at the disposition stage of the juvenile process compared with earlier stages in the process (for example, probable cause hearing, detention hearing, adjudicatory hearing). Clear guidance exists that addresses the need for expressed-interests advocacy for juveniles at *all* stages of the process. For instance, three years after North Carolina's *Role Statement* was published by its Office of the Juvenile Defender, Newman et al. remind us that

> an attorney in a juvenile delinquency proceeding or in an order to show cause against an undisciplined juvenile shall be the juvenile's voice to the court, representing the expressed interests of the juvenile at *every stage* [emphasis added] of the proceedings. (2008, p. 275)

Indeed, the *National Juvenile Defense Standards* directs juvenile defenders to adopt an expressed-interests advocate role, even after their persuasive efforts have failed "throughout the course of the case" (NJDC, 2012, p. 18, Standard 1.2d). In addition, since 2005, North Carolina has required its juvenile defenders to take on an expressed-interests advocate role at *all stages* of the juvenile process (see NCCIDS, 2007; and NCOIDS, 2006).

Despite clear guidelines requiring attorneys to maintain their zealous advocate role throughout *all* stages of the juvenile process, the majority of participants (twenty-two, or 91.7 percent) noted that the *stage* of the juvenile justice process could trigger motivation to depart from the expressed-interests advocate role (see table 5.2). The two participants who did not make this note, 006 and 023, were both in the least experienced group, even though Participant

023 had twice as much experience as Participant 006. Additionally, they could have identified with different types of advocate role; this is difficult to ascertain since Participant 006 declined to answer the question and Participant 023 identified with his clients' "best personal desired interest." Their views of the stage of the juvenile process were discussed during the interview but not during the recorded portion. Participant 006 (declined to identify advocate type) indicated she believed she did not have enough experience to answer the question, and nothing else in her responses suggested a more detailed answer. Participant 023 indicated it was "absolutely not" ever appropriate to depart from the expressed-interests advocate role. He referred to his "prior answers" when asked about stages, but there was nothing concrete to identify as a response, and attempts to follow up were unsuccessful. Participant 006 was the only participant who declined to be audio-recorded, and Participant 023 was one of two participants who passively declined to complete the vignettes exercise.

Participants' comments either specifically referred to the disposition (sentencing) stage as a time in the juvenile process during which they could feel compelled to step out of their expressed-interests advocate role or suggested that was the case. For example, Participant 019 was one of only three participants who did *not* discuss expressed-interests advocacy as central to his meaning of the zealous advocate role. Interestingly, the other two (Participants 007 and 015) who did not indicate expressed-interests advocacy as central to their zealous advocacy meaning were split on whether the disposition stage presented a justifiable departure from the expressed-interests role. Participant 007 commented that it was an acceptable departure. However, Participant 015 commented that such a departure was *not* acceptable at the disposition stage. Participant 019 identified as his clients' best-interests advocate, and even though he viewed role departures as unjustifiable, he appeared to make an exception for the disposition stage. He explained his views:

> Different stages *do* require different ways that I might approach an issue with the client, but I do try to advocate for . . . their best interests at that particular stage [disposition]. At certain stages I can truly advocate for their interests, and sometimes I might have to shift to what is their best interests.

Participant 019 clearly justified departing from the expressed-interests role in favor of a best-interests role at the disposition stage. This could indicate that he either did not understand or did not respect his ethical duties. A likelier explanation is that he believed juvenile defense, particularly at the disposition stage, required a more nuanced approach, as suggested by Birckhead (2010).

Other participants also appeared to believe that juvenile defense requires a more nuanced approach. In fact, a few suggested that the distinction between expressed and best interests at the disposition stage is not so dichotomous. For example, Participant 009 (least experienced, declined to identify advocate type) explained,

> I would say the answer is yes [a defense attorney should depart from advocating for the expressed interests of a client] . . . [but] I would keep that in the context of disposition of the case as opposed to adjudication [fact-finding stage]. So, I think in a [disposition] context alone, yes, in a mild sort of way. In the adjudication process, no. . . . And it's not really in conflict with . . . their expressed interests. . . . I think it's more kind of a compromise position. And that's certainly a form of advocacy, but do I ever depart from advocating their expressed interests? No. Again to answer your question: in disposition, yes, in adjudication, no.

An examination of responses indicated that seven participants (31.8 percent) believed departure from expressed-interests advocacy at the disposition stage was justified, and fifteen (68.2 percent) believed such departure was *not* justified. An interesting difference between these groups emerged in terms of their tenure of experience and advocate type.

The "stage-departure-justifiable" group was mostly made up (85.7 percent) of attorneys from the most experienced group, but they were twice as likely to be best-interests (two out of seven, or 28.6 percent) than expressed-interests (one out of seven, or 14.3 percent) advocates (see table 5.2). On the other hand, those who indicated they did not view a departure from the expressed-interests advocate role as justifiable at the disposition stage had a much lower percentage (53.3 percent) of attorneys from the most experienced group. They also were much likelier to be expressed-interests advocates (eight out of fifteen, or 53.3 percent) (see table 5.2). This result makes sense since it has already been established that the best-interests advocates were twice as likely to be from the most experienced group than were the expressed-interests advocates. This finding raises the questions of whether more experience wore down the resolve of juvenile defenders to succumb to the court's best-interests approach for disposition or whether their experience led them to believe that their expressed-interests efforts were futile. Another perspective could be that, as suggested earlier, the newer juvenile defenders were clearer about their mandated expressed-interests role, given that they were likely to have entered the profession under North Carolina's newly published *Role Statement* (NCOJD, 2005) and therefore more effectively internalized it.

These more experienced attorneys might have learned how to "get along" in the system or might have reached the conclusion that they were not in as good a position as other juvenile courtroom functionaries—namely, the court counselors—to make recommendations so that they might be more willing to defer to court counselors' judgment. In fact, some participants described the pressure they perceived to depart from the expressed-interests advocacy role as a result of how uninformed they felt compared with the court counselor.

Importantly, even though most participants viewed the disposition stage as a potential trigger for role departure, the majority (roughly two-thirds) did *not* view such a departure as justifiable. However, those who did provided similar explanations to Participant 009's. For instance, some participants asserted that the pressure they feel to depart from the expressed-interests advocacy role at this stage specifically stems from their having less information about their clients than court counselors typically do. Participant 001 (most experienced, expressed-interests advocate) explained:

> I think I have a problem ... when we get to the dispositional phase. The juvenile court counselor oftentimes has met with the client and parents and maybe will have gone to the client's house or [will] have a better understanding of the client history than I do, because I just focus on legal issues in the case. So, when they are recommending therapy or that they go to some program to get them involved in the community, that they have some structure after school or that they attend some curriculum assistance at school, lots of times they know more about the client at that point than I do. So, it's hard for me to quibble lots of times with what they're asking for because lots of times they know about the juvenile more than I do.

It would appear that at the disposition stage, Participant 001 might lose sight of his expressed-interests advocate role and feel compelled to defer to the court counselor's recommendation. This information-discrepancy pressure is not necessarily exclusive to the disposition stage. Even still, other participants appeared to falter in the zealous advocate role at this stage for the same reason: they recognized the critical role the court counselor plays and the deeper knowledge court counselors tend to have of the juveniles' lives. Participants thus felt compelled to defer to court counselor recommendations as a result of their deeper knowledge. Because the court counselor's recommendation is designed to prioritize the juvenile's best interests, some participants viewed this deference as an *acceptable* departure from the expressed-interests advocate role. On the other hand, some participants, like Participant 001, viewed this deference as a "weakness."

One of my weaknesses when we get to dispositional phase [is] I probably don't challenge [the court counselor's recommendation]. . . . The court counselor's office does a dispositional court report; they make their recommendations. Lots of times those recommendations seem completely logical and rational to me. Some attorneys do challenge some of the things in the dispositional report more often than I do. . . . So I think some lawyers see their role as, "Let's get the least amount of punishment we can," and . . . when we get to disposition, I don't often change much about what the court counselors are recommending because usually to me it seems to be pretty rational what they're asking.

The excerpts discussed in this section indicate participants' recognition of the potential for role ambiguity at the disposition stage. Participants' responses clearly demonstrate that some experienced difficulty in maintaining their expressed-interests advocate role at this juncture. They also indicate some participants' willingness to depart from the role at this stage and that they viewed such departures as justifiable. Even though Participant 001 referred to his role departure willingness as a "weakness," Participant 009 referred to it as an acceptable "compromise." Perhaps this is a nuance worth considering in future studies, given the implications of role departures for juveniles' due process protections.

Participants reported they were less knowledgeable about their clients than the court counselors, whose recommendations were typically accepted, out of hand, by judges (Participant 011). Participant 011 was one of the few full-time juvenile defenders in the sample and was also one of the most experienced, so this perspective is presumably informed by that long tenure. This knowledge discrepancy between defenders and court counselors appears to make juvenile defenders reluctant to "quibble" (Participant 001) with counselors' recommendations, potentially eroding their adherence to the expressed-interests component of their zealous advocate role. Court counselors are key juvenile courtroom functionaries in that they provide information and assist in establishing relationships (R. Waldrop Rugh, personal communication, July 25, 2015). Yet, despite having no legal training, they appear to exert a great deal of influence on what is, for all intents and purposes, a *legal* process.

This confounding arrangement raises a number of questions. Should this influence be cause for concern, given its apparent impact on the extent to which juvenile defenders fill their critical role? Is the court counselor's input crucial enough to justify potentially subjugating juveniles' due process protections? In other words, does juvenile defenders' failure to "quibble" with the court counselor's recommendations constitute a departure from the zealous advocate role if their clients disagree with those recommendations? These are critical questions for future research.

Some participants appeared to bring to the disposition stage a paternalistic stance toward their clients that encourages them to prioritize their clients' best interests over their expressed interests. Participant 015 (least experienced, best-interests advocate) provided an example of this dynamic:

> I think the time that it changes for me is after the plea or after they are found guilty in a trial. I kind of shift from telling the court what they want and fighting for that into probably, in my opinion, the best [interests] at that point. So, if they're already found guilty and we're trying to figure out what to do with them, whether that be wilderness camp or juvenile detention or just probation or something, I tend to argue more what I think is best and not exactly what the client wants . . . because the client may not want wilderness camp, but if that's what I think is actually best for the child, then I will say, "Absolutely, I think wilderness camp's a good idea." Obviously, that's not what my client wants.

In this situation, Participant 015 appeared to be motivated by an internal humanitarian pull to fight for what he believed was best for his client because the adjudication phase had passed. Recall that Participant 015 was also one of the three participants who did not raise expressed-interests advocacy as central to their definition of zealous advocacy. This apparently justifiable shift in role from expressed to best interests is concerning, given the fact that the disposition phase of the juvenile process has become more punitive and less rehabilitative (Birckhead, 2010). The juvenile court process is like the adult process in that it is adversarial. However, the disposition stage is meant to reflect a rehabilitative approach. If this is not necessarily the case in reality, as Birckhead suggests, it could have severe ramifications for juveniles' due process protections. The ramifications of the punitive realities in the modern-day juvenile court are discussed more thoroughly in chapter 8.

To reiterate, guidelines at the state and national level seem to clearly support the expressed-interests advocate role at *all* stages of the juvenile process. It is therefore puzzling that most participants identified the disposition stage as a role conflict source. It is even more puzzling that almost one-third of those participants viewed role departure at disposition as *acceptable*.

What is it about the disposition stage that prompts some juvenile defenders to become flexible about what seems to be a very clearly delineated role? Are they motivated by their humanity or feelings of compassion toward their clients? Are they being co-opted into the best-interests orientation of the court, believing in the court's "innocuous" impact, as implied by Participant 009, who said, "We're not there to punish; it's not a permanent stigma. The kid obviously needs help"? Do they allow themselves to be co-opted because they see their efforts to serve as the client's voice as futile in the face of judges' heavy deference to court counselors' recommendations and of judges' power? Could it be that attorneys who find such a departure acceptable do not view the ABA's *Model Rules of Professional Conduct* (2013) as controlling when it comes to juvenile representation? And, if this is the case, *why* is it the case? Is there something special about *juvenile* defense as a profession that compels these attorneys to depart from the role they are ethically bound to fill?

Perhaps there is a greater likelihood of internal (person-role) conflict among juvenile defenders when they get to the disposition stage. Attorneys' professional success seems somewhat dependent on their ability to compartmentalize. However, they are still human beings, and some might have children the same age as some of their clients. All of these factors could affect their view of their clients' ability to express an interest, particularly one that involves a suitable state response to bad behavior.

Since more than twice as many participants viewed role departure at the disposition stage as unacceptable (68.2 percent) than acceptable (31.8 percent), it is reasonable to conclude that the discrepancy might not be prevalent. However, the discrepancy exists and is robust, a disturbing fact given North Carolina's tremendous efforts to clarify the juvenile defender role. It is a discrepancy that merits further investigation, particularly with regard to what might diminish it (e.g., relevant training for defenders and/or court counselors, changes in courtroom procedures). Such investigation is beyond the scope of this study, one of whose chief aims was to investigate juvenile defenders' experiences of role conflict from any source, possibly the juvenile court culture itself.

Juvenile Court Culture

As explained in chapter 1, juvenile courts have historically eschewed the adversarial function and minimized the importance of the juvenile defender role. According to recent state assessments, including the North Carolina assessment (Grindall & Puritz, 2003), this "best-interests" culture remains intact (see, for example, Scali et al., 2013). Proponents of this approach use the parens patriae, or rehabilitative, mission, to justify its use, despite the implications for juveniles' due process protections. Even though participants were not directly asked about their views on the juvenile court culture, their responses to other questions revealed that this culture still exists to some extent, as some participants believed it should. However, participants varied on whether they believed that culture should extend to the juvenile defender role. Most appeared to believe it should not, especially considering the court's punitive realities.

Despite the system's espoused rehabilitative orientation, in practice it administers *punishment* to juveniles. The majority of participants seemed to recognize this reality. Participant 008 (most experienced, true-interests advocate) addressed it and its consequences:

> [Prosecutors are] terribly afraid of saying something wrong, and so they just say they've been told, "Push for more punishment," so they do that, and that's often the wrong thing to do in juvenile court. Push for more therapy! Push for more intervention! Push for more anything but just locking the kids up; all [juveniles] do is to get angry.

Participants' discussions of "training school" or, in North Carolina, YDC (Youth Development Center, referred to as "Youth Detention Center" by several participants) indicated that it is perceived as, essentially, a prison for juveniles. Some participants acknowledged that the intention behind training school is rehabilitation but recognized the reality is more punitive. Participant 017 (most experienced, best-interests advocate) acknowledged this when he said, "There's no question YDC is a punishment. You're in a closed, structured program." He further explained,

> Judges may consider [YDC] punishment, but the way it's designed it's supposed to be rehabilitation; that's the emphasis. But the more kids that are there, the more overworked they are, the less counseling sessions they get, [and] then it becomes punishment.

Participant 009 (least experienced, declined to identify advocate type) also considered the rehabilitation mission to be somewhat of a pretext and provided the following explanation:

> That courtroom is set up so we are not stigmatizing with a criminal conviction that will last you forever. [But] the punishments are designed to be punishments. . . . I'm sure it feels like that to the kid. . . . It's meant to be rehabilitative, whereas in the adult system it's meant to be partially rehabilitative, and so there are conflicts in balancing, I think, helping the kid versus defending the kid to some extent. . . . Training school is what we call it, but it's not really a school at all, to be honest.

As explained in earlier chapters and by the US Supreme Court in its *In re Gault* (1967) decision, once the system introduces the possibility of punishment, a defendant, regardless of age, has the right to effective assistance of counsel. Participant 003 remarked that a criminal defense attorney's presence would be unnecessary in a therapeutic system of justice. This point was suggested by a number of other participants and could be the result of the Supreme Court's rationale in *In re Gault*, indicating that punitive outcomes trigger the required presence of defense counsel for defendants. Lawyers and judges are trained to be guided by rules and rationales primarily set forth by statutes and court decisions. Therefore, it is possible that they overlook the need for defense counsel in therapeutic settings, since the requirement of defense counsel for juveniles is justified in part by the loss of freedom associated with punitive outcomes but less so with therapeutic outcomes.

Clearly, punishment exists for juveniles in North Carolina, making the juvenile defender's expressed-interests advocate role a necessary part of the juvenile court system. The possibility of punishment for juveniles in the juvenile court system, traditionally a *rehabilitative* court, could also mean that *any* role conflict could pose a serious problem and thus is a threat to the due process protections juvenile defenders are meant to provide.

Participants did not explicitly identify the juvenile court's best-interests culture as responsible for the role conflict they experience. However, several pointed to court functionaries and their behavior as manifestations of the best-interests culture when asked about their role conflict experiences. Some manifestations were presented earlier in this chapter as examples of role conflict from specific court functionaries. For example, participants recognized the tendency for juvenile judges to automatically accept court counselors' recommendations despite defense attorneys' arguments. And, there were some reports of judges pushing back against defenders' efforts to zealously advocate for their clients' expressed interests. Another example is the expectation of some court counselors and prosecutors that defenders reduce their zealous advocacy in an effort to get the juvenile help. These are quintessential examples of juvenile court functionaries' attempts to co-opt the juvenile defender into the court's best-interests scheme and clearly place defenders at odds with their professional ethics.

Professional Ethics

As explained in the introduction, lawyers' professional conduct is governed by the *Model Rules of Professional Conduct*. These rules require attorneys to advocate for their clients' expressed interests (ABA, 2013, pmbl. § 2). Therefore, the role conflict that juvenile defenders experience can have implications for their professional standing. Even though participants were not directly asked about the ethical implications of their role conflict, their concern over this issue emerged as a theme.

All participants recognized the ethical implications related to their zealous advocate role. In addition, participants acknowledged that all of the vignette scenarios presented them with role conflict and ethical dilemmas. Indeed, one of their main concerns about the impact of role conflict was that it might place them in conflict with the ethical standards they had sworn to uphold. For example, the "Jasmine" vignette (see appendix E) describes a situation where a young girl (age eleven) was being arraigned for an assault with a deadly weapon. She wanted to get her case over with (that is, admit to the charges), but her parents believed she was innocent. The juvenile defender did not have much time with her before the assistant district attorney interrupted to inform the defender that the judge was ready to hear the case. The defender had not had much time to speak with Jasmine and was left to decide how to handle the situation. Participant 002 (most experienced, expressed-interests advocate) indicated he would respond to this dilemma by asking for a continuance and pointing out to the court that

> "my client is receiving ineffective assistance of counsel at this point because I haven't had enough time to fully develop and investigate this case. I need a continuance." I get that on the record—you know, it's kind of a constitutional rights argument or due process argument.

For the purposes of this study, the pressure juvenile defenders faced in this kind of dilemma was also a professional conduct matter. Other participants recognized the ethical implications of the role conflict presented in the "Jasmine" vignette. The ethical implications of participants' responses to this vignette are discussed more thoroughly in chapter 7.

Participant 003 (most experienced, expressed-interests advocate) acknowledged the ethical ramifications of a best-interests approach earlier in his career and changed his approach to expressed interests as a result. The following exchange with Participant 005 (most experienced, declined to identify advocate type) also illustrated the ethical concerns that role conflict raises.

> 005: Been doing this for nearly twenty-five years and, not often, but there have been times when someone would either suggest or request that you take shortcuts . . . and when that happens sometimes it comes from the people that are in power or apparent power, and that's when you need

to go to your moral and ethical compass and say, "No, going to do this the right way no matter what," and stick to your guns.

INTERVIEWER: That's great. What is the right way when it comes to your clients' interests?

005: What's the right way?

I: Mmm-hmm. Because there seem to be a couple of different ideas when it comes to juveniles about what you should be doing.

005: Well, your client is still your client, whether they are juvenile or they are an adult. And you have to listen to your client. . . . If your client is telling you to do something that is immoral, illegal, or unethical, whether adult or juvenile, you tell them "no." If they are doing something that is not in their best interests, I believe that you have an obligation to explain to them the ramifications that go along with that, but they still get to make the ultimate decision. If you get past the point where you feel they should be making the ultimate decision, then instead of you making that ultimate decision you should seek guidance as to whether or not they are competent to help with their own cases, because that's not a decision you get to make. It's still your client's case.

Despite participants' recognition of their ethical mandate to advocate for the expressed interests of their clients, some participants, including Participant 005, viewed the expressed-/best-interests dichotomy as an oversimplification. Immediately after the aforementioned exchange, Participant 005 commented, "I feel you have an ethical obligation to your client to explain both of those [interests] in working toward a resolution for your client." He was one of only three participants who firmly declined to identify with an advocate type. As described previously in this book, this indicates that participants had varying interpretations of their role and views on the extent to which role departures are acceptable or justifiable. Following an ethical mandate, particularly at the disposition stage, might appear to be a factor over which juvenile defenders could exercise *some* choice in practice, even if not in theory. However, factors over which they cannot exercise much choice include the resources that are available to support them in their role.

Resource Availability

Participants were asked, *What kinds of resource pressures—for example, caseload, time, access to resources or service providers—prevent you from being the kind of advocate you would like to be?* What follows is a treatment of topics that are loosely categorized to reflect the kinds of resource pressures participants reported as interfering with their zealous advocate role. As is made clear in the excerpts, these resources are often intertwined with other resources (for example, a lack of time could also mean a heavy caseload or insufficient pay, and so on) or other sources of role conflict.

Participants indicated that resource availability (primarily time), or lack thereof, prevented them from being the kind of advocates they would like to be. More specifically, they identified the following as actual, or potential, resource pressures: time (eighteen participants), caseload (nine), access to service providers (eight), pay/money (eight), and access to sufficient information (six) (see table 5.2). This resonated somewhat with their reports of pressure to prioritize efficiency in the system over their clients' due process rights.

Time (Caseload and Access to Clients)

Time was a difficult source of conflict to address since it seemed so intertwined with several other sources. However, I decided to focus the discussion of time as a source of role conflict in the "system efficiency" section, since that appeared to be where time was most prevalently an issue, according to participants' responses.

Notwithstanding the measurement obstacle, there was some difference between the expressed-interests (seven out of nine, or 77.8 percent) and best-interests (three out of five, or 60 percent) groups in terms of citing time as a source of pressure to depart from the role. This makes some sense because expressed-interests advocates were likelier to have to spend more time coping with the pushback they received from other functionaries. Best-interests advocates might not have needed to fight as hard to accomplish their tasks because they were falling in line with what might have been expected of them by other courtroom functionaries. Even more notably, participants in the least experienced group cited time as a resource pressure at a higher rate (nine out of eleven, or 81.8 percent) than those in the most experienced group (ten out of thirteen, or 76.9 percent). This also makes sense because less experienced attorneys might have still been developing their knowledge and skills, which would have naturally cost them time.

For some participants, insufficient opportunities to connect with their clients created role conflict. For most, this kind of time pressure was intertwined with other pressure sources such as caseload, transportation, parents' schedules, or statutory requirements. Participant 015 (least experienced, best-interests advocate) explained that his struggle with time is tied to caseload:

Yeah [I have faced obstacles or pressures to depart from the zealous advocate role], some of those being time, or maybe not connecting with your client. Things that . . . would, I guess, make you emotionally not want to do the best you could do. . . . Yeah, for me, I think it's going to be time and caseload more than anything.

Participant 022 (least experienced, expressed-interests advocate) found himself in the same boat and astutely noted the strong link between time and caseload. In response to the resource pressures question, he explained how hard it was to tease time apart from caseload:

Caseload can be a big one. . . . I've been practicing law for a couple of years now, and I am starting to handle felonies, and I've been doing that for over a year now, so . . . some have been resolved and some are dragging on and superior court is one of those courts that you take a lot of time away from other courts. I still practice in district [court], I still practice plenty of other types of law, and even in juvenile court there're other clients that need attending to, so you cannot always focus on one person and one set of facts at a time. So, I think caseload and time kind of go hand in hand.

The majority of participants reported "time" as a resource pressure to depart from their role. This seemed to be inextricably intertwined with access to clients, but access to service providers and information emerged as a separate source of role conflict.

Access to Service Providers and Information

Some participants identified access (or lack of access) to service providers (eight, or 33.3 percent) and information (six, or 25 percent) as a resource pressure that interfered with their zealous advocate role. For this kind of resource pressure, there was some difference between participants with the most experience (eight out of thirteen, or 61.5 percent) and the least (five out of eleven, or 45.5 percent). However, there was more difference between the expressed-interests (six out of nine, or 66.7 percent) and best-interests (two out of five, or 40 percent) advocates. In other words, the expressed-interests advocates tended to identify access to resources as a resource pressure to depart from their role more readily than best-interests advocates did. This could mean that juvenile defenders who adhered to the expressed-interests advocate role were faced with less cooperation from other courtroom functionaries to get what they needed for their clients.

Access to service providers could also be intertwined with lack of information, as explained by Participant 008 (most experienced, true-interests advocate), who addressed the frustrations he encountered when trying to procure a private investigator:

> The hardest thing we have, and this is true all through the system, is if you get in a situation where you need a private investigator. . . . If I need an investigator in juvenile court, I probably won't be able to get one. And then I end up going out trying to do something I really don't understand how to do.

Like with time, information as a resource pressure might be hard to tease apart from other sources of role conflict. However, one resource pressure that is relatively clear-cut is compensation.

Pay and Money

At the time of their interviews, all but three participants were nonsalaried attorneys who were paid by appointment. In other words, their income was dependent upon the number of cases a judge assigned them. Eight participants (33.3 percent) reported that they sometimes experienced financial pressure that interfered with their ability to advocate as zealously as they would like (see table 5.2). Participants were subtly divided on this topic. For instance, the more experienced participants were slightly likelier (five out of thirteen, or 38.5 percent) to identify pay as a resource pressure than the less experienced (three out of eleven, or 27.3 percent). This finding makes sense because the more experienced attorneys might anticipate pay increases that simply do not happen. In the following, Participant 015 (least experienced, best-interests advocate) disappointedly notes how juvenile defenders' pay in his jurisdiction had shifted:

> It's really hard to actually bring home any money and pay your bills without having a huge caseload because the money is just not there. When I first became an attorney, it was $75 an hour, and they lowered it back when . . . the economy wasn't doing real well; they lowered it, and they just never put it back up, because that's not very popular to do.

This would have been the case for all participants, since they practice in the same state. The fact that the rate did not shift upward after the economy picked up again likely had some impact on most of this study's participants since twenty-one out of the twenty-four total (87.5 percent) are appointed counsel. But, the shift's plateau would have had its greatest impact on those who managed only a few cases.

Participants also showed a slight difference in terms of type of advocate when it came to pay as a resource pressure. Expressed-interests advocates were somewhat more likely (three out of nine, or 33.3 percent) to identify pay as a resource pressure than were best-interests advocates (one out of five, or 20 percent). This finding resonates because expressed-interests advocates could find themselves getting fewer appointments from the court, having earned a reputation for not "playing along" with the court scheme. The difference between these groups was not large but is one worth investigating in future studies.

Making conclusions about the impact of pay and money is challenging because, as with many other resource restraints, pay and money are tied to other resource pressures, such as the time juvenile defenders spend on their cases. As Participant 004 (least experienced, expressed-interests advocate) noted,

> All . . . defense attorneys in juvenile court are appointed for all practical purposes, and we get paid a pittance, and the judge scrutinizes our time, and if the judge doesn't scrutinize our time the indigent defense services statewide office scrutinizes our time and . . . fairly so.

The same can be said for nearly all other resources addressed in participants' responses, since they also seemed to be intertwined with either time or money.

Role Conflict Conclusion

Not every participant recognized or acknowledged having experienced land mines beneath the jungle gyms over which their clients clambered. In other words, not all participants directly acknowledged experiencing "conflicting expectations" in their expressed-interests advocate role. Likewise, not all participants reported experiencing "pressure to depart" from their role. However, all twenty-four participants were able to identify at least one experience where they felt some form of role conflict.

Most of participants' role conflict examples were stories involving specific cases or experiences where they felt their expressed-interests advocacy efforts were needlessly frustrated or impeded but by forces that were not a regular part of the adversarial process contest. As demonstrated by the examples provided throughout this chapter, pressure/pushback and conflicting expectations come from multiple sources, in various forms, and for numerous reasons. Most important, the prevalence of these experiences indicates the undeniable existence of role conflict for juvenile defenders in 2014 North Carolina.

These findings ultimately imply that someone or something (e.g., judges, the system) might need to change in order to resolve the apparent discrepancy between juvenile defenders' professional mandates (ethical standards and state endorsements) and the expectations of organizational authorities (courtroom functionaries). It would be difficult to suggest solutions, however, without better understanding how role conflict truly affects juvenile defenders and how they cope with it.

7. Navigating Land Mines

Participants have so far provided us with a clear and sometimes colorful picture of the extent to which they encounter "land mines" among the jungle gyms over which they guard their young charges. They have also explained from where the unexpected "explosives" originate and what they look like when triggered. Some of the sources of role conflict might come as a surprise, particularly with regard to other juvenile defenders who would be expected to empathize with their colleagues and avoid placing them in the exact ethical dilemma with which they likely contend. However, this finding was not the only unexpected outcome from participant interviews. *How* participants navigated the role conflict they encountered, and particularly how some have possibly benefited from it, was also rather unexpected.

Role Conflict Impact

As described in chapter 3, role conflict can have serious and detrimental effects on the role incumbent. This study invited participants to share the various ways role conflict has had an impact on them as well as the ways they have coped with it. At best, it is confusing for someone in a role, especially one as complex as a juvenile defender role, to face conflicting messages about his or her tasks and goals. At worst, the experience interferes with role incumbents' effectiveness and negatively affects those they intend to serve.

Assessing the seriousness and impact of role conflict presented some challenges. Some amount of inference is involved when one asks job incumbents the extent to which a phenomenon they might or might not recognize affects them. However, adherence to emergent themes reduced the need for inference to some extent. Ultimately, as seen in table 7.1, four areas of role conflict impact emerged from participants' responses: tension and stress, time, work quality, and case outcomes.

Tension and Stress

Any professional role can present its incumbent with tension or stress. This is particularly true for roles that as a matter of course involve conflict—for

Table 7.1. Role Conflict Impact

Reported impact of role conflict experiences	n	Percentage
Tension and stress (n = 24)		
Yes (100% of most experienced; 7.1% of expressed-interests advocates)	21	87.5
No (100% were least experienced; 27.3% of least experienced)	3	12.5
Time (n = 23)		
A lot (3/3 or 100% were most experienced; 2/3 or 66.7% were best-interests advocates)	3	13.0
Some (88.9% were least experienced; 80% were expressed-interests advocates)	9	39.1
A little (60% were most experienced; 33.3% of expressed-interests advocates)	5	21.7
None (66.7% were most experienced; 16.7% of expressed-interests advocates)	6	26.1
Work quality (n = 24)		
Yes (80% of least experienced; 66.7% of expressed-interests advocates)	17	70.8
No (71.4% of most experienced; 40% of best-interests advocates)	7	29.2
Work quality of yes impacted (n = 17)		
Positive impact (53.9% of most experienced; 30% of expressed-interests advocates)	10	58.8
Negative impact (60% of best-interests advocates)	7	41.2
Case outcomes (n = 24)		
Yes (72.7% of least experienced; 88.9% of expressed-interests advocates)	15	62.5
No (77.8% were most experienced and 53.9% of most experienced; 60% of best-interests advocates)	9	37.5

example, trial lawyers whose job it is to work in an adversarial context. Most participants (twenty-one out of twenty-four, or 87.5 percent) reported experiencing tension or stress as a result of their role conflict experiences (see table 7.1). The participants who reported *not* feeling any tension or stress due to role conflict were all members of the least experienced group, but they all identified as different advocate types (Participants 010, personal interest; 018, expressed interest; and 023, best-personal-desired interest). Interestingly, none of these three identified as a best-interests advocate, which would have made sense since, presumably, a best-interests advocate would *not* encounter a lot of role conflict from which they would experience tension or stress. The three non-stress/tension participants had among the fewest years of experience, ranging from two and a half to five years. Their identified advocate type *could* be interpreted as expressed interests, and they were more recent additions to the cadre of juvenile defenders, so it could be that North Carolina's official expressed-interests mandate had been internalized in the courts where they were working. Or, their lack of tension/stress could be explained by their possession of personal constitutions that allowed them to deflect any stress or tension that role conflict might have caused them.

Participants provided a variety of descriptions of the tension or stress they experienced, including a sense of frustration from facing pushback from parents or getting yelled at by a judge for trying to do their job and feeling discouraged compassion for a client stuck in tragic circumstances. Some participants reported experiencing stress from circumstances where their clients' expressed and best interests conflicted (i.e., "conflicting client-interests" dilemmas).

As explained in previous chapters, role conflict occurs when there are conflicting expectations of a particular role. A number of participants recognized that some of the tension or stress they experienced stemmed from these conflicting expectations. Participant 022 (least experienced, expressed-interests advocate) perfectly illustrated the role-conflict impact identified in organizational literature (Jackson et al., 1987).

> We talked a bit earlier about expectations, and there's of course the expectation that everyone else has and then there's the expectation that you have. . . . There can be a fair amount of stress, both in the stress that [parents] put on me and then in my own expectations for how I would do [my job]. I think whenever you have a job and you find out that the job is not going to go the way that you expect it to, while there are certainly sometimes pleasant surprises, it can often be a source of stress even just to change gears.

Even though most participants did not identify what they believed to be the *specific* root of their stress, Participant 005 (most experienced, declined to identify advocate type) implied a sense of frustration and unfairness over thwarted goals. When asked whether role conflict experiences ever caused him tension or stress, he replied,

> Yeah. It does. I think from a personal side I want to do the very best that I can when I'm in trial and working with a client or working with any project. And the stress for me is I think it's unfair to my client to not allow me to go forward zealously and do the things that I feel need to be done in a case.

It is reasonable to expect that role incumbents want to do well in their role. This is especially true when the purpose of that role is to ensure the system is *fair* to their clients. One could also imagine juvenile defenders feel a still larger sense of purpose, since their role legitimizes the due process guarantees of the justice system; this sense of purpose could magnify the pressure they feel to perform well. Juvenile defenders have presumably inhabited the role out of some desire to make sure juveniles are treated fairly in the justice system. So, if role conflict creates an unfair situation for their clients, juvenile defenders are very likely to experience stress as a result.

Even though other participants did not explain their experiences of stress in the same way as Participant 005, one can imagine that they, too, might feel a sense of frustration or unfairness as a result of conflicting messages about what they are supposed to do in their role. Instead, much of the reason that participants reported experiencing tension or stress appeared to be the result of frustration with individuals, mostly parents, who misunderstood the juvenile defender role, the system itself, or their own role. Participant 008 (most experienced, true-interests advocate) explained that much of his stress came from naive parents who "either [couldn't] accept the fact that their kid did something, which is common, or . . . just [were] not going to see what's going on." Participant 001 (most experienced, expressed-interests advocate) also provided an example of how parent-based role conflict could create stress for him:

> There are certainly times when there's been tension or stress involved when I have sort of conflicting ideas from the parents about what they want to see happen . . . and it goes both ways. . . . [They want] the client not to be adjudicated on anything, or . . . more often . . . the parents come to court and want the juvenile court system to punish the child more than they can be under the statute [such as be] taken out of the home and sent to a group home.

Getting pressure from them to lock the child up when [it's unwarranted] . . . that makes it very difficult.

It is impossible to control someone else's expectations of an individual in his or her role, but what can add to the frustration is when those conflicting expectations reside in the same individual, the role incumbent himself or herself. Despite participants' efforts to compartmentalize their professional role from their role as human beings, a skill at which lawyers are considered so adept it provides fodder for countless lawyer jokes, they still experienced tension or stress from their role. Sometimes, the conflicting expectations of them in their role came from within, as discussed in chapter 5. This type of role conflict presents juvenile defenders with a unique kind of tension or stress. Participant 010 (least experienced, personal-interests advocate) explained,

> I am [conflicted about my role], and it's going to be the same situation where . . . like with the court counselor . . . I want to be the advocate for the client. I'm saying, "Okay, it needs to be dismissed, we can go to trial because you probably cannot hold your burden and prove your case," but I also understand that if the child doesn't get the services they need that they may end up back in court as a juvenile or more likely as an adult where the consequences are going to be more severe. So there are times when it's like, what do I do? Do I advocate for the client and try to get this dismissal, or do I say, "You know what, for the child's best interests we're gonna . . ." How can I get them to plead to this to get the services they need?

Time Spent Managing and Coping

Benjamin Franklin first coined the phrase "time is money" in his 1748 publication "Advice to a Young Tradesman." For juvenile defenders, time is also crucial interaction with clients and the opportunity to meaningfully communicate to them their situation and options. Given their lack of experience, juvenile clients require more time than adults to fully benefit from their assistance of counsel; it takes longer to explain the law and their legal options to them. Adult clients require careful and time-consuming explanation of points of law, but juvenile clients require this even more.

Participants were asked how much time they spend per week coping with role conflict. They struggled with this question more than any other but were able to articulate an estimate of the kind of time they spend managing role conflict situations. Most participants (seventeen, or 73.9 percent) reported spending anywhere from a little to a lot of time coping with role conflict. Six, or 26.1 percent, reported they spent no time at all coping with role conflict experiences (see table 7.1). Participants reported that this time is often expended managing parents or clients.

Participant 003 (most experienced, expressed-interests advocate) indicated that he spent very little time coping with role conflict: "Maybe five or ten minutes, it's hard to say. . . . Probably I'm coping by just getting back to the office and diving into whatever the next [thing is]." Alternatively, Participant 002 (most experienced, expressed-interests advocate) noted, "[Coping with role conflict] might make my stay down at the courthouse a little bit longer; maybe I stay down there two hours instead of one hour if I have a case that week." At the same time, Participant 005 (most experienced, declined to identify advocate type) indicated that coping with role conflict was an ongoing effort:

I guess the real answer is how many hours are there? It's a constant. . . . I think I do deal with it on a very constant basis, because even when you're not directly working with it, it affects your life. However, I think the question is more directed as "How much time is spent negatively affecting you?" And I think that varies; it varies very likely with what you're dealing with and who you're dealing with. I don't know of an attorney that does trial work that doesn't go, "Oh, that's the judge we got? Great!" [sarcastically]. Or, "Oh, we've got them? Oh, that's gonna be fine." It changes from day to day and time to time, as I explain to clients. We're dealing with people, and I may know the way that they react 90 percent of the time, but they're people. And if something happened in their life, bad or good, last night, they may act differently than what we think. And so you have to change within the moment sometimes. So, I don't know that I have a good answer for you on how much [time I spend coping with role conflict].

A notable difference among the participants grouped by time spent is that most of the "some" time participants belonged to the least experienced group and most of the "a little" time participants belonged to the most experienced group. These divisions made sense because the more experienced participants had presumably learned how to either more efficiently handle role conflict or avoid it because they had honed their skills or established reputations as expressed-interests advocates who were unlikely to depart from the role. The more experienced participants would therefore spend less time coping with role conflict.

Another notable difference was that the participants who indicated they spent "a lot" of time coping with role conflict or no longer spent time coping with role conflict were all from the most experienced group of attorneys. In terms of the "no longer" group, this could mean that some of the more experienced attorneys had *learned to cope* with the pushback to save time. Interestingly, two of the three participants who reported spending "a lot" of time coping with role conflict were best-interests advocates; the third declined to identify as an advocate type. This was a surprising finding because one would expect best-interests advocates to spend less time coping with role conflict since they would presumably experience less role conflict. In fact, the findings discussed in chapter 6 indicate this might have been the case. Further research would be helpful to shed light on this puzzling discovery.

Ultimately, participants who reported spending time dealing with role conflict indicated that this time is often spent managing parents or clients and helping them understand the extent to which parental involvement in the case was appropriate. This demonstrates a direct way that role conflict costs juvenile defenders time. On the other hand, there are indirect ways role conflict can cost these attorneys time or effort, such as when it affects the quality of their work.

Work Quality

State assessments have revealed that the quality of juvenile defense is poor and lacking in the states they covered, as explained in previous chapters. At the same time, it is difficult to make conclusions about the true quality of juvenile defense, given how little the assessment authors revealed about the methodology they used to arrive at this conclusion. To be fair to these intrepid professionals, "quality of counsel" could be considered a quagmire of ever-shifting variables at best. In fact, at the heart of the legal realism movement was a jurist by the name of Judge Jerome Frank who cynically attributed legal outcomes to the contents of judges' breakfasts (Frank, 1973, p. 162). Nevertheless, there are extremely dedicated organizations, like the North Carolina Office of Indigent Defense Services and the Indigent Defense Research Association, that seek to accomplish the seemingly impossible assessment of quality of counsel. Despite the challenge of this task, the study at the heart of this book also sought to assess the quality of counsel in some way. It did so by inviting participants to answer the following question: *What is your impression of how these kinds of [role conflict] experiences have affected the quality of your work? What is your impression of how these kinds of experiences have impacted you as a juvenile defender generally?*

Seventeen participants (70.8 percent) reported that role conflict experiences affected the quality of their work (see table 7.1). Interestingly, only seven of those seventeen (41.2 percent) believed the impact was *bad*, and there were no discernible patterns of experience or advocate type among them. The following excerpt demonstrates how role conflict experiences have negatively affected Participant 008's (most experienced, true-interests advocate) attitude, the way he strategized, and the way he viewed his professional development:

> [Role conflict] made me more cynical. And I think I started cynical, so I think I'm a whole lot worse than I ever used to be. . . . What I know is at the start of the case, . . . if I'm gonna win I have to define what that win is *very* carefully. See, I think I came out of law school believing that the cops made all this stuff up. I mean, I really do. . . . I have never had a suppression motion granted by any judge at any level of anything I've ever done. The judge thinks everything's fine . . . and it's like, "No, that's not how it's supposed to work!" The fact that . . . I'm still practicing law [after twenty-four years], that sometimes surprises me. There were a lot of days in the early couple [of] years I didn't think I was going to make it. . . . There's this emotional wall to get through with a new profession, teaching or law or whatever, and if you get through it, you're okay.

Most participants who suggested that role conflict had a negative effect on the quality of their work focused on how it makes them *feel* less effective or on how it *could* negatively affect their work quality. For example, Participant 022 (least experienced, expressed-interests) said, "Any time you find that you have pressure or tension in a case, it always has the potential to have a detrimental effect."

Interestingly, ten of the seventeen participants (58.8 percent) explained they believed their role conflict experiences had a *positive* impact on their work quality. Participant 005 (most experienced, declined to identify advocate type) painted a compelling picture of role conflict's positive effect on his work quality:

> I think it makes [my work quality] better. With adversity comes growth, and we all need a little rain to make the flowers grow. . . . If everything went smoothly all the time, it's probably because no one is questioning the system and it's just a check-off sheet. And that's not what the law is. The law is about real people and real events, and very seldom is it as simple as checking these three boxes . . . [and] I think it's made me a better advocate all around. But . . . on a personal level I think it's helped me to understand how to deal with all of life in a better way; because of it being a trial, [it] is kind of a mirror of life in some ways.

Participant 005 was among several other members of the most experienced participants who made up the "good impact" group; in fact, as shown in table 7.1, participants who reported a positive impact from role conflict on their work quality made up half the most-experienced group. This pattern made sense because one might expect that the more experienced a defender becomes, the better he or she would be at turning an obstacle into an advantage. At the same time, this pattern could reflect that defenders who remain in the profession for a length of time are likelier to have developed the kinds of coping skills that turn "rain into growing flowers," at least more than those who leave the role altogether. There was a similar pattern among the participants who reported that role conflict did *not* impact the quality of their work. The "no impact" group contained a higher percentage (five out of seven, or 71.4 percent) of the most experienced participants than of the least experienced group (two out of seven, or 28.6 percent). This made sense as well for some of the same reasons that participants found that role conflict had a positive effect on their work quality: experience (built by remaining in the role) presumably increased skill or at least effective coping responses. Except, in this case, it could be that more experienced defenders also had become immune to the impact of role conflict.

There appeared to be no pattern among participants with regard to advocate type with the possible exception of the good outcome group, which had a higher percentage of expressed-interests advocates (three out of ten, or 30 percent) than best-interests advocates (zero out of ten). This finding might reflect a difference in experience or in personal characteristics (e.g., fortitude, tenacity, optimism) on the part of expressed-interests advocates, because they seemed to have turned role conflict—a negative experience—into something positive. And, as with other patterns discussed in this chapter, length of service, which might be intertwined with these personal characteristics, appeared to have a significant relationship to participants' view of the impact of role conflict on their work quality, whether good or bad.

The extent to which some juvenile defenders believed their role conflict experiences positively affected their work quality is an interesting finding. Do these particular individuals have personality traits (e.g., resilience, tenacity, confidence) or life circumstances that have made them more immune or resistant to the negative impact of role conflict than others? Do these traits, or does defenders' tenure in the role, enable them to move past the role conflict experience or turn it into something advantageous? Finally, do these particular participants have better interpersonal skills or familiarity with the idiosyncrasies of the court and its functionaries (i.e., social capital) than do the participants who reported experiencing a negative impact from role conflict, or than those who have avoided or withdrawn from the role? These are critical questions for future studies.

Participants who reported the positive impact of role conflict on their work quality deserve admiration, without a doubt. At the same time, there clearly was a negative impact on work quality for several others. The extremely complex and confidential nature of juvenile defense makes work quality an incredibly difficult, if not impossible, phenomenon to measure. As explained in chapter 3, the amount of inference involved in any effort to assess juvenile defenders' work quality through observation could have easily negated any value such efforts would have had. However, this does not render attempts to empirically examine role conflict and its impact futile. This study provides some guidance for current and future efforts to capture juvenile defenders' work quality.

A final point to make about work quality relates to the sample used for the study, which was made up of attorneys who had *not* chosen to withdraw from the juvenile defender role. In other words, the study was made up of participants—with the possible exception of Participant 003, who was on the verge of withdrawing from the role at the time of his interview—who repeatedly chose to remain in the role despite the role conflict they had experienced. As a result, these participants might have been likelier to have traits or perspectives that allowed them to view role conflict as a positive challenge or an opportunity for professional development. Therefore, participants' responses on this topic might not have accurately reflected the nature of role conflict's impact on their work quality. A more concrete way to assess role conflict's impact on juvenile defenders might be found in examining its impact on client outcomes.

Case Outcomes

Most participants recognized that role conflict could, or does, affect the quality of their work and case outcomes. More specifically, fifteen participants (62.5 percent) reported they believed their role conflict experiences had an impact on case outcomes (see table 7.1). For example, Participant 001 (most experienced, expressed-interests advocate) explained that

> clearly it affects case outcomes just because it's difficult to manage what I'm getting . . . from the parents; . . . it's just . . . difficult when the parents want a different outcome than what the juvenile wants.

And Participant 002 (most experienced, expressed-interests advocate) explained that one possible way role conflict affected his case outcomes was by discouraging him from his purpose. He described this indirect process in the following way:

This feeling that lawyers get of losing all the time, it's sort of depressing them. And I think it sort of also makes me perform worse too in situations like this, like what I'm going into tomorrow I'm going to feel like I have no chance of winning, but you know we're going to take a shot at it and maybe the witnesses won't show up or maybe I'll convince the judge that they're lying.

Participant 005 (most experienced, declined to identify advocate type) also indicated that role conflict might serve to discourage juvenile defenders. He explained,

I think . . . if something affects you and keeps you from being zealous, then I think you're going to get a less positive outcome, because you need to be able to put your best foot forward and do whatever needs to be done.

His comment here implies that role conflict suppresses juvenile defenders' ability to put their "best foot forward" and consequently negatively affects their case outcomes.

Participant 013 (least experienced), an expressed-interests advocate who viewed role departures as unjustifiable even at the disposition stage, made an interesting note about role conflict's impact on one of her case outcomes. She described a situation where she advised her client to cooperate with the state to avoid getting transferred to adult court. Unfortunately, her uncooperative client would not take her advice, so she had to make plans to accommodate her client's expressed wishes. While she was planning, Participant 013 and her client "outwaited" the prosecutor, who ultimately removed the threat of transfer. This resulted in a plea agreement where her client admitted to most of the charges.

Participant 013 was asked, *When there are pressures that prevent you from being as zealous an advocate as you would like to be, how does that affect case outcomes?* She referred back to the uncooperative client case and replied, "In order to guarantee the fact that he didn't get transferred [to adult court], we probably pled to some charges that we otherwise might have fought a little harder." The fact that the threat of transfer was removed was a stroke of luck, and Participant 013 was able to convince her client to accept a plea agreement without feeling like she departed from her zealous advocate role. However, she still felt like she would have fought harder had the threat *not* been removed. And, since her client was giving her pushback, the outcome could have been far worse. For instance, he could have been transferred to adult court given his previous uncooperative stance, and this was an outcome Participant 013 very much wanted to avoid.

As previously stated, more than half of participants reported that role conflict affected their case outcomes, and of those, a higher percentage (eight out of eleven, or 72.7 percent) of the least experienced group reported so, with only a little more than half (seven out of thirteen) of the most experienced group reporting so (see table 7.1). Also, just over half were expressed-interests advocates (eight out of fifteen, or 53.3 percent), while only two (13.3 percent) belonged to the best-interests group; the remaining five belonged to a number of different advocate types or declined to identify as any type. These patterns resonate with the notion that less experienced attorneys might still have been building their reputations and skills, so they might have found that, despite their best efforts, their case outcomes were affected by the role conflict they faced. Extrapolating from the pattern of advocate type was a little more difficult, since not every participant identified as either an expressed- or best-interests advocate. However, it stands to reason that a higher percentage of expressed-interests advocates would report that role conflict affected their case outcomes because the outcomes they sought, as expressed by their child clients, might have sometimes flown in the face of the court's best-interests orientation. As with all of these extrapolations, further research with a larger sample would likely be able to determine if these patterns reflect significant differences.

Interesting patterns also emerged among the nine participants who did *not* report such impact. Almost all (seven out of nine, or 77.8 percent) of them belonged to the most experienced group of participants (see table 7.1). This finding is logical because more experienced attorneys were likely to have developed effective coping responses to role conflict that mitigated its impact on their case outcomes. There was also a higher percentage of best-interests advocates (33.3 percent) than expressed-interests advocates (11.1 percent) who indicated they did not believe the role conflict they experienced affected their case outcomes. Four of the remaining five no-outcome-impact participants identified with another type of advocate (such as "true-interests"), and one declined to identify as any. So, it is difficult to draw much meaning from this pattern. However, one might estimate that best-interests advocates would have likely reported less impact of role conflict on their case outcomes because the outcomes they sought might have been more in line with the best-interests orientation of the court and therefore resulted in less role conflict and less interference with their case outcomes. Again, a larger sample would help verify if these hints indicate a real underlying pattern.

Participants' recognition that role conflict affected their case outcomes is poignant. Not every juvenile defender will have developed the skills necessary to prevent role conflict's impact. For instance, judges can be intimidating, and this can discourage zealous advocacy on the part of less experienced or less confident juvenile defenders, possibly leaving their juvenile clients with less-than-effective assistance of counsel.

The consensus that role conflict can have a negative impact on case outcomes reflects the relationship found in the organizational literature between role conflict and work performance (e.g., Wright & Bonett, 1997). It is reasonable to conclude that if the system or its functionaries exhibit pushback behavior beyond what is necessary for the adversarial process, and pushback behavior interferes with juvenile defenders' role, they will likely be less successful than if they did not face such interference. It is therefore also reasonable to conclude that the role conflict that juvenile defenders experience negatively affects their performance or the quality of their work. In fact, such a relationship was found in a study of burnout correlates among public service attorneys (Jackson et al., 1987). Since there is a good deal of overlap between the work of public service attorneys and juvenile defenders, a replication of the study by Jackson and her colleagues might be a suitable follow-up to this one.

Regardless of participants' spin on the ways role conflict affects them, they clearly experienced role conflict, and those who remained in the role must have found ways to cope with it. Understanding how participants coped with role conflict is an important part of setting the stage for future examinations.

Role Conflict Coping Strategies and Consequences

As suggested earlier in this chapter, participants presumably found ways to cope with the role conflict they faced. If they had not, they would have not been presently serving as juvenile defenders and available to participate in this study. Recall that coping has been defined as a response that is intended to change the objective nature of a stressful situation (French et al., 1974). Additionally, it refers to behavior that "protects people from being psychologically harmed by problematic social experience" (Pearlin & Schooler, 1978, p. 2).

Participants reported coping with the phenomenon of role conflict and its effects against the background of the contextual and individual factors discussed in previous chapters. This study invited participants to share the ways in which they coped with role conflict. Four major themes emerged from participants' responses to coping questions and vignette scenarios: client management, parent management, courtroom management, and self-management.

Client Management

Participants provided several examples of coping strategies for managing their client-based role conflict. These strategies emerged under two major themes: using persuasion skills and qualifying the way defenders spoke to the court on behalf of their clients.

PERSUASION SKILLS

Participants reported utilizing their skills of persuasion to convince clients to shift their interests in conflicting-client-interests situations. This type of dilemma is a meaningful and common reality for many juvenile respondents. Participant 024 (most experienced, legal-interests advocate), a juvenile defender for nearly four decades, explained how she would use her persuasion skills to try to convince her clients to change their unreasonable or unrealistic interests:

> Obviously if your client says, "I want [you] to advocate for the fact that my probation should include a trip to Disney World," . . . no, I don't think you should do that, but I think you can always advocate for your client's expressed interests as well as . . . something that's more likely to happen that still would be a benefit to client.

Participant 024 was one of the study's most experienced defenders. She had attended one of the better law schools in the state. Even though she had not participated in her law school's juvenile defense clinic, probably because it did not exist at the time she attended, she had participated in a number of continuing legal education courses that were facilitated by her county's juvenile association and defense lawyers' association. Clearly, Participant 024 seemed to have the confidence and experience to identify when she could try to help her clients without departing from what she believed was her role as a zealous advocate. She had identified her role as her clients' legal-interests advocate and was one of the few participants who said she had not "experienced any outside unwarranted pressure that affects the advocacy." So, confident in her skills as a persuasive counselor and advocate, she seemed to know when to tell her clients "no" without feeling like she was departing from the advocate role.

Another very experienced participant shared the ways he used his persuasion skills to get a client to change his interests, such as when the client wanted to testify or speak to the judge himself. Participant 005 (declined to identify advocate type) explained how he spoke to a client who had been pushing back against the defender's need for the judge to view his client as credible:

One of the things I do with clients [who give me pushback] on a semi-regular basis [is] to try to help them understand when they have a story that doesn't hold together. Many times I will turn the tables and say, "Let's imagine you're the judge, you have a black robe, you just heard the story that you told me. What would you think?" And almost without exception, you know, "I wouldn't believe that!" And I'll kind of go, "And, the judge wouldn't either." So that's been very helpful.

Other participants described the ways they would use persuasion to handle the dilemma presented in one of the study's most realistic vignette scenarios. The "James" scenario first described in chapter 4 (see also appendix E) involved fourteen-year-old James, who had been arrested for heroin possession and was struggling with addiction. The participant, James's juvenile defender, was presented with evidence that the search leading to James's arrest might have been illegal. The defender was asked if he or she would file a motion to suppress evidence found during a potentially illegal search if it meant James would not get help for his addiction that he could not otherwise afford. The vignette was silent about what James wanted. Participants' responses to this vignette scenario generally indicated that it would be difficult, maybe even impossible, for the defender to advocate to the court for something if the client did not truly want it.

In his coping plan for the "James" dilemma, Participant 009 (least experienced, declined to identify advocate type) explained that he would attempt to persuade the client to admit to the problem. He offered, "I think an effective way of reducing that tension is to get the kid to admit the fact that [substance use] might be an issue," yet he explained, "It's hard for me to get up there and say the kid needs drug therapy if he's like, 'What are you talking about?'"

Unlike Participant 024, Participant 009 was one of the study's least experienced juvenile defenders with ten years of experience as an attorney but only three years of experience as a juvenile defender. He had attended a well-respected law school outside of North Carolina and declined to identify as any type of advocate. Participant 009 would have begun his practice of juvenile defense law *after* the North Carolina *Role Statement* (NCOJD, 2005) was released, so he should have had a clear idea of the expressed-interests element of his role, even if he was not willing to identify as any particular type. As revealed in chapter 4, how this participant defined his role made this understanding clear, but it also showed his recognition of the role's nuanced reality. Additionally, it demonstrated his recognition of the importance of using persuasion skills to cope with client-based role conflict. Recall that

Participant 009 said that while he would always advocate precisely what his client wished, he also might "sidestep a little bit" to not contradict his client but identify alternatives he thought would be helpful. He did not view this as necessarily departing from the expressed-interests advocate role but conceded it was possibly "slightly departing" from it.

Other participants' responses to the interview questions indicated their use of persuasion skills to cope with conflicting-client-interests dilemmas. For example, Participant 017 (most experienced, best-interests advocate) stated, "Well, [if what the client wants isn't in his best interests] you zealously argue to your client that [something else] is what his best interests is." He followed up that even though he would hope to convince his client to change his interests, he would ultimately respect the client's expressed wishes. Participant 017 had attended a law school outside of North Carolina and had participated in the juvenile law clinic (i.e., practical coursework) it offered. He had relocated to North Carolina and was aware of the state's prioritization of expressed-interests advocacy since he had attended juvenile defense trainings. So, even though he identified as a best-interests advocate, he still prioritized his clients' expressed interests. This interesting discrepancy might reflect Participant 017's recognition of the nuances inherent in juvenile defense and explain why he used persuasion to try to change his clients' interests.

Participant 014, a far less experienced defender who identified as an expressed-interests advocate, reflected the same approach.

> So there's the counseling aspect to when I'm talking to my juvenile clients . . . about what their expressed interests are and what I may think their best interests are. After we've had that conversation, and if they are adamant in going a certain route, their expressed interests, well, I've satisfied myself and my ethical obligations to counsel them as far as the process, outcomes, and things like that, so . . . now I can go full force and try to accomplish their expressed wishes, even if I personally think that's the worst thing that could happen to them.

Even with only two years of experience as a juvenile defender, Participant 014 had completed a number of trainings offered by the University of North Carolina's School of Government and North Carolina's Indigent Defense Services. Participant 014 was one of three full-time juvenile defenders who participated in the study, so it is easy to see how he would have been able to develop his clear definition of the role. To be sure, even participants who had served as part-time juvenile defenders would have engaged in some training either through logging courtroom observation hours or completing a number of continuing legal education courses (such as Participant 011). Since

Participant 014 was a more recent addition to the cadre of juvenile defenders in his county, having only graduated from a local law school in 2010 (four years prior to data collection), he was likely to have been more influenced by North Carolina's new approach to the juvenile defender role and the plethora of available training opportunities.

As illustrated in Participant 014's excerpt, participants appeared willing to do their best to inform their clients of relevant information and options, even when clients' expressed interests did not make sense to their attorneys. However, once participants felt they had adequately performed their counselor function, they ultimately advocated for their clients' expressed interests. This appears to demonstrate an adherence, at least in 2014, to the expressed-interests role that Grindall and Puritz (2003) reported as so often abandoned.

Recall that participants' responses indicated that the conflicting-client-interests dilemma posed a challenge only to the *advocate* role, the role with which this study was primarily concerned. It is important to reiterate that this study's discussion of role conflict focused only on the advocate function of the juvenile defender role, because persuasion skills are so heavily utilized when juvenile defenders serve as counselors to their clients. So, when juvenile defenders attempt to persuade their clients to change their interests, they are also carrying out the counselor role, and that particular role does not ethically require an expressed-interests focus. However, recall that when juvenile defenders carry out their advocate role, they are required to treat their child clients just as they would treat their adult clients. Previous research and the present study demonstrate that this is not so easily accomplished.

One could argue that the counselor and advocate roles merge a little when juvenile defenders attempt to persuade their clients to change their interests, since they are using persuasion to possibly avoid the ethical dilemma they might face by having to advocate for expressed interests they do not believe are in the client's best interests and therefore are either unlikely to be fulfilled or unlikely to lead to improving the client's life. When juvenile defenders speak to the court on their clients' behalf, however, the role they are supposed to fill is quite a bit clearer; it must be the *advocate* role. The strategies that participants engaged to cope with role conflict situations while speaking on their clients' behalf mostly involved utilizing their considerable communication skills.

QUALIFIED LANGUAGE

As discussed in chapter 4, participants widely recognized that they served as the clients' "voice" to the court. Participant 013 (least experienced, expressed-interests advocate) stated her view:

I am one voice among many, and my voice is going to be my client's voice. And, my client doesn't need me to be looking out for what I personally think is in their best interest; there's lots of other folks in the room that are doing that. And so what's most important to me is that my client's voice be heard, and I have no conflict with that at all.

Participant 013's dedication to serving as her clients' voice to the court is inspiring and shared by several other participants who identified as expressed-interests advocates. If a juvenile has gotten in trouble with the law and there is someone, a lawyer, whose role it is to speak on that juvenile's behalf to the court of law, a context with which he or she has far more familiarity than the child has, that lawyer will articulate to the court what the juvenile's wishes are, not his or hers, not the child's parents', and not some other stakeholder's. That lawyer's job and duty is to speak to the court *for the juvenile*. Nevertheless, some participants, despite recognizing their role as the client's voice to the court *and* their expressed-interests advocate duty, described the ways that they qualified their language to the court while speaking on the juvenile client's behalf. In other words, these participants shared that they would provide verbal or nonverbal cues to the judge to communicate the fact that even though they were speaking on the client's behalf, they simultaneously did not necessarily agree with or approve of what they were saying.

One example is Participant 008 (most experienced, true-interests advocate), one of the study's most articulate and colorful defenders. He described that one of the ways he coped with the impact of role conflict involved signaling to the judge that he disagreed with his client:

> You can code things to a judge when you're in the courtroom. You can say things like, "Your Honor, my *client* [emphasis added] wants you to know the following facts," and then the judge at that point has quit listening to you because it's coming from your client [not from you], but your kid gets to hear you represent them and say their bit, and that really carries a lot of weight with kids.

Here Participant 008 explained how he communicated to the judge his personal disagreement with his client's wishes while still serving as his client's voice. In doing so, Participant 008 ensured that his client saw him speak to the judge on the client's behalf, thereby safeguarding the trust his client has placed in him. At the same time, Participant 008 safeguarded his professional standing with the judge, whom he was likely to encounter when representing other clients. He did this by signaling to the judge that what he was saying came *only* from the client, not from himself. This is a unique coping strategy that technically did not violate the zealous advocate role requirements, though it might draw scrutiny from attorneys who define the role more strictly. Juveniles might be inexperienced, but some are savvy enough to catch on that their attorney is treating their wishes as less than serious. At the same time, it is common knowledge among attorneys that maintaining a positive relationship with the judge is of paramount importance to attorneys *and* their clients. The ethical ambiguity of this issue is addressed more thoroughly in chapter 8.

Another example came from Participant 003 (most experienced, expressed-interests advocate), who found himself needing to qualify his language to the court, in part to preserve his standing in the court:

> I used to take more of a tack that I would act in the best interest of the juvenile. I don't think I ever really did that in regards to the guilt and innocence phase; I probably did that more so in regards to the disposition phase . . . what I felt was actually better for the client. As I got older I realized that there may be some ethical issues, so I think I just more or less kept quiet and let the court realize [by] my wording and my silence that I may not be in approval of what my client was asking for.

Both Participants 008 and 003 genuinely wished to serve as the client's "voice," but they also appeared to recognize the pressure to qualify how they did so because of their concern for the relationship they had with their client or the judge. This demonstrates how role conflict can create situations that, as Stapleton and Teitelbaum asserted, would "sorely press the most adroit of actors" (1972, p. 146). Defense attorneys must advocate for their clients' expressed interests without triggering the judge's ire for being too zealous, all the while trying to create and preserve their clients' trust. This is an understandable concern, given the literature on the trouble juvenile respondents have in trusting their attorneys and the importance of trust to the attorney-client relationship (Pierce & Brodsky, 2002).

Other participants reported qualifying their language to the court for the sake of preserving their clients' feelings and trust, among other things. Participant 011 (most experienced, expressed-interests advocate) shared a story of the struggle she faced when speaking to the court about a client whose mother no longer wanted him:

> I'm standing there saying this is a neglectful mother that doesn't want her kids, and it's true. But how do you say she doesn't want him with him sitting right there, you know? I have to choose my words so that the judge understands it

without saying, "Mom doesn't want him" when he's sitting right there beside me. I get a lot of that, and I just keep going. I have a very thick skin.

Participant 011, like Participant 008, had a long history of working on behalf of juveniles in the court system. Even though her tenure in the juvenile defender role was not as long as Participant 008's, her experience cultivating and nurturing the trust of at-risk juveniles was essentially the same, given her seventeen years as an attorney and decades of experience as a child abuse investigator. Also like Participant 008, 011 had been directly involved in training tool development for other juvenile defenders.

These excerpts raise a number of questions. For example, how many juvenile defenders qualify their language to the courts when speaking on behalf of their clients? Does "coding" things to the judge so he or she knows the defender disagrees with the client comport with "zealous advocacy"? It clearly did for Participant 008. And when Participant 011 limited the way she framed her client's story to the judge in open court so that her client would not hear that his mother simply did not want him, was she departing from her expressed-interests role? One could argue that she was not, unless the client specifically wanted her to explain this to the judge.

Would some juvenile defenders regard this "coding" or qualifying language as role departures or as the defender being "co-opted" into the rehabilitative scheme of the juvenile court, as suggested by the 2003 North Carolina juvenile defense assessment (Grindall & Puritz)? Determining whether the practice of qualifying a client's words to the court constitutes a departure from expressed-interests advocacy is an excellent area for future research.

So far, strategies that participants have used to manage role conflict stemming from their clients has been addressed. Participants also described strategies they used to manage parents who presented them with role conflict.

Parent Management

Representing juvenile respondents in delinquency and criminal court hearings is an especially complicated endeavor due to the fact that the client comes with another individual or two, customarily protective of and more empowered than the client. Participants frequently spoke of strategies used to cope with parent-based role conflict. As described in chapter 5, parents were often combative with juvenile defenders in their oftentimes-misplaced efforts to protect their children. Parents frequently attempted to act as either the client or the lawyer in their child's case. The most prevalent strategies that emerged from participants' parent-based role conflict included affirming the defender's role with the parents and excluding the parents from client meetings.

AFFIRMING THE DEFENDER'S ROLE

As explained in chapter 5, participants believed that parents typically did not understand the juvenile defender role. One of the ways participants often coped with pushback from parents was to use their considerable communication skills to help clarify to parents the true nature of the juvenile defender role.

Participant 001 (most experienced, expressed-interests advocate) explained how he handled difficult parents:

> I typically speak to the parents. I explain to them my role in the court system, which is for the expressed interests of the juvenile. That is, what the parents want ... [is] not necessarily what their child wants, and ... my role is to advocate for the child. .... And if they're not rational then what happens is typically, if I'm really frustrated, I would bring it to the attention of the court.

Participant 001 began in his role as a juvenile defender about nine years prior to the interview he gave for this study. That was about the same time that North Carolina's *Role Statement* (NCOJD, 2005) was disseminated for the first time. Like so many other participants who identified as expressed-interests advocates, Participant 001 availed himself of the continuing legal education courses offered by the state, particularly the juvenile defense training offered through the School of Government at the University of North Carolina at Chapel Hill. These combined experiences might have contributed to his communication skills and confidence to adeptly manage parent-based role conflict.

Participants provided a plethora of examples of how they would communicate information about their role, and the client's, to parents. For example, Participant 005 (most experienced, declined to identify advocate type) explained his way of coping with the dilemma presented in the "Daniel" vignette (see appendix E), in which Daniel's mother wanted her son to admit to the charges against him, even though Daniel wanted to go to trial.

> So [you would] explain to her your ethical obligations and that Daniel is the client and he has to make that decision and possibly remov[e] her from the room because he doesn't need to have that pressure of trying to please her and talk about his case at the same time. So, that is part of it, [and] the way to cope with it is to do exactly that.

Participant 005 was one of the study's most experienced defenders. He had practiced juvenile defense for twenty-three years and engaged in extensive juvenile defense training (i.e., clinics, self-study, continuing legal education). And, while he did not wish to identify as a particular advocate type, his definition of his role included a strong expressed-interests component. Despite having a lot more experience than most other participants, Participant 005's coping strategy in the excerpt reflects that offered by several other participants. However, their efforts were not always successful. In some instances, defenders removed or otherwise excluded parents from their meetings with clients.

EXCLUDING PARENTS

Participant 019 (most experienced, best-interests advocate) provided the following answer to the question about what he had found to be effective in reducing role conflict–based tension or stress:

> Removing the parent or guardian, where normally the problem is, from the interview with the juvenile and just taking some time even before . . . getting into the details to just talk to the juvenile about what their likes and dislikes are, and that kind of opens up the lines of communication and kind of gets them to understand, "Hey, I'm on your side."

Participant 019's willingness to draw boundaries with parents so that he could have more open lines of communication with his clients indicates that he took his zealous advocate role seriously.

Participant 005 (most experienced, declined to identify advocate type) also engaged the coping strategy of drawing boundaries with parents. He explained that, in a pinch, he would not "have any problem asking a parent to leave the room, even when they are very irate about wanting to be there, and explain to them that I have an ethical obligation and I'm going to follow that." However, failing that, he would "go to the [North Carolina state] bar,[1] go to the judge, [and say,] 'Do what you have to do, but I'm going to do it the way that I feel it has to be done.'"

Again, Participant 005 was one of the study's most experienced juvenile defenders. Like Participants 011 and 008, he was well known as a zealous advocate for the juveniles in his county. His willingness to seek help from the judge in a parent-based role conflict situation reflects a type of confidence and professional skill that experienced juvenile defenders might have over inexperienced defenders. At the same time, there might be situations where the judge is unable or unwilling to assist a juvenile defender in this way. Perhaps the judge is reluctant to put his or her foot down with a parent, possibly because the judge does not support or respect the juvenile defender role. Or, the judge might be unsupportive of the role in other ways that tie the hands of a defender. Under those kinds of circumstances, and in situations where juvenile defenders feel they cannot ethically proceed in a case, they might choose to officially withdraw from it. Participant 001 (most experienced, expressed-interests advocate) shared a relevant experience:

> If [parents are] not rational, then what happens is typically, if I'm really frustrated, I would bring it to the attention of the court that this person is . . . you know. . . . I had a mother one time blast me for, I can't remember what the situation was, but just got completely bent out of shape, you know. Sometimes I'll just bring it to the court's attention that this isn't, even though she's not the juvenile, "this is not working out, and based on my compensation in this courtroom, [if] you want to appoint somebody else to this case that's fine."

Participant 017 (most experienced, best-interests advocate) described how a clash between the client's expressed and best interests could lead to withdrawal. He explained that he would zealously argue to his client what he thought was in the client's best interests. But, if it came to a point where his options amounted to the "level of ineffective assistance" of counsel, he would withdraw. Withdrawal from the role is the most extreme role conflict coping response. It is also the most effective at reducing the tension or stress that juvenile defenders experience from role conflict. However, none of the participants reported having actually withdrawn from a case as an immediate response to role conflict.

Withdrawal emerged as a coping response only through participants' sparse comments that recognized it as a coping response option. For example, Participant 003 (most experienced, expressed-interests advocate) was in the process of passively withdrawing from the list of appointed counsel in his county. However, he was still on the appointed counsel list, or I would not have been provided his contact information. His reasons for passively withdrawing had more to do with financial pressures (resource-related source of role conflict) than with other sources of role conflict. He had been practicing juvenile defense for eighteen years and identified himself as an expressed-interests advocate. Even though he was firm about his expressed-interests role and found departures—even at disposition—to be unjustifiable, he still experienced role conflict rarely. Therefore, his passive withdrawal was not necessarily due to overt role conflict or its impact.

It is not surprising that "withdrawal" was not a widely cited coping response to role conflict. The participants, at the time of their interviews, were current job incumbents, so it is reasonable to assume that they had found a way to cope with or adapt to role conflict in a way that enabled them to remain in the role.

Courtroom Management

As with any profession, one might expect to get some pushback from people who do not have a sturdy appreciation of what one's professional role is. At the same time, one might reasonably be surprised when facing role conflict from one's direct workgroup, especially those assuming the same role. As indicated in chapter 5, participants reported courtroom functionary–based role conflict as occurring less frequently than role conflict from clients and parents. Nevertheless, this type of role conflict has the potential for more impact, given the power or authority of its sources: judges, prosecutors, court counselors, and other defense attorneys. Even though participants recognized some support from these functionaries, they also easily provided examples of role conflict they had experienced from them and described corresponding coping strategies. These strategies involved affirming their role definition with functionaries and building a strong reputation and tenure of experience as zealous advocates for juveniles.

AFFIRMING ROLE TO FUNCTIONARIES

Participants, typically more experienced defenders, would sometimes explicitly remind courtroom functionaries of the defender role definition. Participant 011 (most experienced, expressed-interests advocate), one of the study's full-time juvenile defenders, described in chapter 5 how she would constantly have to do this with court counselors:

> I've had court counselors tell me that I'm not really working in the kid's best interests. And I repeatedly say, "That's not my job; that's yours. . . . That's not mine." And . . . I have to keep saying it over and over again.

Even though Participant 011 had previously been a child abuse investigator (best-interests role) for over two decades, she demonstrated a clear understanding of the expressed-interests component of her juvenile defender role. This is true despite the fact that she had inhabited the role for only seven years. What likely explained this clear understanding was that she had previous experience prosecuting juvenile cases. She also openly recognized that court counselors' reports are often "rubber-stamp[ed]" by judges, yet she still asserted her zealous advocate (expressed-interests) role in the face of pushback from court counselors *and* judges:

Two [judges of three] very much [support me in my role]. . . . We do have a judge [who] still doesn't get that. Bless his heart. And I just have to continually say, you know, "Your Honor, I'm here for my client, and this is what he wants." And [then] he rubber-stamps what the court counselor asks for.

Other participants were also willing to remind the judge of the responsibilities of the juvenile defender role. Participant 018 (least experienced, expressed-interests advocate) had only one year of experience as a juvenile defender but found himself in the confusing, and politically dangerous, position of reminding the judge of the defender role's true meaning:

I actually recently had a judge inquire about what my actual role was as an attorney in court, and it was a little bit concerning because my job is to act in the expressed interest of the juvenile, and I had to refresh the judge's memory that it wasn't best interests but it was expressed interest.

Even though Participant 018 did not have Participant 011's years of experience in the defender role, he, like her, identified himself as an expressed-interests advocate *and* had engaged in some additional juvenile defense training, specifically, continuing legal education courses. This is a background shared with Participant 022 (least experienced, expressed-interests advocate), who explained how he handled role conflict from prosecutors:

If I'm having a problem with the DA, I always remind the DA what my job is, that I am advocating for the expressed interests of my child, of my client. And . . . my job is to inform them, . . . to help them, . . . to listen to them, and to not judge them.

Participant 022 had practiced juvenile defense for only four years. However, his experience with juvenile defense professional development activities like continuing legal education courses and the juvenile justice clinic at his law school likely increased his awareness of the North Carolina *Role Statement* (NCOJD, 2005) emphasizing expressed-interests advocacy; these experiences also likely instilled in him the confidence to adhere to the *Role Statement*.

So far, juvenile defenders' coping strategies for *person*-based role conflict have been discussed. However, recall that the findings revealed that participants also held *system*-based factors (for example, pressure for efficiency and the stage of the process) responsible for the role conflict they experience.

System Push for Efficiency: Even though the system's push for efficiency typically manifests through a courtroom functionary's behavior (for example, the judge getting impatient and urging defenders to "move things along"), this type of role conflict was recognized as its own source because it came from multiple courtroom functionaries (see table 5.2). Also, one of the vignette scenarios showcased the system's push for efficiency. The "Jasmine" scenario involved an eleven-year-old girl who was being arraigned for assault with a deadly weapon (see appendix E). Her parents insisted that she was innocent, but Jasmine wanted to get the whole thing over with. The defender's information led him to conclude that she needed a trial. While the defender was speaking with Jasmine and her parents, the assistant district attorney knocked on the conference room door and informed the defender that the judge was ready to hear Jasmine's case.

Participants' coping responses to the "Jasmine" vignette invariably included a request to the judge to continue the case to another date so the defender could have more time to prepare. Participant 003 (most experienced, expressed-interests advocacy) explained a situation where he requested a continuance as a result of this kind of push for efficiency:

> This [scenario] is probably one that makes my stress level rise, . . . when the assistant DA [tries to push forward] because the judge is ready to hear a case. . . . I've had at least one example of when I walked out and said, "Your Honor, this is the first time that I've met with the juvenile and we need additional, I need additional, time to be able to talk to some possible witnesses."

The "request for continuance" coping response poses a bit of an analytical challenge. A request for a continuance could be construed as a departure from the expressed-interests component of the zealous advocate role because Jasmine had clearly indicated she wanted to expedite her case—in other words, admit to the charges. But, if defenders do not *automatically* advocate for their clients' expressed wishes, does that necessarily mean they have departed from the zealous advocate role? As explained in previous chapters, there are ethical implications for *not* advocating for a client's expressed interests. However, there are also ethical implications for advocating for a client's expressed interests in such an automatic fashion, as indicated by several participants.

Participant 011 (most experienced, expressed-interests advocate) illustrated how she would cope with the "Jasmine" vignette by mentioning her ethical duties. "I would say, 'Your Honor, at this point I have not been given the time to do my ethical duties as effective assistance of counsel in this case; therefore, I request a continuance.'" Although somewhat reluctant to request a continuance, given the system's emphasis on efficient case processing, participants indicated they regularly did so when it was critical to making sure their clients made informed decisions with respect to defense strategy. This is likely the most critical when it comes to the disposition stage. Recall that this was the sentencing phase of the juvenile court process, which appeared to trigger internal role conflict for some participants. In fact, participants specifically addressed strategies they used to cope with role conflict they encountered at the disposition stage.

Disposition Stage: Participants' responses to disposition-based role conflict indicated that they would use the same coping strategies addressed previously in this chapter. At the same time, some participants, particularly those who viewed the disposition stage as a justifiable reason for zealous advocate role departure, indicated they would adjust their zealous advocacy role. To elaborate on an earlier quote from Participant 009,

> I think I would always say my client's thoughts, and then if I had thoughts that were slightly alternative or maybe in direct conflict, . . . I think I might say, "Here are some ideas, some alternatives, that maybe historically worked better in the past." . . . And oftentimes it's that it's actually a form of advocacy, because if you have a kid who's charged with something somewhat brutal and wants to be on unsupervised probation, the judge isn't going to do that. So, to kind of meet halfway . . . [is] not really in conflict with what their expressed interests [are]. . . . I think it's more kind of a compromise position. And that's certainly a form of advocacy, but do I ever depart from advocating their expressed interests? . . . In disposition, yes, in adjudication, no.

Other participants who viewed the disposition stage as a justifiable reason for role departures indicated they would "step outside" the role (Participant 007—most experienced, best-defense advocate) and think "about a lot more than [the client's] expressed interest" (Participant 016—most experienced, best-interests advocate). Like a number of others, Participant 008 (most experienced, true-interests advocate) shared that his goals with his client shift at the disposition stage; he explained, "Once we're in the system [meaning the client has been adjudicated "guilty" or "responsible"], my goal is to get the kid to address whatever got [him or her in trouble] and then straighten that out and get out." Others argued that because clients were so young (Participant 019—most experienced, best-interests advocate), they did not understand and did not know (Participant 020—least experienced, legal-interests advocate) what their expressed interests were. Participant 020 explained his view on the reason for the dilemma many juvenile defenders faced at disposition:

If they want to admit or deny [responsibility in] a case, you know that's not going to be something [where] I'm ever going to deviate from what they say, but as for sentencing . . . there's not a whole lot to go on. They're not giving me much to work with as to what they want to [get] help [for], and . . . *then* I will be thinking in terms of best interests.

Most participants responded to disposition-based role conflict by affirming their role, often using their persuasion skills to do so. Nevertheless, even some who viewed role departures at the disposition stage as unjustifiable admitted that the juvenile defender role "doesn't end" with adjudication and that "what [they] do in disposition is at least as important" (004—least experienced, expressed-interests advocate). Participant 004 regarded juvenile court as a "problem-solving" court. Even though he was an expressed-interests advocate and viewed disposition-based role departures as unjustifiable, he appeared to have developed, over the course of his six-year career, a view of the juvenile defender role that implied compromise:

I think most of us who practice defense . . . view one of our primary roles as trying to find alternatives for disposition that will benefit our clients . . . [such as] make recommendations to the court counselors and try to represent to the judges . . . the kinds of information on disposition [that] will help them look favorably upon whatever it is our client wants to see happen.

Participant 005 (most experienced, declined to identify advocate type), like Participant 004, viewed disposition-based departures as unjustifiable. Nevertheless, he stated that he understood why juvenile defenders might view their role as changing at the disposition stage and that best and expressed interests should "go hand in hand" and "mesh in your mind." He explained, "It may be that your strategy changes or your client's mind changes as the process goes along, but it should be based upon working those two issues together as opposed to separately." Again, Participant 005 was one of the most experienced and widely respected juvenile defenders in his county. He, along with a number of other participants, seemed to have developed an understanding of how nuanced his role is as a juvenile defender. In fact, a number of participants identified building experience and a reputation as one of their coping strategies.

BUILDING REPUTATION AND EXPERIENCE

Participants indicated that they coped with role conflict and its effects by building a strong reputation as a zealous advocate and learning from their experiences in the role. Their commitment to the role despite role conflict incidents had allowed them to gain confidence and courage to either effectively cope with role conflict or avoid it altogether. Participant 008 (true-interests advocate), one of the most experienced and highly regarded juvenile defenders, asserted the following about building experience:

> I think the most effective thing any lawyer does is just catch onto that stuff [informal norms and practices in the courtroom], and that's just a matter of doing it. . . . They can't teach you this stuff in law school because you don't have professors who spent twenty to twenty-five years in a courtroom. They spent twenty-five years in the classroom. Nothing wrong with that, but in terms of learning how to practice law, you need to come out and get bloodied yourself. Get into the trench, take out your knife, and go kill someone.

Participant 008's insistence that lawyers need to "catch onto stuff" could hold one of the keys to how juvenile defenders navigate the murky waters of the role conflict that so clearly exists. Participant 008 admitted at one point in his interview that early in his career he was not sure he would "make it" in his chosen profession. But, he was able to "catch onto stuff," which might have played a critical part in his remaining committed to the role. It also might have paved the way for him to succeed in the role for as long as he had—twenty-four years as of 2014, the year he was interviewed—and as well as he had. Participant 008's confidence in the face of role conflict experiences and ability to use subtle communications to the judge without feeling as though he was departing from his expressed-interests advocate role also appeared to have been pivotal to his success as an attorney. What also helped Participant 008, and other participants like 005 and 011, was his ability to develop a reputation for being a zealous advocate for his clients.

A law professional's reputation is critical to his or her success; a reputation cannot be built if one is not willing to put in the time and practice. Participant 013 (least experienced, expressed-interests advocate) explained how her reputation might have allowed her to avoid role conflict. She also implied that her reputation was built, in part, because she was able to effectively cope with internal conflict.

> I think from my experiences that the folks that I work with know where I stand, and so inside I might have a conflict [about what my role is], but on the outside nobody knows that I have a conflict with it. I'll be doing what my client wants, and they know that, and I have not had any issues with that.

Participant 013 appeared to have built enough of a reputation in her five years of practice by the time she was interviewed to possibly avoid much courtroom-based role conflict and its impact. She had remained committed to her expressed-interests advocate role and avoided showing hesitation or conflict in doing so.

Self-Management

It is reasonable to assume that regardless of one's professional role, most people engage in activities that help them find relief from daily tensions and stressors. Participants described ways they coped with role conflict by identifying strategies they used to reduce stress or decompress. These strategies were categorized as redirecting attention, creating work-life balance, and building a support network.

REDIRECTING ATTENTION

Some participants described the creative ways they handled role conflict when it happened in open court. Even though lawyers are trained to think on their feet and exhibit good poker faces, experiencing role conflict in the middle of their most public professional tasks can be very stressful for them. Some participants shared that in order to deal with this type of stress, they would redirect their attention to buy time during court proceedings. Participant 022 (least experienced, expressed-interests advocate) explained that in order to effectively reduce the tension or stress one got from role conflict,

> you can't just say, "Your Honor, I need a fifteen-minute recess" and drive home and play with my dog for a while. What you can do is turn to your client, if you've got even just a couple moments, and kind of explain things to them, and when you hear yourself explaining things to a client it will also help you think about it. I have had this happen numerous times where something happens in court and I say, "Your Honor, I need a moment to explain this to my client." As I'm talking to him I'm saying, "All right, they're allowing this evidence that I didn't think was admissible; here's what I think we should do." [In] my mind, as I'm explaining it to them I am hearing myself say it, and I'm already thinking about what I can do to reassess the situation.

This is a coping response that requires the ability to think quickly on one's feet, a necessary skill for any litigation attorney; this is especially true for those safeguarding due process rights in a court culture that pushes for efficiency and might not recognize the value of the defender role. Participant 022, with four years of experience as a juvenile defender, might have been less experienced than most of the other participants, but he had attended law school and its juvenile law clinic in the same county where he practiced. These experiences likely provided him with opportunities to develop the skills he displayed in the above scenario, not to mention critical professional networking.

CREATING WORK-LIFE BALANCE

Several participants implicitly addressed the importance of work-life balance, and one, Participant 016 (most experienced, best-interests advocate), explicitly noted it when she said, "I try to work out and run a lot. I think it just helps me to kind of get a work-life balance [and] to not . . . let the stress build up." Other participants recognized the ameliorative effects of exercise, such as Participant 002 (most experienced, expressed-interests advocate), who used physical and mental exercises to reduce his role conflict–based stress.

> I exercise a lot. That's the biggest thing that I do. I'm a long-distance runner, and that has really helped, I think, over the years just keeping me calm, keeping the blood pressure down, being better, and . . . then just the other techniques, [telling yourself to] "be calm," even if a judge is railing at you and you completely think they are wrong, just "be calm." You know, ride it out. . . . I think the being calm and the exercise are probably two of the most effective things in terms of reducing stress in my job.

Like Participant 002, Participant 022 (least experienced, expressed-interests advocate) suggested a mental exercise he used to reduce his role conflict–based stress. He explained,

> Well just briefly, and I think this is something that every attorney should do, but not every attorney has time for, is to take a step back. . . . Obviously, not in court. I go all the way in court as I can, but when I am no longer meeting with the client, and I am no longer in court, then I take a step back. I do not take my work home with me if I don't have to.

BUILDING A SUPPORT NETWORK

Participants' considerable communication skills helped them in their efforts to resolve personal tension or stress. These skills were used to develop positive work relationships with others who could lend support during difficult times. Many participants appeared to rely a great deal on the strong relationships they had developed with their colleagues and other professionals to cope with the role conflict they face. Participants heavily identified talking to others, specifically colleagues and mentors, as a way to relieve their role conflict–based tension or stress. Participant 002 (most experienced, expressed-interests advocate) explained,

169

It helps to go talk to other people and say, "Here's my dilemma, here is my problem, is my thinking about this wrong, what [do] you think with your fresh eyes?" I get some good info that way. . . . That's therapy in itself, you know, just going and talking to somebody else and saying, "Hey, what am I doing wrong here?" And it's okay if somebody says, . . . "You're being unreasonable, let it go . . . it's not worth it" or whatever. . . . "Pick your battles," or what have you. "Don't let that judge get to you, don't let that parent get to you . . . [don't let that] prosecutor get to you, just deal with it."

Even though a small number of participants mentioned talking to their significant others while honoring their duty of confidentiality to their clients, most of them indicated that they talked to colleagues or other professionals to vent about role conflict experiences or get validation for their perspectives or coping responses. As indicated by Participant 002's comments, he was doing more than simply *talking* to other people; he was also receiving solace, guidance, and mentorship.

Participants also identified mentors or mentorship relationships as sources of solace, validation, and guidance. Participant 008 (most experienced, true-interests advocate) found guidance merely by witnessing the steadfastness of another attorney in the same role. One type of mentorship is certainly to simply act as a model of effective behavior. However, most participants identified engaging in mentorship relationships that were more direct and interactive. For example, Participant 013 (least experienced, expressed-interests advocate) discussed the way a mentorship group provided her with a venue in which she could "debrief" about role conflict experiences:

[To cope with a role conflict experience] I debriefed with folks like —— [an Alpha County defender] who understand. We have a lunch group that every so often meet[s]. . . . We go out to lunch, and people talk about their stuff and make sure you're doing what you're supposed to be, doing everything you can do, and some things are just out of your control. . . . Yeah, they help.

Over half of the participants referred to mentorship as part of their continued management of cases and professional lives. Participant 007 (most experienced, best-defense advocate) described his process of leaning on past mentors in order to cope with role conflict:

I just thought back to the attorneys that I worked under and watched them in court, watched them butt heads with prosecutors and judges that wanted it done a certain way, and I just kind of leaned on that. So, it was more a matter of what I experienced, the formative years of law practice and law school, that sort of got me through that.

The importance of participants' relationships with others, particularly with those who served to guide juvenile defenders through the dilemmas they inevitably faced in their work, cannot be overemphasized. Some participants even suggested mentorship relationships could improve training for juvenile defenders. Mentorship during training could certainly increase one's chances of developing the skills needed to perform the job well, and it could build the confidence juvenile defenders need to weather the role conflict they face. It could also build the kinds of skills and networking relationships (i.e., social capital) required for a juvenile defender to effectively turn a role conflict encounter into a learning experience.

Whatever coping strategies juvenile defenders enlist when facing role conflict, the picture painted by this study's participants was far from that of the co-opted juvenile defenders portrayed in Grindall and Puritz's 2003 assessment. With a few exceptions, like those who viewed the disposition stage as a justifiable time to depart from their role, North Carolina's juvenile defenders appeared quite dedicated to the expressed-interests component of the zealous advocate role. Participants who utilized coping strategies that seemed most in line with expressed-interests advocacy—for instance, standing up to the judge and court counselors—appeared to have internalized North Carolina's *Role Statement* the most (NCOJD, 2005). There appears to be some relationship between participants' coping strategy, type of advocacy, and the extent to which they have engaged in juvenile defense training (for example, clinics, self-study, continuing legal education). The sample's small size made it difficult to identify these relationships with any confidence, but there certainly appeared to be some connections among these factors. Nevertheless, participants of all advocate types and training experiences demonstrated great dedication to their clients and commitment to developing strategies to resisting role conflict's impact. These strategies, however, were not without their consequences.

Role Conflict Coping Consequences

Participants used a number of different strategies to cope with the role conflict they encountered. These strategies provided participants with ways of relieving the tension or stress that accompanied the role conflict they experienced from other juvenile justice system stakeholders or from the system's pressures and proceedings. These strategies, for the most part, allowed participants to continue to function in a role from which they might otherwise have withdrawn. Nevertheless, these strategies also generated consequences that had either detrimental or beneficial effects on juvenile defenders.

Sometimes participants' coping strategies led to additional role conflict, creating a vicious cycle for them. Sometimes the consequences involved improving a child's life. And sometimes the strategies brought about learning as well as a sense of affirmation and purpose.

Juvenile Court Stakeholders

Most coping consequences that emerged from participants' responses involved negative responses from courtroom functionaries, primarily judges and other lawyers. The most common scenario that participants recounted entailed judges showing their displeasure at the defenders' display of zealous advocate behaviors. For example, Participant 011 (most experienced, expressed-interests advocate) described a judge who persisted in pushing back against her role as an expressed-interests advocate. As can be surmised from the following excerpt, her coping response to him in that situation was not without consequence:

> We've had a judge in there that still doesn't get that I'm not there for the best interest of the child. And I just have to reeducate him, routinely. My job is to ask for what the kid wants. . . . [When the judges push back] you can tell because . . . one judge in particular, although I do love him, gets this real angry look, and sometimes I'm worried that because he's angry at me, he's going to take it out on my kid.

Participant 002 (most experienced, expressed-interests advocate) remarked that "judges and DAs start[ed] getting mad at me" when he tried to get a continuance request "on the record" because he believed he had not been granted enough time with his client and was concerned his client would consequently receive "ineffective assistance of counsel." Participant 003 (most experienced, expressed-interests advocate) admitted that he had "probably incurred the wrath of a judge because I said in one of those conversations, 'I'm going to recommend my client maybe not answer the question.' And they don't like that." Participant 003's example was particularly compelling because the US Supreme Court only a few years prior to this study decided a *Miranda* (1966) rights case based in North Carolina (*J. D. B. vs. North Carolina*, 2011). Even though the case held that police officers should take a juvenile's age into account for the purposes of mirandizing, it recognized that juveniles enjoy due process rights, including the right to remain silent. That Participant 003's judge outwardly disapproved of his protecting his juvenile clients' right to remain silent was certainly cause for concern.

Participant 007 (most experienced, best-defense advocate) shared an experience from a multiple respondent case where the consequences came from the judge *and* his fellow defenders. In this particular situation he encountered a cycle of pushback from other defense attorneys for attempting to discredit a weak piece of evidence on behalf of his client. Participant 007 zealously cross-examined a police officer about charging his client for drug possession despite the fact that there was no concrete evidence that what his client possessed was a controlled substance. As a result, Participant 007 "got talked to later in the week [by] the other attorneys about, you know, . . . we all gotta get along here and stuff like that."

It is important to point out that participants' coping responses to judge-based role conflict did not always result in igniting the judge's ire. In the following excerpt, Participant 003 (most experienced, expressed-interests advocate) describes how his affirming his role to a judge as a coping response to role conflict ultimately benefited him. However, it did not appear that way at first.

> I had a district court judge regularly serve in juvenile court who constantly would compliment me to my clients about [how] I would represent them zealously. We had a couple run-ins because he would do what he thought was in the best interest of the child, and sometimes I think that violated their constitutional rights. I would speak out to that, and . . . he had a pretty loud outbreak. I kept my mouth shut. I walked out very angry, but I didn't let him know about it. Later he didn't so much apologize[,] but he did say, "We're good, we're fine."

When I replied that such a comment was remarkable, the participant agreed: "Yeah, from a judge."

Participants also recognized when their coping responses to role conflict had positive consequences for their clients. An example from earlier in this chapter is illustrative. Participant 019 (most experienced, best-interests advocate) shared that "removing the parent or guardian, where normally the problem is, from the interview with the juvenile," as well as "taking some time even before . . . getting into the details to just talk to the juvenile about what their likes and dislikes are," resulted in opening up "the lines of communication and kind of gets [clients] to understand, 'Hey, I'm on your side.'"

Participant 008 (most experienced, true-interests advocate) described how he would use his time in the courtroom to "out" an abusive parent. In other words, he would cope with role conflict by qualifying his language to the court in such a way that the judge would be alerted to a major issue that Participant 008 believed would ultimately help his client.

> Often, if the problem is the parent, it's very important that the judge see that, and so what you do is piss off the parent in the courtroom so the parent flares up at you. And then the judge sees that.... If you get the problem, the issue, to flare up in court and let a judge see that, then you say to the judge, "I think you've seen what you need to see, Judge," and sit down. It drives the point home.

However, consequences of coping with role conflict did not always result in positive things for clients. Participant 003 (most experienced, expressed-interests advocate) described an experience where his request for a continuance so that he could have more time to prepare his client's case was denied. This denial compounded the stress he already felt from having so little time to prepare for his client.

> [A refusal] doesn't usually happen, but it did happen on at least one occasion. ... I ended up pleading the client ... I don't know that I would do that again today. But it would be up to the client and what the ramifications ... would be [to] pleading guilty as opposed to pushing it and appealing the case because you weren't provided an opportunity to represent your client.

Self

The judge-based pushback that Participant 003 experienced appears to have been very influential. The fact that the judge with whom he seemed to receive the most pushback ultimately sang his praises might have reinforced 003's decision to convert from a best-interests to an expressed-interests advocate, despite the growing pains of getting yelled at by the judge. During his interview, Participant 003 shared that he used to view his role as a *best*-interests advocate but after recognizing the ethical implications of that approach switched to an expressed-interests approach. He explained, "After some time I thought maybe that's not really zealously representing my client as I should, so even though it might be my personal feelings, it's not what I was there for." So, *learning* appears to be one of the consequences of the role conflict coping strategies participants use.

Stress-relief seems to have been an important consequence of the coping strategies used by participants. Participant 020 (least experienced, legal-interests advocate) frankly explained how overtly complaining did a lot to clear the air and relieve his stress. He also noted the importance of perspective when he said,

I . . . rant. . . . [I'm] not saying I don't take it home, but I'm a believer in getting things off your chest, and when . . . things happen . . . things aren't happening to me, they're happening to my clients. . . . I get to go home at the end of the day, so I do okay with it, but if I'm feeling bummed out about the prosecutor, about the judge, we just rant and rave. And that's about it.

Finally, Participant 022 (least experienced, expressed-interests advocate) explained how taking a "step back" or busying himself with alternative activities served to provide him with a fresh outlook on role conflict that was causing him stress.

I do not take my work home with me if I don't have to. I have interests . . . that I turn to in these sorts of situations . . . but I turn away from it, and then when I come back to it I am refreshed. I have perhaps a more objective point [of view] . . . and when I come back to it, after doing these other things and I have . . . more of a clean slate, more of a fresh outlook, then I can think of things that I couldn't see before simply because I was in the moment, I had to deal with them, I had to deal with the judge. Perhaps . . . when you're in the thick of it you can't see the forest for the trees, if you follow. And then so I think while certainly there are attorneys I know that are working eighty-hour weeks, and I bless them for that because . . . they're doing a great job, I have the perhaps luxury of having a family life, and I really turn to that when I can, and it allows me to unwind and come back and be more focused than I would've been if I'd simply just kept going full tilt.

Participants involved in this study seemed to be able to take some of the role conflict they experienced and turn it into learning experiences. They drew professional development opportunities from the role conflict they experienced. They even found learning opportunities in the negative consequences from their coping strategies. Is it possible that participants' fortitude to persevere through role conflict and the resulting negative consequences was due, in part, to the attitude that inspired Participant 005 (most experienced, declined to identify advocate type) to say, "With adversity comes growth, and we all need a little rain to make the flowers grow"? As with most foundational research like this study, this is a question ripe for additional research.

8. Concluding Thoughts and Future Research

*A*s has been suggested throughout this book, juvenile defenders face a unique challenge when attempting to follow a strictly expressed-interests-advocate mandate in the context of a best-interests system (Birckhead, 2010; Henning, 2005). Birckhead observes that defense attorneys are pressed by other courtroom functionaries and by clients' parents to depart from advocacy norms and might feel internally conflicted about their role, even if they are absolutely devoted to the most zealous expressed-interests form of advocacy. She also argues that the quality of juvenile defense suffers as a result of the unique challenges inherent in expressed-interests advocacy for juveniles (2010). Her assertions were confirmed by the present study.

Nature of the Role

We saw in previous chapters that juvenile defenders struggled with role confusion or role ambiguity, which is consistent with Grindall and Puritz's 2003 state assessment. That so many participants in this study did *not* identify as expressed-interests advocates suggests that the NCOJD's 2005 *Role Statement* message promulgated by the North Carolina Office of the Juvenile Defender had not yet fully reached them at the time of their interviews. It might also mean that juvenile defenders were unwilling to adopt a strict expressed-interests approach out of principle or apparent necessity. Perhaps the expressed-/best-interests dichotomy oversimplifies the realities of the juvenile defender role, as both legal scholars and juvenile defenders have suggested.

Overall, however, participants reported adhering to the expressed-interests component of their zealous advocate role despite the challenges of doing so. Most had a clear idea of what the role was *supposed* to be. This is encouraging, given that the 2003 state assessment reported a "misapprehension of the role of defense counsel in juvenile proceedings," which resulted in an "uneven state of defense representation . . . in North Carolina" (Grindall & Puritz, 2003, p. 2).

Role Conflict Impact

Despite the admirable pluck of those participants who reported that role conflict had a positive impact on the quality of their work—largely by motivating them to work harder or smarter—there was still a negative impact on work quality for others. The extremely complex and confidential nature of juvenile defense makes work quality an incredibly difficult phenomenon to measure. As mentioned earlier, the amount of inference involved in any effort to assess juvenile defenders' work quality through observation could easily negate any value such efforts could offer. However, this does not render attempts to empirically examine role conflict and its impact on work quality futile. Future efforts could make better use of triangulation techniques by supplementing interviews with participant-specific shadowing or courtroom observations to discover more role conflict dynamics.

With regard to role conflict *prevalence*, participants indicated a full spectrum; some never, or rarely, experienced it; others did so on a regular basis. However, even participants who *reported* never having experienced role conflict indicated they had faced it without realizing the experience was role conflict.

Push for Efficiency

The majority of role conflict that juvenile defenders faced appeared to originate with external forces, primarily clients, parents, and the system's push for efficiency. Oftentimes, the role conflict that participants experienced from other courtroom functionaries—namely the judge, prosecutors, and other defense attorneys—seemed to relate to the concern about efficient processing of cases. Even though this finding comes as no surprise, given how crowded court dockets are known to be, it is also rather disturbing. The primary purpose of the juvenile defender is to safeguard juveniles' due process rights against abuses of power by the system's functionaries. A court's push for efficiency, instead of careful consideration, could be construed as an abuse of power. A court's primary purpose is unlike that of any other organization: to achieve *justice*. Justice is a goal that cannot be accomplished without vigilant application of the US Constitution's due process protections, chief among which is the effective assistance of a zealous advocate for the respondent. This is even more the case with juvenile courts, given the need for accurate fact-finding and *careful* consideration of juveniles' personal circumstances in light of their tender years. This approach would be extremely difficult to honor if the process were rushed. Additionally, if the court's operations impede a key figure, the one who serves as the solitary check against abuse of power or error by the system's functionaries, the justice goal cannot be achieved.

That juvenile defenders faced pushback from so many sources and in a context that regularly imposes actual punishment (e.g., restriction of an individual's freedom) on juveniles calls into question the system's fairness, credibility, and legitimacy. The court has the power to mete out punishment to juveniles, individuals who are entitled to effective assistance of counsel. But how effective can that counsel be if such powerful forces are working against him or her *beyond* what is necessary for the adversarial process? As explained previously, even though several participants appeared to have a clear idea of what their role was supposed to be, more identified their advocate role as something *other* than expressed interests. Additionally, even the best-interests advocates reported experiencing some form of role conflict. Role ambiguity exists and role conflict occurs as a result of courtroom functionaries' actions or the system's push for efficiency (or both). These findings imply that when effective assistance of counsel is unnecessarily impeded by the system or its functionaries, due process guarantees are compromised as a result. This result heavily affects the system's efficacy as a whole and likely undermines its credibility, legitimacy, and ultimate goal of reducing recidivism by the juveniles it processes.

Negative Impact of Role Conflict

Participants reported facing negative effects from their role conflict experiences. Even though some said they felt motivated to work harder or smarter as a result of pushback or conflicting expectations, not all did. The tension and stress that participants reported experiencing drew attention, energy, and time away from their clients with whom they already had limited time. In addition, some participants believed that their role conflict negatively affected case outcomes. Given the clear expressed-interests-advocacy mandate, the existence of any pushback for defenders beyond what is necessary for an adversarial contest is likely to be detrimental to juveniles and the system at large. For example, if child clients witness their advocates getting pushback from other courtroom functionaries (such as the judge or prosecutor acting in a dismissive or overly cooperative way toward the defense attorney), they might not feel confident enough in their advocates to be honest with them about their circumstances or wishes. As suggested by Pierce and Brodsky (2002), "defendants who believe that their lawyer works for the judge or 'the system' might believe that anything that they tell their attorney will be shared with the judge and possibly the prosecutor of the policy" (p. 102). Pierce and

Brodsky further note that respondents' lack of trust in their attorneys could lead to a "disparity in the quality of defense" (p. 102). Yet, since in jurisdictions like the ones targeted for this study many juvenile defenders are paid through the system, the problem of role conflict for juvenile defenders could be far more serious than this study indicates.

How serious a problem role conflict is for a juvenile defender appears to depend on multiple factors. These include, but are not limited to, advocate type, tenure of experience, access to mentorship, willingness to take on juvenile defense–specific training (for example, self-study), personality, and persuasion skills. It also depends on a better picture of the pushback they receive that is beyond what is reasonably expected, and necessary, to the traditional adversarial contest of the court system.

Juvenile defenders reasonably expect some level of conflict in an adversarial process; however, they cannot be expected to provide effective assistance of counsel if they are faced with the kind and degree of role conflict reported by this study's participants. Participants unanimously faced role conflict with parents and clients, and the majority experienced role conflict at the disposition stage, with several viewing departures from the expressed-interests role at this stage as *justifiable* despite clearly stated standards that such departure is *not* acceptable. In addition, several participants, as a result of role conflict, incurred a negative impact on themselves (e.g., feeling tension or stress), on their case outcomes (e.g., a "responsible" plea for an offense the juvenile did not commit in order to avoid a more severe punishment if the attorney had pushed for a trial), and on the quality of their work as juvenile defenders (e.g., failing to seek supportive witnesses because the defender lacks resources for an investigation).

Prior research indicates that role conflict can lead to role turnover (withdrawal) and burnout (including emotional exhaustion) (Cordes & Dougherty, 1993; Jackson et al., 1987). It is true that participants found ways to cope with role conflict and that some drew benefits from it. However, this says nothing about those who were unable to do the same or who withdrew from the role, leaving an already overburdened juvenile justice system with fewer capable juvenile defenders. Additional research is necessary to determine what truly makes the difference between those who remain in the role and those who leave. Arbitrary barriers to the defense function did not appear to benefit these attorneys (notwithstanding those who turned challenges into advantages), the juvenile respondents they seek to serve, or the society that relies on the justice system to be fair. As already indicated, the weakness of the argument that role conflict is not such a big deal because some juvenile

179

defenders are able to turn it into a positive experience naively dismisses the reality that doing so unnecessarily takes time and energy from the client who already typically has too little time with his or her attorney. Allowing these barriers to persist might create unnecessary and undeserved hardship for juvenile defenders; this naturally translates into a worse experience for their clients. In addition, it diminishes the benefit the role is designed to bestow upon juveniles, unnecessarily frustrates the system and its purpose, and erodes society's confidence in the system to be fair, just, and effective.

Defender Factors versus Context

All participants at some point felt internally conflicted about their role, and several identified the conflicting-client-interests dilemma (the difference between a client's expressed interests and best interests) as responsible for that internal conflict. This tendency indicates a relatively clear understanding of the expressed-interests-advocacy mandate. It also reflects some discernment between client conditions that might justify role departures. Either way, participants sometimes experienced a conflict between their duty as expressed-interests advocates and their desire to do what they believed was best for the client. This was most clearly demonstrated at disposition, where the tendency was to defer to the expertise of the court counselor.

Some of this study's most controversial findings were the extent to which the disposition stage was viewed as a source of role conflict and the extent to which participants viewed role departures at disposition as justifiable. As explained in chapter 2, North Carolina's *Role Statement* (NCOJD, 2005) and "Performance Guidelines" (Newman et al., 2008) clearly state that juvenile defenders are expected to provide expressed-interests advocacy at *all* stages of the process. These official publications were disseminated at least partially in response to the 2003 state assessment, which found that juvenile defenders were regularly co-opted into the juvenile court's best-interests scheme (Grindall & Puritz). Even though the assessment found this phenomenon at all stages of the process, the present study's findings confirm that this discrepancy was prevalent at the disposition stage, even a decade after the *Role Statement*'s dissemination.

Coping and Social Capital

Juvenile defenders coped with role conflict in a variety of ways. They primarily relied upon their professional skills, training, and relationships, particularly with mentors. Participants' identification of their most effective coping responses to role conflict suggests that familiarity with the juvenile court's networks, norms, and nuances is at least partially responsible for their success in coping with role conflict. These responses somewhat align with Burke and Belcourt's seminal work (1974) on coping responses to role stress. Burke and Belcourt found that the most common effective coping responses were, in descending order of frequency, talking with others, analyzing the situation and changing the strategy of attack, and working harder and longer (a distant third). Additional research on the nuances of how juvenile defenders cope with role stress would be useful in contributing to the literature. The present study's findings appear to deviate from Burke and Belcourt's in that juvenile defenders' coping responses emphasized their ability to build their interpersonal, communication, and networking skills and pick up on informal cultural norms such as social capital, also known as the informal norms and values of the court that facilitate networking and cooperation among its functionaries.

One of the most notable findings of the study presented in this book is that some participants turned the challenge of role conflict into something advantageous, like an opportunity to learn a new professional skill or network. As demonstrated earlier, juvenile defenders could often be left with having to decide just how far they wanted to push for their clients without incurring the wrath of certain judges. Learning this takes experience, finesse, and possibly social capital (Putnam, 1995; Fukuyama, 1997).

Social capital is an intangible force that, among other things, "exists in the *relations* among persons" (Coleman, 1988, p. S100). It is a concept that has many definitions and is often used in the literature to answer questions confronted by organizations (Adler & Kwon, 2002). The term is sometimes used to refer to "the good will that is engendered by the fabric of social relations and that can be mobilized to facilitate action" (p. 17). Fukuyama offers one of the most relevant definitions, stating, "Social capital can be defined simply as the existence of a certain set of informal values or norms shared among members of a group that permit cooperation among them" (1997, as cited in Adler & Kwon, 2002, p. 20[1]). Putnam provides another; he views social capital as "features of a social organization such as networks, norms, and social trust that facilitate coordination and cooperation for mutual benefit" (1995, p. 67).

Facility with social capital has been found to be an influential factor in explaining organizational phenomena in two areas that relate to this study. First, social capital can influence career success (Gabbay & Zuckerman, 1998; Podolny & Baron, 1997). Second, it can decrease turnover (i.e., withdrawal) rates (Krackhardt & Hanson, 1993).

181

Participants' identification of their most effective coping responses to role conflict suggests that facility with social capital is at least partially responsible for their success in coping with it. This suggestion indicates the need for closer scrutiny of juvenile defenders' ability to pick up on informal cultural norms ("catch onto stuff," as mentioned by Participant 008) and to build their interpersonal, communication, and networking skills in order to better understand their role conflict and coping responses.

Even though this study's findings indicated that social capital might play an important role in juvenile defenders' navigating and effectively coping with role conflict, other courtroom functionaries still need to cooperate with those efforts. Is it enough to expect juvenile defenders to seek out mentors; engage in extra training; and spend valuable time "butting heads" with parents, judges, prosecutors, court counselors, and other defense attorneys when they already struggle to spend enough time with their clients? How is the system to achieve justice if juvenile defenders are expected to rush through their cases in order to avoid triggering the judge's ire so that future cases with the same judge will not be jeopardized or they will not be passed over for other court appointments? If building experience and reputation have such an impact on the likelihood that juvenile defenders will face or be affected by role conflict, as the findings here suggested, what else can be done to support newer, less experienced attorneys to help them through their growing pains?

Further investigation of the juvenile court culture, juvenile court functionary beliefs/views, and social capital is necessary to begin answering these questions. These factors were not formally investigated in the present study, but this absence is a limitation that could easily be remedied in future investigations. It is thus not the study's most irremediable limitation.

The Future of the Juvenile Defender Role

Given the variety of role conflict factors that emerged from this study, there is ample evidence to suggest that the expressed-interests advocate role in the juvenile system is far more nuanced than it seems. Birckhead (2010) argues that defense attorneys are caught in the middle of competing norms from family, criminal defense, and juvenile court cultures. She argues that juvenile defenders face "competing systemic pressures" (p. 959) and that these pressures have a negative impact on defenders' "effective representation of juveniles" (p. 982).

Birckhead offers a number of suggestions to respond to this situation (2010). Among them is a critical first step: encourage juvenile defenders to acknowledge that expressed-interests advocacy of juveniles presents them with a unique problem, given the competing forces (Birckhead refers to them as "cultures") involved. Such recognition would legitimate the problem and provide defenders some solace, an excellent start to further solutions. The present study did much to accomplish this first step.

Birckhead further suggests that law schools and state bar associations should provide courses and clinics geared toward raising awareness of the "culture clash" and encouraging cross-cultural lawyering (2010, p. 959). She also recommends that members of the legal community, including legislators and policy makers, change the juvenile system culture by challenging the common but incorrect attitude that juvenile court does not merit serious attention and has outcomes that do not negatively impact the juvenile's future. This is an especially critical suggestion since a number of modern-day juvenile defenders hold this view of juvenile court.

Another of Birckhead's suggestions involves a cross-cultural perspective of law practice referred to as the "Five Habits of Cross-Cultural Lawyering" (2010, p. 982). These "five habits" encourage attorneys to be, among other things, more reflective, flexible, and culturally aware in their practice of law (Bryant, 2001). Some of the five habits address the need for lawyers to be sensitive and responsive communicators as well as more mindful of cultural differences and similarities among courtroom functionaries. Bryant also recommends that these efforts should aim to build rapport, understanding, and trust between lawyers and their clients (p. 33). Bryant's suggestions make sense but would be difficult to implement without some level of facility in the juvenile court's informal norms and practices.

This study's findings indicated that, among other things, juvenile defenders' ability to develop, or tap into, the court's informal norms and practices might play an important role in their navigating, and effectively coping with, role conflict. At the same time, they would need some cooperation from other courtroom functionaries who might need to change their attitudes and beliefs about the juvenile defender role. Such changes would be difficult given the juvenile court's best-interests culture, an approach clearly entailing informal values and norms that contravene the officially endorsed juvenile defender role.

While the question of whether a strictly expressed-interests approach to juvenile defense is more appropriate for legal scholars, further empirical investigation of the juvenile court culture, juvenile defender role, role conflict, and coping responses is necessary to assess the validity of this study's conclusions.

Training, Practice, and Policy Improvements

This book has attempted to describe an empirical investigation of a widely recognized problem and reveal how juvenile defenders have tried to manage that problem. It will conclude with recommendations for future research, as do many reports on investigations of this nature. However, because the problem here investigated is an applied problem, practical solutions should also be addressed. Participants were therefore asked for suggestions about training opportunities and changes to policies or practices they believe would help them with their juvenile advocacy efforts.

Participants provided suggestions for training opportunities that covered form and subject matter. For the most part, participants believed that on-the-job or practical training, including courtroom observations, would be very beneficial. Several also suggested that increased opportunities for mentorship would help them improve their advocacy. These suggestions make sense, given the centrality of experience in human development and learning (Kolb & Kolb, 2005).

At the same time, participants widely recognized the value of more formal learning experiences, as typically conveyed in continuing legal education courses. Several recommended that there be more such courses and proffered specific topics to be addressed. The most prevalently suggested topics were information on dispositional options (i.e., services and punishments, but mostly services), adolescent behavior, juvenile case law and procedure information updates, adolescent development, and the differences between representing juveniles and adults.

These suggested topics reflect participants' sincere and deep dedication to the well-being of their juvenile clients. They also demonstrate participants' recognition of the unique nature of their role as counselors and advocates of individuals who, while entitled to the same constitutional protections as their adult counterparts, are qualitatively different decision makers. Other topics, while proffered by only a few participants, reflected the same recognition. Examples included how to communicate/relate to kids; more explanations of roles of other functionaries, particularly the court counselors; how a case affects juveniles' families; and how to handle conflicting-client-interests and other ethical dilemmas.

Participants' dedication to their role and the demographic they serve is also seen in their suggestions for policy and practice changes. These suggestions could be categorized into the following areas: legislative, organizational, service to kids, and resources. The most frequent suggestion overall was for legislators to raise the eligibility age for delinquency court to include sixteen- and seventeen-year-olds. This makes sense, given present, widely recognized developmental, cognitive, and experiential disadvantages this age group has when compared with full-grown adults.

Participants also recognized the practical barriers of limited resources, particularly the low pay and lack of resources for the system, including dispositional options. Recall that several participants suggested more training on disposition options and information; in fact, this was the most prevalent of the suggestions for training topics or policy/practice changes. Relatedly, some participants identified the pitfalls of policies like those that ban juveniles with felony convictions from playing school sports or that take a "zero tolerance" approach to what some might argue are less criminal actions and more growing pains of immature individuals in a society with ever-changing norms, values, and technology (e.g., cyberbullying, relational aggression).

Finally, a number of participants proposed that juvenile courtroom functionaries facilitate more connection, trust, and involvement with juveniles who come through the court system. Related recommendations were more organizational. Participants wished that they were allowed to see their clients earlier in the process; that the court—in practice, not just in policy—would exhaust nonpunitive responses before using punitive options; and that the court would provide them with the better communication they viewed court counselors as having from the court.

Future studies of the juvenile defender role should closely consider these suggestions. The juvenile justice system appears to contain a number of contradictory forces that seem to interfere with its efficacy and possibly create more problems than it solves. At the gate of the efficiency momentum driven by a best-interests/rehabilitation mission stand the juvenile defenders, who are tasked with ensuring that our most vulnerable citizens receive due process. They are also beset with inconsistent, and possibly incompatible, messages from powerful sources about their duties to their clients. Given the tragic consequences that can befall children lost in the justice system and the growing concern over the impact of the school-to-prison pipeline (Christle, Jolivette, & Nelson, 2005), making sure juvenile defenders have a clear and consistent message about their role and duties is paramount. Ensuring accurate information regarding the role confusion and conflict problems they face is also critical and can be best investigated through carefully constructed empirical research. The study central to this book is only the beginning of a much-needed and, hopefully, long body of empirical literature on juvenile defender role conflict. Yet despite its foundational role, the study is not without its limitations.

Limitations

One of the major limitations to this study, besides those addressed in chapter 3 that relate to its methodology, is that it focused on a matter of some delicacy for the participants. Juvenile defenders are ethically required to advocate for the expressed interests of a client. Yet, they are tasked with advocating for clients who might not be mature or experienced enough to form and express their intentions and desires. This places juvenile defenders in a uniquely conflicted position that could easily result in unwitting violation of their ethical duties. Participants might have been reluctant to openly acknowledge their struggles with adhering to their ethical rules, even though they operate in a context that pressures them to disregard those rules. This is especially true because law is a profession where even the appearance of impropriety can be grounds for scrutiny and possibly sanction. The following statement by Participant 022 reflects the nature of this reluctance.

> Well, I try not to let [role conflict] affect case outcomes at all . . . and I'm sure every person you ask that will say that, because we want to believe that we will be as effective as possible.

A related limitation is the fact that not all participants might have recognized certain experiences as manifestations of role conflict or as relevant to the expressed-interests advocate role. Making this matter even more difficult was the ambiguity surrounding what type of advocate juvenile defenders identified with. In other words, if participants viewed themselves as best-interests advocates, was it really the expressed-interests role they viewed themselves as pressured to depart from? Several participants, at the end of an hour-long interview (at minimum) discussing topics related to the expressed-/best-interests dichotomy, identified themselves as an advocate of neither expressed nor best interests. That so many participants deliberately avoided identifying themselves as one of the two types of advocate, and that three firmly declined to answer the question, was important on its own. This avoidance could reflect participants' reluctance to be pigeonholed, frustration over role ambiguity, or recognition of the complicated nature of juvenile defense. Additional research would likely shed light on these dynamics.

There was certainly some difficulty in teasing out role conflict manifestations from what was considered normal adversarial process conflict. Even though the juvenile court uses euphemisms to create a less stigmatizing atmosphere for juveniles than criminal court (for example, referring to juvenile probation officers as "court counselors"), the nature of the juvenile process is adversarial, and punishment is actually administered. Were punishment not a reality in juvenile court, the US Supreme Court would not have used it to justify juveniles' right to assistance of counsel in *In re Gault* (1967). However, it is unlikely that the adversarial nature of a court proceeding fully explains the role conflict that juvenile defenders experience from judges and prosecutors. This is especially true because, as discussed previously, the juvenile court is often nowhere near as adversarial as adult criminal court. In addition, the adversarial nature of the court process does not explain the role conflict that juvenile defenders experience from court counselors, whose critical role is more informational than legal.

Another limitation to this study is the fact that it involved interviews only with *practicing* juvenile defenders. At their most impactful, role conflict experiences could lead a role incumbent to withdraw from the role. In fact, that could have been the case for sample members who declined to participate in the study because they no longer represented juveniles. While withdrawal is a coping response that should not be overlooked, the purpose of this study was to assess coping techniques of juvenile defenders *remaining* in the role. One of the reasons for this was to identify successful forms of coping with the hope of eventually deriving training tools. Individuals who have permanently discontinued serving in the juvenile defender role were not included in the study. As a result, it provides an incomplete picture of role conflict's impact.

The coping measure used in this study might have had some limitations, particularly with regard to the question "How much time per week would you say you spend coping with these kinds of [role conflict] experiences?" Participants did not indicate that they spent a great deal of time coping with role conflict, but there are two major problems with using this information to conclude that role conflict is *not* a serious or prevalent issue among juvenile defenders. First, participants struggled with the question, indicating they might not readily recognize the time they spend coping with role conflict. Second, given the sensitive nature of juveniles and their legal status as children (that is, individuals who typically cannot transport themselves to meetings or hearings or contact their attorneys on their own, and so on), one could argue that *any* time that juvenile defenders spent managing role conflict—especially role conflict that originates outside the juvenile—is time taken away from addressing their clients' needs. The "time spent" question might not have accurately captured what it was designed to capture, and what was captured is likely an underestimate of the problem's seriousness and prevalence.

A final limitation of this study relates to me as investigator. I was the only investigator in this study and served as the sole interviewer and analyst.

Therefore, any biases I might have as a result of my own professional and personal experiences could have influenced the interpretations and inferences made.

Notwithstanding these limitations, this study helped to close some of the gap in the empirical literature on juvenile defense. Until now, there appears to have been no empirical study that has systematically assessed the nature and impact of role conflict experienced by juvenile defenders or their coping responses. Given the considerable debate surrounding the nature and definition of the juvenile defender role, such a study is timely and essential to shedding light on the challenges these attorneys face as well as on some of the obstacles to their noble endeavors. This study also provided an important view of the inner workings and consequences of the juvenile justice system as it navigates competing paradigmatic and challenging politico-socio-economic transitions (e.g., shifts in political power, public views on juveniles or crime, funding sources) and raised several questions that are now ripe for further investigation.

Directions for Future Research

This study produced an incredibly rich data set. The numerous quotes provided in these chapters do not approach an exhaustive list of relevant excerpts. Not only were there abundant additional illustrations of the concepts and phenomena discussed, but there were a great many more topics that simply did not relate enough to the central questions of the study to justify inclusion in the book.

The study also leaves several unanswered questions. For instance, the sample size was too small for more than a modest descriptive analysis, but there are constructs that are quite suitable for quantitative measurement and analysis. As seen in charts 8.1 and 8.2, these constructs could be converted into quantitative instruments, pilot tested, and more widely disseminated to achieve a broader understanding of the extent and impact of role conflict for juvenile defenders.

Charts 8.1 and 8.2 organize concepts that emerged from this study into variables that appear to predict or result from role conflict. For instance, if juvenile defenders do not view their role as "tempering the system" but as "helping the juvenile," they might not experience as much role conflict as juvenile defenders who prioritize their role as a system check over their role as a juvenile helper. Or, if juvenile defenders view their role as a best-interests advocate, they might not be as aware of role conflict manifestations. So, future

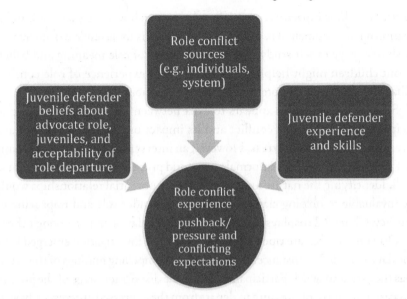

Chart 8.1. Role Conflict Antecedents for Future Research

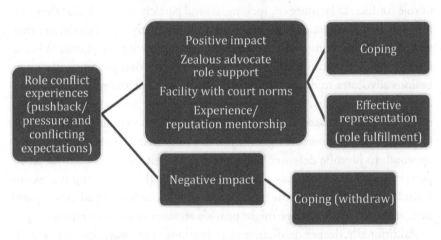

Chart 8.2. Role Conflict Outcomes for Future Research

research could involve more, and more varied, questions targeting role conflict or involve alternative techniques that raise participants' awareness of role conflict manifestations. There also might be some predictive value in a juvenile defender's beliefs about the capacity of children to make decisions and articulate their own interests. The same can be said about the extent to which a defender finds role departures at the disposition stage justifiable. The predictive value in examining juvenile defenders' beliefs about children's decision-making capacity is especially salient given how widely available information on developmental psychology information is for juvenile defenders who wish to engage in self-study. Therefore, nuances of role meaning and beliefs about children might help predict a defender's experience of role conflict. Chart 8.1 displays this potential relationship, among others.

Some association also appears to exist between the extent to which participants experience role conflict and its impact on their work quality and experience of tension or stress. However, an intervening factor of mentorship or facility with the court's informal norms and practices seems to be present as well. Identifying the nature and power of these potential relationships would be invaluable to helping clarify the juvenile defender role and improving its efficacy. Chart 8.2 displays this potential set of relationships, among others.

Other topics that are ripe for further qualitative investigation emerged from the data analysis. For instance, one of the most compelling findings of this study was the extent to which participants viewed the disposition stage of the juvenile process as a source of pressure to depart from the expressed-interests advocate role; most—in fact, all but two—identified the disposition stage as a source of role conflict. Even more compelling, several participants indicated they saw role departures at this stage as justifiable, despite clearly stated guidelines that such departures are not. This finding raises the following questions: What is it about the disposition stage of the juvenile process that prompts otherwise zealous advocates to depart from their officially mandated role? Could it be, as Birckhead suggests, that the juvenile defense function is far too nuanced, rendering the expressed-/best-interests dichotomy overly simplistic (2010)? Could juveniles' due process rights be just as well protected with a more blended approach to juvenile defense? Or, is the court's best-interests orientation so powerful that it actually has a negative impact on the very group it seeks to assist? A study examining the implications of role conflict and advocacy practices at the disposition stage might provide answers to these questions.

Additionally, deeper qualitative examinations of the ways juvenile defenders experience role conflict as a result of their relationships with other juvenile court stakeholders, particularly their clients, would be useful in identifying correlates of role conflict. A closer study of other stakeholders' attitudes toward the juvenile defender role would balance scientific understanding of juvenile defender role conflict. This is particularly true with regard to the attitudes of other juvenile court functionaries like judges, prosecutors, and court counselors.

Participants' qualification of their language to the court, asserting their position with role conflict sources, use of persuasion and networking skills, and facility with the court's informal norms and practices appear to be critical in how juvenile defenders experience, are impacted by, and cope with role conflict. The emergence of these factors was another of this study's more compelling findings. A logical next step in the development of research on the prevalence and impact of role conflict on juvenile defenders would be to develop relevant quantitative measures.

Participants' responses hint at a relationship between their coping skills and juvenile defense training experiences. Recall that most participants gave suggestions for improving juvenile defender training, such as more on-the-job training, more courtroom time and in-service training with other juvenile defenders, more training on how to deal with problem clients, and more training on the juvenile mindset. Some suggested additional training on understanding the roles of other court functionaries, specifically the court counselors. And Participant 002 suggested

> just general CLE's [continuing legal education courses] that talk about the process, talk about ethical dilemmas you face, talk about the child's desires versus the child's best interests[, since this] is a common dilemma you face in juvenile delinquency court.

A study examining the impact of some of these professional development experiences could shed light on the ways juvenile defenders develop and utilize their most necessary skills, including those that help them avoid or cope with role conflict.

Some participants emphasized the need for mentorship, and others, like Participant 012, believed, "You have to learn how to communicate to be an effective defender of juveniles—period. It's all about communication." These responses reinforce the notion that some of the emerging factors discussed in chapter 7 (such as using persuasion skills or building a support group) merit additional investigation.

Finally, the present study could be replicated in other jurisdictions to shed comparative light on the prevalence and impact of juvenile defender role conflict and coping responses. It would be interesting to see if jurisdictions that made lesser or greater efforts to encourage strictly expressed-interests advocacy reflect differences in role conflict prevalence. This would be especially important to study in the states that underwent the same kind of assessment that North Carolina did in 2003. Since these assessments tended to report that defenders demonstrated role confusion, and since many defenders articulated that they felt a lack of support in their role as well as pressure to depart from it, determining which jurisdictions have made role definition changes would have its own importance (Grindall & Puritz, 2003). A comparison of states that have implemented changes like North Carolina's and those that have not could inform future policy and practice.

Conclusions and Recommendations

This study represents the first assessment of role conflict among North Carolina juvenile defenders since the 2003 Grindall and Puritz assessment brought the matter to light and the NCOJD's 2005 *Role Statement* clarified the state's policy on the juvenile defender role. This study reflects an in-depth examination of what could be considered the most critical and least respected role in the juvenile justice system: the juvenile defender. These attorneys serve as the *only* voice of the juvenile in the justice system, a system that, despite its noble intentions, exercises actual punitive power over juveniles. What is more, it is a system that espouses and pushes a rehabilitative orientation even at the cost of the due process rights of those it seeks to serve.

Despite North Carolina's efforts to promote expressed-interests advocacy among its juvenile defenders, the majority of participants in this study still reported experiencing role conflict from forces that could compel them to depart from their expressed-interests advocate role. Some of those forces originated within the juvenile defender and some created justification for role departure (such as the client's mental capacity and the like), but most were external (parents, clients, the push for efficiency, and so on).

Notwithstanding these pressures, the juvenile defenders who participated in this study exhibited a great deal of passion and dedication to their clients, the juvenile court, and the US Constitution. They were very clear in their praise for other functionaries in their home courts. They reported interacting with incredibly supportive courtroom functionaries who not only understood and supported the juvenile defender role but also commended them for their zealous efforts. As encouraging as these remarks are, there remain strong forces that work *against* juvenile defenders' carrying out their zealous advocate role.

This study's findings made clear that the expressed-/best-interests dichotomy for juvenile defense might not be as simple as with adult defense. However, the best response to this dilemma is *unlikely* to be co-opting juvenile defenders, the sole voice for the juvenile, into the best-interests orientation of the juvenile court. Doing so would seriously undermine the juvenile defender's role as guardian of juvenile clients' due process rights and the efficacy of the system itself. The time might be ripe for creating another solution, making additional research on these topics important and necessary.

This study's findings led to the following recommendations:

1. After refinement of this study, conduct more empirical research on juvenile defenders' role conflict and coping responses (including replications of the present study) in other jurisdictions, including assessments using quantitative measures of the target constructs and applied to larger samples (see charts 8.1 and 8.2).
2. Conduct a role definition assessment of juvenile justice defender systems throughout the United States.
3. Identify NJDC assessment states that have implemented role clarification changes and replicate this study within those states. Compare the results to those of states without role clarification changes.
4. Conduct qualitative examinations of juvenile courtroom functionaries' attitudes, definitions, and expectations of the juvenile defender role. Do the same for other stakeholders (such as parents, clients, and service providers).
5. Conduct an assessment of juvenile court functionaries' attitudes toward the disposition stage of the process and *actual* nature of outcomes. Address implications for the juvenile defender role; do the same for other stakeholders (such as parents, clients, and service providers).
6. Assess and foster clarity about the juvenile defender role among juvenile justice system stakeholders (courtroom functionaries, parents, clients, service providers, and so on).
7. Conduct qualitative examinations of the influence of the following juvenile defender factors on their role conflict experiences, responses, and impact: advocate type, length of experience (tenure), reputation, interpersonal/communication skills, and facility with informal norms and practices ("social capital").
8. Conduct continuing legal education workshops designed to foster clarity and support for the juvenile defender role, role conflict source identification, and coping response options.
9. Identify, assess, and foster mentorship programs for juvenile defenders.
10. Collaborate with the NJDC to develop and disseminate materials (print and electronic) to foster clarity and support for the juvenile

defender role, role conflict source identification, and coping response options.

11. Collaborate with the NJDC to establish a clearinghouse of best practices, information, and "war stories" to foster clarity and support for the juvenile defender role, role conflict source identification, and coping response options.

Further empirical investigations including, but not limited to, these recommendations is critical. Without it, and without seeking ways to resolve the nefarious problems that are juvenile defender role ambiguity and conflict, juveniles might be left with a game of chance as to what type of advocate they are assigned. Based on the implications of the state assessments and this study's findings, not all juveniles will be assigned a defense attorney, let alone one who is dedicated and passionate enough to navigate role conflict. They also might not be assigned an attorney who can navigate it long enough to develop strong skills or a solid reputation or to have the time and desire to mentor others. If the system cannot correct itself and at least hold its own functionaries to the same adversarial and due process standards expected in the adult system, juvenile defenders could be in the same gambling position as their clients.

When it comes to due process protections in the justice system, is it acceptable that the best that kids can hope for are well-intentioned advocates who are beleaguered with unnecessary pushback from those who should support them in their role? In the words of one such advocate,

> We brought them here and *we owe it to them* [emphasis added] [to zealously advocate for them]. . . . [The] kid needs it done, so I'm going to do it. . . . But, [it's] not fair [to not zealously advocate for the kid]; [I] don't [want to] let the poor [kid] down. (Maine juvenile defender, personal communication, July 28, 2011)

As long as juvenile defenders must contend with role ambiguity and conflict from the very system tasked with helping these kids, we are all letting them down. In other words, if our justice system is going to promise children the right to guardians of their "jungle gym" time, we certainly owe it to them *and* their guardians to ensure there are no "land mines" lurking beneath.

Appendixes
Notes
References
Index

Analysis

A social constructivist orientation informed this study's data analysis. Social constructivism assumes veracity in respondents' retelling of their individual experiences (Guba & Lincoln, 1989). Respondents might have shared components of their lived experience of juvenile defender role meaning, role conflict, and related pressures and coping responses. An additional assumption is that this shared experience has informative value (Patton, 2002; Van Manen, 1990).

In order to analyze the data, an initial thematic framework was developed using the research questions. Similar themes were clustered into higher order categories to identify underlying patterns of meaning and interpretation (Strauss & Corbin, 1994). The initial thematic framework was amended and adapted several times during analysis as each interview was coded. The framework was finalized after the last interview was coded, and previously coded interviews were reviewed and recoded to include emerging themes. Interpretive themes were developed, redefined, and retroactively applied as necessary to accommodate emerging meanings in the data, as suggested by Miles and Huberman (1994). Coping strategies in response to role conflict were analyzed using a previously established coping rubric (Hall, 1972) and category set (Burke & Belcourt, 1974).

Validity

The investigator-involved nature of qualitative research can make establishing validity a challenge. In qualitative research, the quality and credibility of the data are highly dependent on several factors, including investigator subjectivity, trustworthiness, authenticity, and triangulation (Patton, 2002, p. 544). I was the only interviewer and analyst for this study and was, therefore, the only instrument through which data were collected and analyzed. This makes for more consistent data analysis, but the analysis might suffer from investigator bias. It was thus incumbent upon me to be persistently mindful of any predisposed notions about juvenile defenders' experiences of role conflict, relevant pressures, and resultant coping. I also needed to be mindful of any predisposed notions about juvenile justice matters overall, such as critical or supportive thoughts regarding the juvenile court's orientation (i.e., parens patriae versus due process).

Additionally, in order to ensure reliability, I read each question to each participant verbatim from the interview protocols, unless the answer had already been given in response to another question, or unless the question was asked in edited form as a follow-up to a relevant response to another question. In these instances, I attempted to use wording as close as possible to the written question without impeding the flow of the interview. Also, paper (in-person interviews) or electronic (phone interviews) copies of the interview protocols were provided to the participants so they could read along throughout the interview. Additional follow-up questions were asked depending on participant responses. The "disposition stage" question was not part of the *written* protocol because pilot responses indicated little variance on this item, but all participants were asked about role departure due to stage if they did not raise the topic themselves. Only two participants' responses (006 and 023) were not captured in their transcripts, but their responses are briefly discussed in the book's main text.

I designed this study because of my beliefs about the value of the US Constitution, due process protections, human development, and the professional development of law practitioners, particularly of those who safeguard the due process rights of minors. These beliefs could have affected my objectivity throughout the study. However, my experience and rigorous training in scientific method have allowed me to develop the skills necessary to manage bias resulting from my beliefs or perspectives. I have spent several years in training as a social science researcher, have conducted and published my own research, and have been trained as a lawyer and industrial/organizational psychologist. I also have several years of experience conducting interviews and working with courtroom workgroup members in a variety of roles. I lack direct experience in the juvenile defender role. Not having performed that role, however, could allow me more objectivity.

Since 2004, I have made the professional development of lawyers my primary research agenda. In order to counteract investigator subjectivity, I relied on my ethics training, research experience, and the study's instruments. I also implemented member checks, providing each participant the opportunity to review his or her interview transcript and make changes. Participants had two weeks to make changes, but only one made any.

ID# _____

> Your responses to the following questions are
> *voluntary* and will be kept *confidential*.

Demographics

I identify with the following:

Age _____

Sex

    Female _____

    Male _____

Race

    Caucasian/white _____

    Hispanic _____

    African American/black _____

    Asian/Pacific Islander _____

    Other (please specify) _____

Marital status

    Married _____

    Single _____

    Divorced/separated _____

    Widowed _____

Annual income

    $0–25,000 _____

    $25,001–35,000 _____

    $35,001–45,000 _____

    $45,001–55,000 _____

    $55,001–65,000 _____

    $65,001+ _____

Professional Background

Current job title _____

Years of service as juvenile defense attorney _____

Years of service in related role (e.g., juvenile prosecutor, indigent counsel, court counselor, etc.) _____

Title of related role(s) _____

Years of service as attorney (of any type) _____

Law school attended _____

Year of law school graduation _____

Juvenile defense practice training (certifications, CLEs, clinics, workshops, self-study, etc.)

_____

_____

_____

_____

_____

Other relevant background

_____

_____

_____

_____

I view myself as an advocate for my client's _____ interests.

Thank you for your participation!

Juvenile Defender Role Conflict
Interview Protocol

1. What does zealous advocacy mean to you in terms of advocating for your client's interests?
2. Have you ever faced obstacles or pressures to depart from the zealous advocate role? What were they?
3. Who or what do you think is responsible for any pressure you experience to depart from the zealous advocate role? Can you make a list?
4. In your experience, do you think judges support your role as a zealous advocate of the *expressed* interests of your juvenile client? Why or why not?
5. In your experience, do you think other courtroom workgroup members support your role as a zealous advocate of the *expressed* interests of your juvenile client? Why or why not?
6. In your opinion, should a defense attorney ever depart from advocating for the *expressed* interests of a client?
7. Do you ever feel like there are conflicting expectations of you in your role as a zealous advocate for juveniles? How so?
8. What do you think is the source or sources of these conflicting expectations?
9. Do you ever feel like you, personally, are conflicted about your role as a zealous advocate for juveniles, or what it requires you to do? How so?
10. Does having a very young, or special-needs, client ever affect your zealous advocacy role? How so?

Follow-Up Questions
1. What kinds of verbal or nonverbal pressures from others prevent you from being the kind of advocate you would like to be? From whom do you experience these pressures?
2. What kinds of resource pressures—for example, caseload, time, access to resources or service providers—prevent you from being the kind of advocate you would like to be?

3. What kinds of training opportunities do you think would help you improve your advocacy for juveniles?
4. Are there any other policy or practice changes you think would help you improve your advocacy for juveniles?
5. When there are pressures that prevent you from being as zealous an advocate as you would like to be, how does that affect case outcomes?

Appendix D
Coping Responses to Role Conflict: Interview Protocol

When thinking about the experiences you shared earlier in this interview:

1. Would you please describe if those experiences caused you any tension or stress?
2. Would you please describe what you have done that you found particularly *effective* at reducing that tension or stress?
3. Would you please describe a specific example of those kinds of experiences?
4. Would you please describe specifically how you coped with that experience?
5. What is your impression of how these kinds of experiences have affected the quality of your work?
6. What is your impression of how these kinds of experiences have impacted you as a juvenile defender generally?
7. How much time per week would you say you spend coping with these kinds of experiences?

Appendix E
Coping Vignettes

Please consider the following scenarios. Please explain how you
would cope with any ethical dilemma(s) the scenario presents.
Please remember that there are no right or wrong answers.

1. *Daniel.* He is a fourteen-year-old charged with disorderly conduct at school.
He wants to go to trial. There are some triable issues, and you think there is
a fairly good chance of prevailing. He also wants to testify, though you think
this is not advisable, as he tends to laugh nervously at most questions, and
his story doesn't completely hold together. His mother wants him to admit,
as she feels he needs the structure offered by supervised probation.

What is the main dilemma, and how would you cope with it?

2. *LaToya.* She is a fifteen-year-old girl charged with three counts of assault.
Two of the alleged victims were seriously injured. The prosecutor and the
court counselor will be recommending an out-of-home placement and/or
wilderness camp at disposition. Meanwhile, there's a very good defense based
on mistaken identity; you and your supervisor feel very optimistic about your
chances at trial.

LaToya is quite meek and defers to her parents on everything. It has been
difficult to have interviews alone with her, as her parents have demanded to
be present and she hasn't said anything to counter that. Her parents say that
she "confessed" to them soon after they were contacted regarding the juvenile
petition, and they say it is her "moral duty" to admit to the charges in court
and to suffer the consequences, whatever they might be. LaToya is very quiet
during your interviews and says only that she'll do what her parents want. She
does admit that she didn't have anything to do with the incident and that she
"confessed" to her parents because they said if she didn't, they would punish her.

What is the main dilemma, and how would you cope with it?

3. *Michael.* He is a thirteen-year-old charged with possession with intent to
distribute marijuana. He was found with ten baggies of weed, cash, a pager,

and a list of "buyers." He says that he is "guilty" and just wants to get it over with in court but that he's afraid of what his aunt—who is his guardian—will say, as he has denied the whole thing to her. His aunt wants him to go to trial. She says he was "set up" and that she doesn't want to see him following in the footsteps of his father (her brother), who is currently doing time for drug trafficking.

What is the main dilemma, and how would you cope with it?

4. *John.* He is a fifteen-year-old with an IQ of sixty-eight and diagnosed with attention deficit hyperactivity disorder. Let's say that the prosecutor has offered a plea to a misdemeanor, which ensures that the case will remain in juvenile court. The DA also says that should John refuse to admit to the misdemeanor, she will seek a transfer hearing and try John as an adult. In your professional judgment, John should accept the plea. If he is convicted of the class B1 felony, his presumptive range is 192–240 months, mitigated range is 144–192 months, and aggravated range is 240–300 months. All sentences must be an active sentence. When you give John your advice, he tells you that he's not admitting to anything and that he wants a jury trial.

What is the main dilemma, and how would you cope with it?

5. *Sonya.* She is charged with two counts each of felony breaking and entering and felony larceny. Both the assistant district attorney and Sonya's court counselor have advised you that they plan to strenuously recommend commitment. At Sonya's last hearing, the judge warned her that "any more slip-ups" would result in her commitment to the youth development center.

Sonya's cousin who is nineteen and is familiar with the system recommends to Sonya (though she's unsure) that Sonya can waive her juvenile jurisdiction and enter a plea of guilty in adult criminal court because it is unlikely that Sonya will receive prison time as a first offender. Although Sonya has never been detained long-term, she attempted suicide during her most recent stay in detention because she "couldn't take" being locked up.

What is the main dilemma, and how would you cope with it?

6. *Steven.* He is a fourteen-year-old juvenile who is in the seventh grade and has been held in detention for five days while he waits for a detention hearing on Monday. He is being held because he is charged in a petition alleging simple assault. The alleged victim is his mother. The juvenile has a history of mental health problems; he is diagnosed with attention deficit disorder, intermittent explosive disorder, and oppositional defiant disorder; and it is believed he is

bipolar (though he is too young for that diagnosis). The juvenile's mother tells you at the detention hearing that she wants to be present with you when you talk to her son because she wants to make sure you don't put words in his mouth. She also tells you that he is going to plead because "he did it." She also tells you that he cannot come home because she's tired of him and wants the court to do something about him or lock him up. He has had numerous suspensions from school and has not been evaluated by the school, though she has asked repeatedly since he was in the fifth grade. You learn from your client just before the detention hearing that there is a history of domestic violence in the home and that he believes that he acted in "self-defense." He wants to go home with his mother despite what his mother says. You know of alternative placements that could be available rather than detention.

What is the main dilemma, and how would you cope with it?

7. *Jasmine*. It is arraignment day for your client, eleven-year-old Jasmine. She has a petition for assault with a deadly weapon. You have eight cases on that morning. You do not have a lot of time to talk with the parents, who need to talk to you. Your client tells you that she is guilty. You talk with your client about the details. You conclude that based on the information she provides that she needs a trial. As you are talking to your client and parents, the assistant district attorney knocks and says that the judge is ready for your case to be heard. The parents tell you that their daughter is innocent and you need to investigate. Your client wants to get it over with.

What is the main dilemma, and how would you cope with it?

8. *James*. James is fourteen years old and has been arrested for possession of heroin. In the course of preparing his case, you learn he is an addict. You also come across evidence that the search leading to his arrest may have been illegal. Do you file a motion to suppress, knowing James won't get treatment for his addiction? His mother doesn't have insurance, and the only way for him to get treatment is for him to be adjudicated delinquent.

What is the main dilemma, and how would you cope with it?

2. The Modern-Day Juvenile Defender

1. See also ABA Juvenile Justice Center & New England Juvenile Defender Center, 2003 (ME); Ainsworth, 1990; Albin et al., 2003 (MT); Calvin, 2003 (WA); Cumming et al., 2003 (MD); Puritz & Brooks, 2002 (KY); and Puritz, Scali, & Picou, 2002 (VA).

2. ABA Juvenile Justice Center & New England Juvenile Defender Center, 2003 (ME); Albin et al., 2003 (MT); Beck et al., 2009 (NE); Brooks & Kamine, 2003 (OH); Calvin, 2003 (WA); Celeste & Puritz, 2001 (LA); Crawford et al., 2007 (IL); Cumming et al., 2003 (MD); Grindall & Puritz, 2003 (NC); Kehoe & Tandy, 2006 (IN); Miller-Wilson, 2003 (PA); Puritz, 2012 (CO); Puritz et al., 2002 (VA); Puritz et al., 2007 (MS); Puritz & Brooks, 2002 (KY); Puritz & Crawford, 2006 (FL); Puritz & Sterling, 2010 (WV); Puritz & Sun, 2001 (GA); Scali et al., 2010 (SC); Scali et al., 2013 (MO); Stewart et al., 2000 (TX).

3. My efforts to procure detailed information on samples and assessment measures, such as interview protocols, were unsuccessful. When I requested these details from the National Juvenile Defender Center, it was explained that those details could not be released in order to protect the authors' intellectual property rights.

4. See, for example, Beck et al., 2009 (NE); Crawford et al., 2007 (IL); Puritz, 2012 (CO); Puritz et al., 2007 (MS); Puritz & Sterling, 2010 (WV); Scali et al., 2010 (SC); Scali et al., 2013 (MO), etc.

5. See, for instance, Beck et al., 2009 (NE); Celeste & Puritz, 2001 (LA); Puritz et al., 2007 (MS); Puritz & Brooks, 2002 (KY); Puritz & Sterling, 2010 (WV); Scali et al., 2010 (SC); Scali et al., 2013 (MO).

6. ABA Juvenile Justice Center & New England Juvenile Defender Center, 2003 (ME); Albin et al., 2003 (MT); Beck et al., 2009 (NE); Brooks & Kamine, 2003 (OH); Calvin, 2003 (WA); Celeste & Puritz, 2001 (LA); Crawford et al., 2007 (IL); Cumming et al., 2003 (MD); Grindall & Puritz, 2003 (NC); Kehoe & Tandy, 2006 (IN); Miller-Wilson, 2003 (PA); Puritz, 2012 (CO); Puritz et al., 2002 (VA); Puritz et al., 2007 (MS); Puritz & Brooks,

2002 (KY); Puritz & Crawford, 2006 (FL); Puritz & Sterling, 2010 (WV); Puritz & Sun, 2001 (GA); Scali et al., 2010 (SC); Scali et al., 2013 (MO); Stewart et al., 2000 (TX).

7. ABA Juvenile Justice Center & New England Juvenile Defender Center, 2003 (ME); Albin et al., 2003 (MT); Beck et al., 2009 (NE); Brooks & Kamine, 2003 (OH); Calvin, 2003 (WA); Celeste & Puritz, 2001 (LA); Crawford et al., 2007 (IL); Cumming et al., 2003 (MD); Grindall & Puritz, 2003 (NC); Kehoe & Tandy, 2006 (IN); Miller-Wilson, 2003 (PA); Puritz, 2012 (CO); Puritz et al., 2002 (VA); Puritz et al., 2007 (MS); Puritz & Brooks, 2002 (KY); Puritz & Crawford, 2006 (FL); Puritz & Sterling, 2010 (WV); Puritz & Sun, 2001 (GA); Scali et al., 2010 (SC); Scali et al., 2013 (MO); Stewart et al., 2000 (TX).

7. Navigating Land Mines

1. Each state "bar" is an organization responsible for the licensure and training of attorneys as well as the management of those whose ethics or practices do not meet certain standards.

8. Concluding Thoughts and Future Research

1. Adler and Kwon's article does not provide a page number for this quote, despite having the language in quotation marks. Efforts to procure the page number, and article, through Northeastern University's library staff have proved unsuccessful as of this time. An electronic mail from Dr. Fukuyama dated June 7, 2015, indicates that the definition was likely the result of a transcript of a talk he gave at the Stern School.

ABA Juvenile Justice Center & New England Juvenile Defender Center. (2003). *Maine: An assessment of access to counsel and quality of representation in delinquency proceedings.* Washington, DC: ABA Juvenile Justice Center.

Adler, Paul S., & Kwon, Seok-Woo. (2002). Social capital: Prospects for a new concept. *Academy of Management Review, 27*(1), 17–40.

Ainsworth, Janet E. (1990). Re-imagining childhood and reconstructing the legal order: The case for abolishing the juvenile court. *N.C. L. Rev., 69,* 1083–1133.

Albin, B., Albin, M., Gladden, E., Ropelato, S., & Stroll, G. (2003). *Montana: An assessment of access to counsel and quality of representation in delinquency proceedings.* Washington, DC: ABA Juvenile Justice Center.

American Bar Association. (2013). *Model rules of professional conduct.* Washington, DC: American Bar Association.

Beck, J., Puritz, P., & Sterling, R. W. (2009). *Nebraska: Juvenile Legal Defense: A report on access to counsel and quality of representation for children in Nebraska.* Washington, DC: National Juvenile Defender Center.

Birckhead, Tamar R. (2004). Unpublished training materials, including hypothetical vignettes depicting ethical dilemmas faced by juvenile defense attorneys. Provided to Dr. Anne M. Corbin via email on October 24, 2013.

Birckhead, Tamar R. (2010). Culture clash: The challenge of lawyering across difference in juvenile court. *Rutgers L. Rev., 62,* 959–991.

Bishop, Donna M., & Feld, Barry C. (2012). Trends in juvenile justice policy and practice. In B. C. Feld and D. M. Bishop (Eds.), *The Oxford handbook of juvenile crime and juvenile justice* (pp. 898–921). New York: Oxford University Press.

Brooks, K., & Kamine, D. (2003). *Justice cut short: An assessment of access to counsel and quality of representation in delinquency proceedings in Ohio.* Washington, DC: American Bar Association.

Bryant, Susan. (2001). The five habits: Building cross-culture competence in lawyers. *Clinical L. Rev., 8,* 33–107.

Burke, Ronald J., & Belcourt, Monica L. (1974). Managerial role stress and coping responses. *Journal of Business Administration, 5*(2), 55–68.

Burruss, George W., Jr., & Kempf-Leonard, Kimberly. (2002). The questionable advantage of defense counsel in juvenile court. *Justice Quarterly, 19*(1), 37–68.

Buss, Emily. (1995). You're my what?—The problem of children's misperceptions of their lawyers' roles. *Fordham L. Rev., 64*, 1699.

Buss, Emily. (1998). Confronting developmental barriers to the empowerment of child clients. *Cornell L. Rev., 84*, 895–966.

Buss, Emily. (2000). Role of lawyers in promoting juveniles' competence as defendants. In T. Grisso and R. G. Schwartz (Eds.), *Youth on trial: A developmental perspective on juvenile justice* (pp. 243–265). Chicago: University of Chicago Press.

Calvin, E. M. (2003). *Washington: An assessment of access to counsel and quality of representation in delinquency proceedings.* Washington, DC: American Bar Association.

Celeste, G., & Puritz, P. (2001). *The children left behind: An assessment of access to counsel and quality of representation in delinquency proceedings in Louisiana.* Washington, DC: American Bar Association.

Christle, Christine A., Jolivette, Kristine, & Nelson, C. Michael. (2005). Breaking the school-to-prison pipeline: Identifying school risk and protective factors for youth delinquency. *Exceptionality, 13*(2), 69–88.

Clarke, Stevens H., & Koch, Gary G. (1980). Juvenile court: Therapy or crime control, and do lawyers make a difference? *Law and Soc'y Rev., 14*, 263–308.

Cohen, Fred. (1965). Function of the attorney and the commitment of the mentally ill. *Tex. L. Rev., 44*, 424–469.

Coleman, James S. (1988). Social capital in the creation of human capital. *American Journal of Sociology, 94*, S95–S120.

Cordes, Cynthia L., & Dougherty, Thomas W. (1993). A review and an integration of research on job burnout. *Academy of Management Review, 18*(4), 621–656.

Crawford, C., Dohrn, B., Geraghty, T. F., Moss, M. B, & Puritz, P. (2007). *Illinois: An assessment of access to counsel and quality of representation in delinquency proceedings.* Washington, DC: National Juvenile Defender Center.

Crotty, Michael. (1998). *The foundations of social research: Meaning and perspective in the research process.* London: Sage.

Cumming, E., Finley, M., Hall, S., Humphrey, A., & Picou, I. (2003). *Maryland: An assessment of access to counsel and quality of representation in delinquency proceedings.* Washington, DC: American Bar Association.

Dickerson v. United States, 530 US 428 (2000).

Fedders, Barbara. (2010). Losing hold on the guiding hand: Ineffective assistance of counsel in juvenile delinquency representation. *Lewis & Clark L. Rev., 14,* 771–819.

Fedders, Barbara. (2012). Defining the role of counsel in the sentencing phase of a juvenile delinquency case. *Child. Legal Rts. J., 32,* 25–51.

Feld, Barry C. (1988). *In re Gault* revisited: A cross-state comparison of the right to counsel in juvenile court. *Crime & Delinquency, 34*(4), 393–424.

Feld, Barry C. (1989). The right to counsel in juvenile court: An empirical study of when lawyers appear and the difference they make. *J. Crim. L. & Criminology (1973–), 79*(4), 1185–1346.

Feld, Barry C. (1993). Criminalizing the American juvenile court. *Crime and Justice, 17,* 197–280.

Feld, Barry C. (1999). *Bad kids: Race and the transformation of the juvenile court.* New York: Oxford University Press.

Feld, Barry C. (2000). *Cases and materials on juvenile justice administration.* Eagan, MN: West Group.

Feld, Barry C. (2012). Procedural rights in juvenile courts: Competence and consequences. In B. C. Feld and D. M. Bishop (Eds.), *The Oxford handbook of juvenile crime and juvenile justice* (pp. 664–691). New York: Oxford University Press.

Finkelstein, M. M., Weiss, A., Cohen, S., & Fisher, S. (1973). *Prosecution in the juvenile courts: Guidelines for the future.* [Boston assessment.] Washington, DC: US Department of Justice.

Fox, S. J. (1970). Juvenile justice reform: An historical perspective. *Stan. L. Rev., 22*(6), 1187–1239.

Frank, Jerome. (1973). *Courts on trial: Myth and reality in American justice.* Princeton: Princeton University Press.

Franklin, Benjamin. (1748). "Advice to a young tradesman." In *George Fisher: The American instructor: or Young man's best companion. . . . The ninth edition revised and corrected,* 375–377. Philadelphia: Printed by B. Franklin and D. Hall.

French, John R. P., Rodgers, Willard, & Cobb, Sidney. (1974). Adjustment as person-environment fit. In G. V. Coelho, D. A. Hamburg, & J. E. Adams (Eds.), *Coping and Adaptation* (pp. 316–333). New York: Basic Books.

Fukuyama, Francis. (1997). Social capital and the modern capitalist economy: Creating a high trust workplace. *Stern Business Magazine, 4*(1), 1–16.

Gabbay, Shaul M., & Zuckerman, Ezra W. (1998). Social capital and opportunity in corporate R&D: The contingent effect of contact density on mobility expectations. *Social Science Research, 27*(2), 189–217.

Garner, B. A., & Black, H. C. (2006). *Black's law dictionary.* St. Paul, MN: Thomson/West.

Geertz, Clifford. (1973). *The interpretation of cultures: Selected essays.* New York: Basic Books.

Getzels, Jacob W., & Guba, Egon G. (1954). Role, role conflict, and effectiveness: An empirical study. *American Sociological Review, 19*(2), 164–175.

Gideon v. Wainwright, 372 US 335 (1963).

Green, Bruce A., & Dohrn, Bernardine. (1995). Foreword: Children and the ethical practice of law. *Fordham L. Rev., 64,* 1281–1298.

Grindall, L., & Puritz, P. (2003). *North Carolina: An assessment of access to counsel and quality of representation in delinquency proceedings.* Washington, DC: ABA Juvenile Justice Center and Southern Juvenile Defender Center.

Grisso, Thomas. (1997). The competence of adolescents as trial defendants. *Psychol. Pub. Pol'y & Law, 3*(1), 3–32.

Guba, Egon G., & Lincoln, Yvonna S. (1989). *Fourth generation evaluation.* Newbury Park, CA: Sage.

Guggenheim, Martin. (1984). The right to be represented but not heard: Reflections on legal representation for children. *N.Y.U. L. Rev., 59,* 76–155.

Hall, Douglas T. (1972). A model of coping with role conflict: The role behavior of college educated women. *Administrative Science Quarterly, 17*(4), 471–486.

Henning, Kristin. (2005). Loyalty, paternalism, and rights: Client counseling theory and the role of child's counsel in delinquency cases. *Notre Dame L. Rev., 81,* 245–324.

In re Gault, 367 US 1 (1967).

In re RD, 499 N.E.2d 478 (Ill. App. Ct. 1986).

Institute of Judicial Administration and the American Bar Association. (1980). *Juvenile justice standards relating to counsel for private parties.* Cambridge, MA: Ballinger.

Jackson, Susan E., Turner, Jon A., & Brief, Arthur P. (1987). Correlates of burnout among public service lawyers. *Journal of Organizational Behavior, 8*(4), 339–349.

J. D. B. v. North Carolina, 131 S. Ct. 2394 (2011).

Katz, Daniel, & Kahn, Robert L. (1966). *The social psychology of organizations.* New York: Wiley.

Kehoe, E. G., & Tandy, K. B. (2006). *Indiana: An assessment of access to counsel and quality of representation in delinquency proceedings.* Washington, DC: National Juvenile Defender Center.

Knitzer, Jane, & Sobie, Merril. (1984). *Law guardians in New York State: A study of the legal representation of children.* New York: New York State Bar Association.

Kolb, Alice Y., & Kolb, David A. (2005). Learning styles and learning spaces: Enhancing experiential learning in higher education. *Academy of Management Learning & Education, 4*(2), 193–212.

Krackhardt, David, & Hanson, Jeffrey R. (1993). Informal networks. *Harvard Business Review, 71*(4), 104–111.

Laub, John H., & Mac Murray, Bruce K. (1987). Increasing the prosecutor's role in juvenile court: Expectations and realities. *Justice System Journal, 12*(2), 196–209.

Lawrence, Richard A. (1983). Role of legal counsel in juveniles' understanding of their rights. *Juv. & Fam. Ct. J., 34,* 49–58.

Levy, Paul. (2010). Industrial organizational psychology: Understanding the workplace. New York: Worth.

Lynch, David R. (1997). The nature of occupational stress among public defenders. *Justice System Journal, 19*(1), 17–35.

Marrus, Ellen. (2003). Best interests equals zealous advocacy: A not-so-radical view of holistic representation for children accused of crime. *Md. L. Rev., 62,* 288–360.

McKeiver v. Pennsylvania, 403 US 528 (1971).

Mennel, Robert M. (1972). Origins of the juvenile court: Changing perspectives on the legal rights of juvenile delinquents. *NPPA Journal, 18*(1), 68–78.

Miles, Matthew B., & Huberman, A. Michael. (1994). *Qualitative data analysis: An expanded sourcebook.* Newbury Park, CA: Sage.

Miller-Wilson, L. S. (2003). *Pennsylvania: An assessment of access to counsel and quality of representation in delinquency proceedings.* Washington, DC: ABA Juvenile Justice Center.

Miranda v. Arizona, 384 US 436 (1966).

Mlyniec, Wallace. (1995). Who decides: Decision making in juvenile delinquency proceedings. In R. J. Uphoff (Ed.), *Ethical problems facing the criminal defense lawyer: Practical answers to tough questions.* Washington, DC: American Bar Association.

Moss, Debra Cassens. (1987). *In re Gault* Now 20, but . . . : Juveniles still underrepresented by lawyers in proceedings. *ABA J., 73*(8), 29.

National Juvenile Defender Center. (2012). *National juvenile defense standards.* Washington, DC: National Juvenile Defense Center.

National Juvenile Defender Center. (2014). *State profiles.* Washington, DC: National Juvenile Defender Center.

Newman, L. A., Grine, A., & Zogry, E. J. (2008). Performance guidelines. In *North Carolina juvenile defender manual* (pp. 269–300). Chapel Hill: UNC School of Government.

North Carolina Commission on Indigent Defense Services. (2007). *Performance guidelines for appointed counsel in juvenile delinquency proceedings at the trial level*. Adopted December 14, 2007. Durham: NCCIDS.

North Carolina Office of Indigent Defense Services. (2006). Ethics and role of defense counsel. In *Role of Defense Counsel*, by Phillip J. Penn, from Regional Juvenile Defender Workshops, February–May. Durham: NCCIDS.

North Carolina Office of Indigent Defense Services. (2014). Advanced juvenile defender training: Client-centered representation through all stages of the case. Presentation by Tamar Birckhead. Chapel Hill, NC: UNC School of Government. Formerly posted as training materials on NCOIDS website.

North Carolina Office of the Juvenile Defender. (2005). *Role of defense counsel in juvenile delinquency proceedings* (referred to as *Role Statement* throughout the text). Raleigh: North Carolina Office of the Juvenile Defender.

North Carolina Office of the Juvenile Defender. (2013). *North Carolina Office of the Juvenile Defender Strategic Plan report*. Unpublished report, April. Raleigh, NC: NCOJD.

Patton, Michael Quinn. (2002). Qualitative interviewing. *Qualitative Research and Evaluation Methods, 3*, 344–347.

Pearlin, Leonard I., & Schooler, Carmi. (1978). The structure of coping. *Journal of Health and Social Behavior, 19*(1), 2–21.

Pierce, Christine Schnyder, & Brodsky, Stanley L. (2002). Trust and understanding in the attorney–juvenile relationship. *Behavioral Sciences & the Law, 20*(1–2), 89–107.

Platt, Anthony M. (1977). *The child savers: The invention of delinquency*. Chicago: University of Chicago Press.

Podolny, Joel M., & Baron, James N. (1997). Resources and relationships: Social networks and mobility in the workplace. *American Sociological Review, 62*, 673–693.

Powell v. Alabama, 287 US 45 (1932).

Puritz, P. (2012). *Colorado: An assessment of access to counsel and quality of representation in delinquency proceedings*. Washington, DC: National Juvenile Defender Center.

Puritz, P., & Brooks, K. (2002). *Kentucky: Advancing justice—an assessment of access to counsel and quality of representation in delinquency proceedings*. Washington, DC: National Juvenile Defender Center.

Puritz, P., Burrell, S., Schwartz, R., Soler, M., & Warboys, L. (2002). *A call for justice: An assessment of access to counsel and quality of representation in delinquency proceedings.* (Original work published in 1996). Washington, DC: American Bar Association.

Puritz, P., & Crawford, C. (2006). *Florida: An assessment of access to counsel and quality of representation in delinquency proceedings.* Washington, DC: National Juvenile Defender Center.

Puritz, P., & Majd, K. (2007). Ensuring authentic youth participation in delinquency cases: Creating a paradigm for specialized juvenile defense practice. *Family Court Review, 45*(3), 466–484.

Puritz, P., Scali, M., & Picou, I. (2002). *Virginia: An assessment of access to counsel and quality of representation in delinquency proceedings.* Washington, DC: American Bar Association.

Puritz, P., & Sterling, R. W. (2010). *West Virginia: An assessment of access to counsel and quality of representation in juvenile delinquency court.* Washington, DC: National Juvenile Defender Center.

Puritz, P., & Sun, T. (2001). *Georgia: An assessment of access to counsel and quality of representation in delinquency proceedings.* Washington, DC: American Bar Association, Juvenile Justice Center.

Puritz, P., Walker, R., Riley-Collins, J., & Bedi, S. A. (2007). *Mississippi: An assessment of access to counsel and quality of representation in delinquency proceedings.* Washington, DC: National Juvenile Defender Center.

Putnam, Robert D. (1995). Bowling alone: America's declining social capital. *Journal of Democracy, 6*(1), 65–78.

Rizzo, John R., House, Robert J., & Lirtzman, Sidney I. (1970). Role conflict and ambiguity in complex organizations. *Administrative Science Quarterly, 15*(2), 150–163.

Roper v. Simmons, 543 US 551 (2005).

Rosenthal, Bernard. (1995). *Salem story: Reading the witch trials of 1692.* No. 73. Cambridge: Cambridge University Press.

Rothman, David J. (1980). *Conscience and convenience: The asylum and its alternatives in progressive America.* Piscataway, NJ: Transaction.

Sagatun, Inger J., & Edwards, Leonard P. (1979). The role of the district attorney in juvenile court: Is the juvenile court becoming just like adult court? *Juv. & Fam. Ct. J., 30,* 17–23.

Sanborn, Joseph B., Jr. (1995). Guardian of the public and/or the child: Policy questions and conflicts for the juvenile court prosecutor. *Justice System Journal, 18*(2), 141–156.

Scali, M. A., Song, J. S., & Puritz, P. (2010). *South Carolina: Juvenile indigent defense: A report on access to and quality of representation in delinquency proceedings.* Washington, DC: National Juvenile Defender Center.

Scali, M. A., Tandy, K., Michel, J. & Pauluhn, J. (2013). *Missouri: Justice rationed: An assessment of access to counsel and quality of representation in delinquency proceedings.* Washington, DC: National Juvenile Defender Center.

Schmidt, Melinda G., Reppucci, N. Dickon, & Woolard, Jennifer L. (2003). Effectiveness of participation as a defendant: The attorney–juvenile client relationship. *Behavioral Sciences & the Law, 21*(2), 175–198.

Shelden, R. G. (1999). *Detention diversion advocacy: An evaluation.* Washington, DC: US Department of Justice, Office of Justice Programs, Office of Juvenile Justice and Delinquency Prevention.

Shepard, Robert E., Jr., & Volenik, Adrienne. (1987). Juvenile justice. *Crim. Just., 2,* 33–35.

Shine, James, & Price, Dwight. (1992). Prosecutors and juvenile justice: New roles and perspectives. In I. M. Schwartz (Ed.), *Juvenile justice and public policy: Toward a national agenda* (pp. 101–133). New York: Lexington.

Singer, Simon I. (1997). *Recriminalizing delinquency: Violent juvenile crime and juvenile justice reform.* Cambridge: Cambridge University Press.

Spangenberg, Robert L., & Beeman, Marea L. (1995). Indigent defense systems in the United States. *Law and Contemp. Probs., 58*(1), 31–49.

Stapleton, William Vaughn, & Teitelbaum, Lee E. (1972). *In defense of youth: A study of the role of counsel in American juvenile courts.* New York: Russell Sage Foundation.

Steinberg, Laurence, & Schwartz, Robert G. (2000). Developmental psychology goes to court. *Youth on Trial: A Developmental Perspective on Juvenile Justice, 1,* 9–10.

Stewart, C. E., Celeste, G., Marrus, E., Picou, I., Puritz, P., & Utler, D. (2000). *A report by the Texas Appleseed Fair Defense Project on indigent defense practices in Texas—juvenile chapter.* Washington, DC: American Bar Association.

Stranger, Lisa A. (1996). Conflicts between attorneys and social workers representing children in delinquency proceedings. *Fordham L. Rev., 65,* 1123–1160.

Strauss, Anselm, & Corbin, Juliet. (1994). Grounded theory methodology. *Handbook of Qualitative Research, 17,* 273–85.

US Census Bureau. (2014). *County Population Totals Tables 2010–2015, April 1, 2010 Estimates Base.* Washington, DC: US Census Bureau.

Van Manen, M. (1990). *Researching lived experience*. New York: State University of New York Press.

Van Sell, Mary, Brief, Arthur P., & Schuler, Randall S. (1981). Role conflict and role ambiguity: Integration of the literature and directions for future research. *Human Relations, 34*(1), 43–71.

Wright, Thomas A., & Bonett, Douglas G. (1997). The contribution of burnout to work performance. *Journal of Organizational Behavior, 18*(5), 491–499.

Index

Italicized page numbers indicate full-page tables.

Anne M. Corbin is a law-trained social scientist whose research centers on the professional development of lawyers. She has consulted periodically for the Police Foundation and taught at the University of Massachusetts Lowell, Thomas College in Maine, Elon University, and Michigan State University. She currently serves the state of Vermont's professional development needs and resides there with her family.

PERSPECTIVES
ON CRIME AND JUSTICE

Open, inclusive, and broad in focus, the series covers scholarship on a wide range of crime and justice issues, including the exploration of understudied subjects relating to crime, its causes, and attendant social responses. Of particular interest are works that examine emerging topics or shed new light on more richly studied subjects. Volumes in the series explore emerging forms of deviance and crime, critical perspectives on crime and justice, international and transnational considerations of and responses to crime, innovative crime reduction strategies, and alternate forms of response by the community and justice system to disorder, delinquency, and criminality. Both single-authored studies and collections of original edited content are welcome.

Board of Advisers
Beth M. Huebner, University of Missouri–St. Louis
John P. Jarvis, Federal Bureau of Investigation
Natalie Kroovand Hipple, Indiana University
Justin W. Patchin, University of Wisconsin–Eau Claire
Sean P. Varano, Roger Williams University

QUERIES *and* SUBMISSIONS
Joseph A. Schafer, Series Editor
Department of Criminology and Criminal Justice
Southern Illinois University Carbondale
Carbondale, IL 62901-4504
jschafer@siu.edu
618-453-6376